Reflections on English Word-Formation

We are all familiar with coming across a new word, whether it has just been invented or whether we have just not met it before. How do we invent new words? How do we understand words that we have never heard before? What are the limits on the kinds of words we produce? How have linguists and grammarians dealt with the phenomenon of creating new words, and how justified are their ways of viewing such words? In this concise and compelling book, Professor Bauer, one of the world's best-known morphologists, looks back over fifty years of his work, seeking out overlooked patterns in word-formation, and offering new solutions to recurrent problems. Each chapter deals with a different morphological problem, meaning that the book can either be read from start to finish, or alternatively used as a concise reference work on the key issues and problems in the field.

LAURIE BAUER is Emeritus Professor of Linguistics, Victoria University of Wellington, New Zealand. He is the author of many books on linguistics, including *The Oxford Reference Guide to English Morphology* (with Lieber and Plag), which won the LSA's Leonard Bloomfield Prize. He won the Royal Society of New Zealand's Humanities medal in 2017.

Reflections on English Word-Formation

Laurie Bauer
Victoria University of Wellington

CAMBRIDGE
UNIVERSITY PRESS

Shaftesbury Road, Cambridge CB2 8EA, United Kingdom

One Liberty Plaza, 20th Floor, New York, NY 10006, USA

477 Williamstown Road, Port Melbourne, VIC 3207, Australia

314–321, 3rd Floor, Plot 3, Splendor Forum, Jasola District Centre, New Delhi – 110025, India

103 Penang Road, #05–06/07, Visioncrest Commercial, Singapore 238467

Cambridge University Press is part of Cambridge University Press & Assessment, a department of the University of Cambridge.

We share the University's mission to contribute to society through the pursuit of education, learning and research at the highest international levels of excellence.

www.cambridge.org
Information on this title: www.cambridge.org/9781009559973
DOI: 10.1017/9781009559935

© Laurie Bauer 2025

This publication is in copyright. Subject to statutory exception and to the provisions of relevant collective licensing agreements, no reproduction of any part may take place without the written permission of Cambridge University Press & Assessment.

When citing this work, please include a reference to the DOI 10.1017/9781009559935

First published 2025

Ronnie Li/500px/Getty Images

A catalogue record for this publication is available from the British Library

Library of Congress Cataloging-in-Publication Data
Names: Bauer, Laurie, 1949– author.
Title: Reflections on English word-formation / Laurie Bauer, Victoria University of Wellington.
Description: Cambridge, United Kingdom ; New York, NY : Cambridge University Press, 2025. | Includes bibliographical references and index.
Identifiers: LCCN 2025000454 (print) | LCCN 2025000455 (ebook) | ISBN 9781009559973 (hardback) | ISBN 9781009559966 (paperback) | ISBN 9781009559935 (ebook)
Subjects: LCSH: English language – Word formation.
Classification: LCC PE1175 .B286 2025 (print) | LCC PE1175 (ebook) | DDC 425/.92–dc23/eng/20250520
LC record available at https://lccn.loc.gov/2025000454
LC ebook record available at https://lccn.loc.gov/2025000455

ISBN 978-1-009-55997-3 Hardback
ISBN 978-1-009-55996-6 Paperback

Cambridge University Press & Assessment has no responsibility for the persistence or accuracy of URLs for external or third-party internet websites referred to in this publication and does not guarantee that any content on such websites is, or will remain, accurate or appropriate.

For EU product safety concerns, contact us at Calle de José Abascal, 56, 1°, 28003 Madrid, Spain, or email eugpsr@cambridge.org.

Contents

Acknowledgements *page* vii
Conventions and Abbreviations viii

1 Introduction   1

Part I Basic Questions   11

2 Reflections on the Background to the Study of Word-Formation   13
3 Reflections on Why We Need Word-Formation   35
4 Reflections on the Recognition of Novelty in Words   39
5 Reflections on Blocking and Competition   43
6 Reflections on Potential and Norm   50
7 Reflections on Definition by Stipulation and on Word-Classes   56
8 Reflections on Analogical Word-Formation   64
9 Reflections on the Nature of the Lexeme   69

Part II Semantic Questions   75

10 Reflections on How Words Bear Meaning, and What This
    Implies for Complex Words   77
11 Reflections on Tautology and Redundancy   90

Part III Syntactic Questions   95

12 Reflections on Recursion   97
13 Reflections on Problems with Heads in Word-Formation   102
14 Reflections on Coordination in Word-Formation   110

Part IV Interfaces — 117

15 Reflections on the Interface between Word-Formation and Phonology: Morphophonemics — 119

16 Reflections on the Interface between Word-Formation and Syntax — 131

17 Reflections on the Interface between Word-Formation and Phonetics — 138

18 Reflections on the Interface between Word-Formation and Orthography — 144

19 Reflections on the Interface between Word-Formation and Borrowing — 148

Part V Patterns of Word-Formation in English — 153

20 Reflections on the Limits of Conversion — 155

21 Reflections on Back-Formation — 164

22 Reflections on Coordinative Compounds — 168

23 Reflections on the Irregularity of Prepositions — 174

24 Reflections on Reduplication — 179

Part VI Historical Questions — 185

25 Reflections on Dead Morphology — 187

26 Reflections on Compounds in English and in Wider Germanic — 193

Part VII Questions Involving Inflection — 207

27 Reflections on Inflection inside Word-Formation — 209

28 Reflections on Canonical Form — 218

29 Reflections on the Spread of Regular Inflection to Simple and Derived Forms — 225

30 Conclusion — 232

Index of Topics — 238
Index of English Word-Forming Elements — 241

Acknowledgements

I should like to thank the team at Cambridge University Press for their enthusiasm for the project and their professional approach to this (and, in my experience, every) book project. They were instrumental, among other things, in finding referees for the work when it was first proposed, who provided extremely thoughtful and helpful feedback. I should also like to thank Liza Tarasova and Natalia Beliaeva for reading and commenting on an earlier draft, and providing invaluable criticism, insights and suggestions.

Conventions and Abbreviations

Conventions and Abbreviations

' ... '	round (a) meanings/glosses, (b) technical terms being discussed
" ... "	round direct quotations
· [decimal point]	in glosses, boundary between morphs not indicated by the spelling (also used in the corresponding gloss)
[...]	to indicate morphosyntactic bracketing; to indicate a phonetic transcription
*	to indicate an impossible formation; to show the position of a missing letter
/ ... /	to enclose phonemic transcriptions
. [full stop/period]	to divide words in glosses
~	replaces the meaning of the base in a gloss, or allows for a blank to be filled in by the reader
italics	for cited words, phrases, sentences, affixes not in displays
SMALL CAPITALS	(where needed) (a) for lexemes and (b) in glosses

Abbreviations in Glosses

1, 2, 3	1st, 2nd, 3rd person
ABL	ablative
ACC	accusative
ADV	adverb
DIMIN	diminutive
GEN	genitive
LE	linking element
NMLZ	nominalization
NOM	nominative
N, V, A	noun, verb, adjective
PL	plural
POSS	possessive
SG	singular

1 Introduction

1.1 What Is Word-Formation?

'Word-formation' is the standard label for the way in which words are built up from smaller recurrent formal elements. These smaller formal elements are generally presumed to be linked in a fairly direct way to the meaning of the word that is formed from them. Word-formation is widely assumed to be made up of at least two distinct types: compounding or composition, the way in which compounds like *molehill* and *threadbare* are constructed from smaller words; and derivation, the way in which derivatives like *unfriendly* and *discovery* are constructed from prefixes, suffixes and a word which is their base.

Given the well-known ambiguity of the term 'word' in modern linguistics, it might be better if word-formation were termed 'lexeme-formation'. However, the term 'word-formation' was established before the term 'lexeme' became normal, so 'word-formation' is the usual term. But the term 'word-formation' is also sometimes used to include inflectional morphology, and so to deal with the construction of word-forms such as *covered* and *elephants*; this means that precisely what is included under word-formation is not necessarily fixed (see Chapter 2). The standard notation is that *covered* (in italics) is a word-form belonging to the paradigm of the lexeme COVER (in small capital letters), but this depends on several assumptions being agreed to (see Section 2.4).

Some people prefer the term 'lexical morphology' to 'word-formation' (e.g. Coates 1987). This seems to imply that there is nothing in word-formation that is not part of morphology. The difficulty with this is that there is not necessarily agreement on what the term 'morphology' encompasses, either. While everyone agrees that compounding, inflection and derivation are part of morphology, it is not necessarily true that everyone agrees that the formation of words by conversion (e.g. the link between the verb *to cuddle* and the noun *a cuddle*) is part of morphology, and neither is necessarily true that everyone agrees that the formation of initialisms such as *MIT* from *Massachusetts Institute of Technology* (note that the initialism is not *MIOT*) is part of morphology. Yet both of these might well be included as part of word-formation.

We can already see that word-formation is plagued by terminological problems, and some of these will be expressly addressed in this book (see e.g. Chapters 9, 20 and 22). Terminological problems cannot be solved by fiat. But if they are made explicit, authors can position themselves in regard to the major points of contention involved.

Word-formation can be viewed from at least two different viewpoints. It can be viewed as dealing with the analysis of known words, or it can be viewed as dealing with the ways in which new words are created by speakers. Since the 1970s – possibly before – the predominant approach has been the latter, at least overtly. However, most handbooks provide many examples of the former, and the two viewpoints are not necessarily kept strictly apart. Both approaches will be considered here in different chapters. The latter perspective gives rise to the question of productivity, whether and to what extent individual morphological processes (including compounding and the use of prefixes and suffixes) are used to create previously unknown words. Productivity has proved to be a very difficult area of study (see Bauer 2001). Despite arguments made, for instance by Bauer (1983), productivity is often seen as being one of the ways in which the creation of new words differs from the creation of new sentences. But just how variable productivity works, how it can be measured (if at all) and how it may be constrained are still questions that can be debated, and some of these questions will be raised below (e.g. in Chapter 5).

1.2 Is English Word-Formation Different from Word-Formation in Other Languages?

The short answer to the question raised in the heading here is 'yes'. All languages differ in the details of how their word-formation works, what semantic categories are marked in the word-formation (Japanese and Swahili mark causatives overtly in their morphology, while English tends not to), what kinds of formal means are used in the creation of words (English tends not to use infixation or reduplicating prefixes while many other languages do), and what kinds of pattern are found frequently and what kinds are found rarely. But that is not the reason for having a book about English word-formation. In principle, I could have written about word-formation in a different language, or across languages, and either of those topics might have made a useful contribution. But English is not only a familiar language for many linguists for whom it is not a first language, it is a language for which a great deal of data is available, in the form of dictionaries (most notably the *Oxford English Dictionary*), corpora illustrating usage, wordlists, coverage of word-formation specifically and easily available examples of real usage by language users. It is also the language for which I have the best intuitions (however dangerous intuitions on usage may be). For all these reasons, focusing on English provides materials which allow me to do what I want to do in this book, namely examine the ways in which word-formation can be described and the problems associated with them. This also means, I hope, that many of the questions that are raised here with specific reference to English will actually be of relevance to other languages and allow for discussions on the ways in which languages can differ. Sometimes, for clarity, comparisons are made with other languages (as has already been done above, see, in particular, Chapter 26), but the focus is on the way in which these shed light on what happens in English.

1.3 The Historical Context

Any book is written in a context that is constantly changing. In particular that context involves the way in which scholars understand the topic that they are dealing with, involving the theories they believe in, the terminology they use and the elements that they perceive as being relevant. The historical context, however, is not necessarily uniform across a field such as linguistics. Ideas which are no longer viewed as current in one area of linguistics may still be considered standard in another. This is inevitable in any subject in which the theories that were dominant when one generation of scholars was trained are no longer dominant when new scholars are trained one or two generations later. In the case of word-formation, the perceived importance of morphology in a grammar has changed markedly over just a few generations, going from being a central aspect of grammar to a marginalized area of study and back to a central topic of focus within linguistics (Coates 1987). There is little point in going through the changes in underlying philosophy which have led to this position, but to consider the different structures and fundamental notions that have been left behind might clarify some of the ways in which word-formation has been dealt with.

The twentieth century provides a textbook example of the way in which linguistic entities can come into and go out of fashion, when we consider the notion of the morpheme. The morpheme seems to have been named in the late nineteenth century, although the notion had been available before then. There were two views of the morpheme, a European one and a North American one, but they merged on the North American pattern. A morpheme is a meaningful element of a word. If we consider the word *unfriendly*, we can see that the word is made up of three elements. The core of the word is *friend*, *friend* is turned into an adjective by the addition of the suffix *-ly*, and *friendly* is made negative by the addition of the prefix *un-*. Each of *friend*, *-ly* and *un-* either is a morpheme or, in slightly later analyses, represents a morpheme. If we follow the latter view, a morpheme is an abstract unit (not a form which can be heard or written), realized by one or more forms. If we follow the European tradition (following Saussure 1916), the morpheme is a minimal sign: it has a form and it has a meaning, but contains nothing smaller with the same qualities. If we follow the North American tradition (following Bloomfield 1935), a morpheme is a minimal unit of grammatical analysis; again, it contains nothing with the same qualities. In both cases, the notion of the morpheme was modelled on the notion of the phoneme. In the European tradition, it might have bound variants, in the North American tradition it can be viewed as having allomorphs. The bound variants or allomorphs are variant forms which are restricted to particular environments. Consider the words *embark* and *entrain* meaning, respectively, 'to put onto a ship' and 'to put onto a train'. Each is made up of two forms, *em-* and *bark*, *en-* and *train*. The difference between *em-* and *en-* has nothing to do with the meaning, but the bilabial nasal appears before a bilabial consonant, while the alveolar nasal (at least in the written form) is the default case, occurring where there is no need for *em-*. Because of their distribution, the two do not contrast and they also share a meaning, and so can be seen as variants of the same abstract item. They are distinct morphs representing the same morpheme. (Actually, I have simplified a little, because we find *enmesh* more frequently than we find *emmesh*, because /nm/ is a permissible medial consonant sequence – e.g. in *enmity* – while /nb/ would not be possible in *enbark.) By the 1950s, the morpheme was a standard element of grammatical description, and worked brilliantly for a great deal of English word-formation (and morphology more generally in many languages), exploiting the very strong notion of allomorphy, very much in the structuralist tradition.

Scholars of the time knew that there were problems with this picture, but felt that the notion was valuable enough for it to be worthwhile working round the difficulties these caused. However, more and more problems were found, and as scholars wanted to write explicit grammars in the innovative Chomskyan tradition that became dominant in the 1960s, the problems became viewed as insuperable. This happened first in the description of inflectional systems, although similar examples from derivational morphology could be used to make the same points. The problems were raised and elaborated in works such as the hugely influential Matthews (1972) and Anderson (1992), and can be found summarized in works such as Anderson (2015) and Bauer (2016, 2019). The result was that by the 1990s, the morpheme as it had been presented by the structuralists was no longer considered to be a tenable theoretical notion, at least within theoretical morphological studies, though psycholinguists continued to work with the notion.

Although this is not the place to rehearse all the arguments against the morpheme, we can say briefly that we find instances where a single morph is associated with more than just one meaning, instances where a single meaning is associated with several morphs; we find instances where we have a recognizable morph, but the meaning usually associated with it is not associated with a particular word in which it occurs; we find morphs which do not appear to carry any meaning at all and meanings which do not appear to have any morph for them to be associated with; we have instances where a meaning appears to be associated with a process rather than with a form, and many instances where it is not clear how far we can stretch the notion of allomorphy. This cumulation of problems leads to difficulties in applying the notion of morpheme to many languages, but then the question becomes what can we replace the morpheme with.

In some instances, particularly in cases of complex inflectional systems, it seems to be possible to build up some morphs by the application of phonological rules (Matthews 1972). Meanings can be associated with whole words or sequences of words rather than with individual morphs (Matthews 1972, Booij 2010). In other cases, we might observe formal patterns which do not directly correlate with particular meanings, but which nevertheless tend to be meaning-bearing (Aronoff 1994) or, if not, at least important in morphological patterning and sometimes more diachronically stable than the individual words that instantiate them. Note in all this that while morphemes may not be used, morphs – the formal side of morphemes – tend to persist, and what is lost is the direct link between individual forms and individual meanings.

Ironically, against such a background, the study of word-formation in English, with its concentration of prefixes and suffixes, seems stuck on the idea of the morpheme. There is still a view that words are made up of formal elements, to each of which can be attributed a meaning or a function. This looks remarkably like analysis into morphemes except that there is recognition that not all morphs have meaning (the *-t-* in *dramatist* is either a meaningless extender or is part of an allomorph of *drama* which occurs before certain suffixes), that not all morphs have a consistent meaning (the *-er* in *dishwasher* can denote either a person or an instrument, although some less specific meaning may allow for a single gloss to cover both), we can have meaning spread over multiple morphs (as in *enliven* where prefix and suffix together provide the causative meaning) and more than one meaning in a single morph (as in *song*, which can be seen as containing the meaning of 'sing' as well as the meaning of 'noun') and we can have meanings not associated with any morph (as with the difference between the verb to *whisk* and the noun a *whisk*). That is, those who study word-formation seem more willing than those who study inflection to work round the problems associated with the morpheme rather than simply discarding the notion. Discussions which seem to assume a morpheme-like unit will also be found in this book.

Developments in semantic theory have also had a strong influence on the study of word-formation. The notion of prototype (Rosch 1973, Taylor 2003) has influenced the way in which we view not only the meanings of words, but also the way in which we envisage categories. For instance, we can now think of the suffix *-er* as having a prototypical meaning centring on the notion of agency (*discoverer*), but fading off into instruments (*sharpener*), experiencers (*lover*), locations (*diner*) and even patients (*keeper*) rather than as having a set of fundamentally unrelated meanings. Where categories are concerned, we can think of a class such as compounds having more central members and less central members, rather than being defined by a fixed set of criteria or tests. If *girl Friday* is a compound, it is not as central a compound as *flower-girl*, because *girl Friday* is left-headed (see further Chapter 13). An alternative is to see a category such as compound as a canonical category, again with more and less central members of the category (Corbett 2010). Within Cognitive Linguistics, the importance of figures of speech has been seen as central for the semantics of word-formation because so many words involve figures of speech. For instance, a *whirlybird* 'helicopter' is not literally a bird, but resembles a bird in that it can fly, a *jailbird* 'prisoner' is not literally a bird, but is like a budgerigar in that he or she is kept in a cage, and a *thunderbird* is not a bird because it is a mythical creature, once believed to cause thunder. Recognizing the figurative expressions for what they are makes it easier to explain the often complex meanings of words created by word-formation, as well as the meanings of simplex words.

Corresponding to these various developments, there have been many different theoretical approaches to morphological study. In the early 1960s, within Chomskyan generative grammar, morphology was seen as part of syntax, in line with the view of morphemes that was still current at the time. Lees (1960) provides an illustration of this general approach. Later (most obviously in Chomsky and Halle 1968, but much discussed before that date), some of the workings of morphology were subsumed in phonological rules, in a movement that eventually led to Lexical Phonology and Morphology. Viewing morphology as syntactic persists in Distributed Morphology (Halle and Marantz 1994 and a large amount of more recent work). This contrasts with a movement towards seeing morphology as an independent area of linguistics, not just part of other larger fields, a view which is made overt in the title of Aronoff (1994), but is also to be seen in a lot of works where the notion of morphological paradigm is given a central position, both in inflection and in derivation. This point of view is found in various theoretical positions starting with Bybee (1985) and is increasingly important today.

While this brief outline does not cover all the theoretical positions that have been taken over the last century or so (for more detailed coverage, see Stewart 2015), readers can expect to find individual scholars taking positions which call on several of these approaches in slightly different ways, and giving focus to different aspects of the ways in which word-formation can be dealt with. There is no consensus, but there is much to be learned from studies which take different perspectives on the topic.

1.4 Why Study Word-Formation in Particular?

We could ask why we study anything at all, from how earthworms mate to why the universe is expanding, and I imagine that the answer would be much the same: because it's fascinating and we are curious about how the universe works. One of the topics within the range that we could wonder about is why we should study language. Again, its fascination could be part of the answer, but we might have some extra reasons (just as there might be extra reasons for the study of anything). In the case of language, we could argue that one of the strangest things about human beings is not only that they communicate by means of language, but that it is hard to stop them talking! While other species undoubtedly communicate, the human communication system is far more complex than any other we understand, and it is definitional of human beings. We might be classified as *Homo loquens*. Studying language is therefore one way to try to understand part of what it is that makes us human. More than that, most of us speak more than one language, and those people who do not are at least aware that although language may be a part of what defines humankind, it is not always the same language, and that various languages may well be totally incomprehensible to people who have at least one language to help them communicate with others. Most of us, however many or how few languages we speak, will also be aware that if we cannot use language to communicate, our ability to communicate at all drops drastically. Such observations raise many questions, including: what do languages share? Are all languages really just dialects of Human? Or are they so radically different that knowing one is little help in learning another? Is it always possible to translate between languages? Can we learn Dog and can dogs understand Human (see Anderson 2004)?

Once we have decided to study language, we still have a huge problem: languages have so many properties that it is hard to know where to start studying them. Do we treat languages as organized sound (gesture in the case of sign languages), as words chained together, as a means of transferring meaning by having different ways of expressing a huge number of meanings, as a way of organizing human interaction in such a way as to promote a coherent society, as a way of reflecting the societal structures within which we operate, as some kind of code that keeps changing? Language has all those aspects. Reducing our focus to word-formation has some benefits as a way into this morass of complex interactions: it concerns words, which speakers of European languages at least think they have some understanding of; it deals not only with forms but also with meanings; although we can invent new words, most messages are made up of familiar ones, while most sentences (at least in academic discussions) are not at all familiar; and last but not least, words are fun. Many a comedian has asked questions like if a vegetarian eats vegetables, what does a humanitarian do, or if *sink*, *sank* and *sunk* are all related words, are *think*, *thank* and *thunk* related in the same way? Language is endlessly fascinating, and word-formation, quite apart from being interesting in its own right, makes a good entry point into the wider field of study.

1.5 This Book

Although this book is about word-formation, specifically about word-formation in English, it is not a textbook in the sense that it does not attempt to provide a systematic and thorough discussion of the topic. The title *Reflections* is intended to signify that it covers topics that I have found to be of particular interest in the fifty years I have been thinking and writing about the area, but also that the aim is to provide new insights or points of discussion, not just to provide a summary of the state of the art. The topics covered are loosely collected into thematic groupings, but are quasi-independent: the chapters can be read in isolation, although places where the individual chapters are linked are indicated, as they already have been above. Some matters which may appear minor are covered, some which may seem more important are not. But while topics which are vital to various theories about the way word-formation might work are covered, explanation of individual theories are in general not covered: theories come and go, but how word-formation is actually used lies at the heart of the theories.

Challenge

Find examples from English derivational morphology where the morpheme does not function in the way that is expected, as set out in this chapter. How important are these examples in the general scope of word-formation?

References

Anderson, Stephen R. (1992). *A-morphous Morphology*. Cambridge: Cambridge University Press.
  (2004). *Dr Dolittle's Delusion: Animals and the Uniqueness of Human Communication*. New Haven, CT: Yale University Press.
  (2015). The morpheme: Its nature and use. In Matthew Baermann (ed.), *The Oxford Handbook of Inflection*. Oxford: Oxford University Press, 11–33.
Aronoff, Mark. (1994). *Morphology by Itself*. Cambridge, MA: MIT Press.
Bauer, Laurie. (1983). *English Word-Formation*. Cambridge: Cambridge University Press.
  (2001). *Morphological Productivity*. Cambridge: Cambridge University Press.

(2016). Classical morphemics: Assumptions, extensions, and alternatives. In Andrew Hippisley & Gregory Stump (eds.), *The Cambridge Handbook of Morphology*. Cambridge: Cambridge University Press, 331–55.

(2019). *Rethinking Morphology*. Edinburgh: Edinburgh University Press.

Bloomfield, Leonard. (1935). *Language*. London: Allen & Unwin.

Booij, Geert. (2010). *Construction Morphology*. Oxford: Oxford University Press.

Bybee, Joan. (1985). *Morphology*. Amsterdam: Benjamins.

Chomsky, Noam & Morris Halle. (1968). *The Sound Pattern of English*. New York: Harper & Row.

Coates, Richard. (1987). Lexical morphology. In John Lyons, Richard Coates, Margaret Deuchar & Gerald Gazdar (eds.), *New Horizons in Linguistics 2*. London: Pelican, 103–21.

Corbett, Greville G. (2010). Canonical derivational morphology. *Word Structure* 3, 141–55.

Halle, Morris & Alex Marantz. (1994). Distributed Morphology and the pieces of inflection. In Kenneth Hale & Samuel J. Keyser (eds.), *The View from Building 20*. Cambridge, MA: MIT Press, 111–76.

Lees, Robert B. (1960). *The Grammar of English Nominalizations*. Bloomington: Indiana University Press.

Matthews, P.H. (1972). *Inflectional Morphology*. Cambridge: Cambridge University Press.

Rosch, Eleanor H. (1973). On the internal structure of perceptual and semantic categories. In T.E. Moore (ed.), *Cognitive Development and the Acquisition of Language*, New York: Academic Press, 111–44.

Saussure, Ferdinand de. (1916). *Cours de linguistique générale*. Paris: Payot.

Stewart, Thomas W. (2015). *Contemporary Morphological Theories*. Edinburgh: Edinburgh University Press.

Taylor, John. (2003). *Linguistic Categorization*. 3rd ed. Oxford: Oxford University Press.

Part I

Basic Questions

2 Reflections on the Background to the Study of Word-Formation

2.1 Introduction

To study word-formation is to investigate the way in which words are formed. But that does not allow us to say precisely what is included in word-formation. Although the word *cat* is made up of the phonemes /k/, /æ/ and /t/, we would probably not call this word-formation. So a fundamental question about word-formation is what it covers. Although there is a great deal of dispute as to how best to deal with word-formation in a grammar, there is probably rather less dispute as to what the problems facing an attempt to do so are. Many of these problems will be dealt with, in one way or another, later in the book. Here, the aim is simply to raise the issues.

2.2 Two Traditions

Word-formation has been studied in two main traditions, reflecting the way in which the study of linguistic structure as a whole has been discussed. There is the tradition of considering the patterns, exemplifying them, considering limits on them and what they mean. In relatively recent linguistic terminology, we might call such approaches 'structuralist', although many such discussions pre-date the era which we now think of as the time of structuralist linguistics, starting with Saussure. (We might alternatively use the term 'taxonomic', if this term had not been debased in the linguistics of the early 1960s.) Then there is a tradition of viewing the patterns of word-formation as the output of a series of formal rules. Such approaches go back to the precursors of Panini, and continue today in many formal models including the A-morphous Morphology of Anderson (1992) and Distributed Morphology (Halle and Marantz 1993). The fact that one of these examples focuses on the phonological make-up of words and the other sees words as being made up of elements that are linked by syntactic rules is not really relevant to this fundamental division. In principle, works in the structuralist and rule-based traditions can be translated into the other, though the focus is rather different. The formal mechanisms involved in the second of these approaches may vary considerably, and in doing so may capture different generalizations, but all such approaches share the view that word-formation is underlyingly regular and productive in that new words (new lexemes) can be created by means of the already known rules.

There is a third, more modern, tradition for studying language structures, though it does not translate easily into the other two. It is the tradition of Cognitive Linguistics, with various branches including Construction Grammar, Usage-Based Linguistics and Exemplar Grammar (for a useful introduction, see Bybee 2023). What these share is that they see the patterns of language emerging from the cognitive structures of the human brain and the way in which language is used by its speakers, and they see meaning as the central driver of linguistic structure. Where this influences the study of word-formation, it brings the focus onto networks of words and partial resemblances between words. For many working in this tradition, the use of nominalizations might be more important than the way in a which a particular affix forms nominalizations. This includes the importance of paradigms in various ways. Those who study constructions look at the ways in which sequences of elements are built up, and how their meanings may be idiosyncratic to the construction rather than derived entirely from the meanings of the smaller elements in the sequence.

Whichever of these traditions the individual scholar may wish to pursue, there are three questions which need to be answered before the description is undertaken: what is formed in word-formation? Is word-formation a coherent object of study? And what are the limits of word-formation? None of these is as simple as it might appear.

2.3 What Is a Word?

It is well known that we have no universal definition of what a word is (Bauer 2000, Dixon and Aikhenvald 2002, Hippisley 2015, Wray 2015). Neither do we have a definition of a word which will help us where English is concerned. Most authorities end up using a modified orthographic criterion: a word is surrounded by spaces or punctuation marks in a written text. Quite apart from the places where this does not give a reasonable outcome, it is back to front. As a general principle, we would expect that the place where we write the spaces should derive from the nature of the spoken language, not vice versa. Such a criterion gives a good practical guide, but one that started from the spoken language would be preferable. This is made more difficult, however, by the fact that phonological words and morphosyntactic words do not necessarily coincide – as well as by the fact that definitions for both are inconsistent in the literature (Aikhenvald et al. 2020). For example, for some scholars, prefixes are not part of the same phonological word as their bases, for others, some words like *brokenness* consist of two phonological words because of the geminate /nn/ which can occur only over morphological boundaries. From a semantic point of view, *on the up and up* ('continually improving') and *kick the bucket* ('die') seem to be single words, although the spelling system marks them as being made up of multiple words. And from an orthographic point of view, the fact that we can write *wordformation*, *word-formation* or *word formation* indicates that spaces are not necessarily reliably indicative of status. Where nouns and verbs are concerned, an inflectional marker (where there is one) typically shows the end of the word, but there are huge numbers of words where this does not apply, and care must be taken with *-ing* and *-ed* (or its irregular congeners) because it is not clear whether participles count as inflectional. There are also problems with items such as *ladies-in-waiting* where the inflection does not occur on the right-hand edge of the item, and so leaves it unclear as to whether this should be treated as a word or not. All of this provides a huge theoretical problem, which is rarely seen as a practical problem. That is because word-formation is defined in its own terms, without reference to the word as such.

2.4 Inflections versus Derivation

There is a long tradition of word-formation studies which sees word-formation as embracing derivation and compounding (and possibly some less regular minor patterns) but excluding inflection. Standard descriptive grammars of Indo-European languages, when they mention word-formation, tend to make such assumptions, and the notion is entrenched in the title of the classic text by Marchand (1969) (*The Categories and Types of Present-Day English Word-Formation*), which does not include inflectional morphology. There is a more recent tradition, in which word-formation involves all patterns (or all rules leading to patterns) of elements smaller than the word, including inflection (Baker and Hengeveld 2012: 23, Lieber 2022: 106). The difference hangs on the researcher's view of the split morphology hypothesis (Perlmutter 1988, Booij 1996). The split morphology hypothesis holds that inflection is distinct from (is split off from) derivation, and those who believe in split morphology see inflection as categorially different from derivation; those who reject split morphology do so on the basis that inflection and derivation have more in common than they have distinguishing them, so that they should be treated the same way in a grammar.

Arguments can be provided on both sides of the issue, and have important theoretical implications, but there does not seem to be any absolutely decisive factor which can be used to determine the answer. Some of the arguments are sketched below.

Against split morphology:

- Both inflectional and derivational morphology make use of the same set of formal processes (though not necessarily in any individual language – all

prefixes in English are derivational), processes such as prefixation, suffixation, apophony, reduplication.
- Although there are many criteria which have been presented for distinguishing between inflection and derivation (see, notably, Plank 1994), they are not always easy to apply, they do not always agree, and the borderline between them is often fuzzy – there is dispute in the literature as to whether the *-ly* that forms English adverbs is inflectional or derivational; the result is that there may be dispute as to whether individual processes in a given language are inflectional or derivational, and it may not be clear how to distinguish inflection from derivation in a given language, if it is possible at all (see Bauer and Bauer 2012 on Māori, for instance).
- There appear to be languages with morphological structures that do not distinguish inflection and derivation in any clear way.
- Many apparently inflectional markers can have uses which appear to be derivational, including plural markers in a language like English with *bellow* versus *bellows*, *glass* versus *glasses* ('spectacles'), *look* versus *looks*, and also including participial forms.

For split morphology:

- Without split morphology, there can be no notion of the lexeme, which is defined in terms of inflection, and which is a widely accepted notion in morphological studies as well as in lexicography (where the term 'lemma' is often used).
- All the criteria that distinguish between inflection and derivation lead us to believe that there is at least a canonical difference between them, because although they do not always agree, they do align in many instances.
- Although subsidiarily, all the arguments which lead to the establishment of the lexeme also lead to the adoption of the split morphology hypothesis.

2.5 The Limits of Word-Formation

The next question concerns the limits of word-formation. If derivation and compounding are at the core of word-formation, how far does it extend? On the one hand we have phonaesthemes (Firth [1930] 1965), which are pieces of phonology whose influence in the meaning of a word is diffuse, such as the /gl/ at the beginning of *glum* and *gloom* (see Section 17.1), at another extreme we have phrasal verbs like *look up* in *look up the answer*, which in English are usually treated as being at the intersection of syntax and idiomaticity. Somewhere between these extremes we have back-formation, clipping, conversion, reduplication, internal modification, acronyms, initialisms and possibly neoclassical compounds and closely related forms. Even within compounding, we may argue as to whether, for example, *Paris–Rome* in *the Paris–Rome flight* is or is not a compound (see Chapter 22). If we do not accept the split morphology hypothesis, we also have to consider inflection. And there are vast numbers of multiple word expressions (MWEs) such as *up to date*, *by and large*, *black and blue*, which in some ways are more like lexical items than like freely constructed syntactic phrases, whatever their etymological origins might be. Bauer (2019a) presents a view of word-formation in which all these things might be seen as relevant, but that view is intentionally provocative, and many, perhaps most, scholars would want to be more conservative in what word-formation deals with. Note that there is no claim here than any one answer is 'right' and others are 'wrong', merely that there are many possibilities, and that what is included may influence the form of the theory that is used to discuss such matters.

Another way in which scholars of word-formation have to determine what is and is not relevant to their study is in deciding what the limits are to a synchronic description of word-formation. Bauer (1983) (see also Bauer 2001) spends a lot of space discussing lexicalization and productivity: productivity is involved in whether and to what extent a morphological pattern can be extended to create new forms, and words which are established in the community but which have features (forms, meanings, etc.) which cannot be attributed to the word-formation pattern are lexicalized to some extent. (I have formulated this statement here in terms of patterns, but in Bauer 2001 it is formulated in terms of rules.) To use some well-discussed examples, *lady* (derived historically from elements meaning 'loaf kneader'), *Arabic* (with stress on the initial syllable despite stress normally falling on the syllable preceding the suffix *-ic*), *blackmail* (where *mail* used to mean 'coin' but no longer does), *bishopric* (where the suffix *-ric* does not occur except when attached to *bishop*), *depth* (where the suffix *-th* is not used any more to create new words and where the vowel of the base is not predictable) are all lexicalized in one way or another. The question is: which of these (if any) should be included in the synchronic description of English word-formation (or, to formulate in perhaps a more challenging way, should the synchronic rules of English word-formation allow the generation of any of these forms)? If such words are not part of the productive patterns of English, which is the implication of the challenge just issued, how should they be treated in a description of English and what, if any, part do such words have to play in the description of current English word-formation?

A certain amount of terminology will help with the discussion. Bauer (1983) introduces the term 'institutionalization'. A word is institutionalized when it is recognized in the speech community even though it is in principle in line with productive patterns and could be created by them. The word *hunter* is institutionalized as a 'person who kills wild animals for food', because the term is familiar in the community and could be created from *hunt + er* as a pattern or as a rule. The same is true of *hunter* meaning 'a horse used in hunting'. However, *hunter* is lexicalized in the sense 'pocket watch whose face is protected by a lid' because in the current state of the language we cannot relate that use to the elements *hunt + er*. Bauer (1983) also uses the term 'established' for words which are either lexicalized or institutionalized.

A word is analysable to the extent that the language specialist (perhaps the speaker of the language, though that is less clear) can see the elements which make it up and see that they might be relevant to the interpretation of the word. *Blackmail* is analysable in this sense: we may not know what *mail* is supposed to mean in *blackmail*, but we are not in doubt as to it being a relevant element in the make-up of the word.

A word is transparent to the extent that the linguist or speaker can see what the elements in the word are and what they mean, and thus how they contribute to the overall meaning of the word. *Warmth* is analysable and transparent, *health* might be analysable, but is not transparent, at least not for most speakers. This is despite the fact that *-th* is not productive, and thus *health* is not institutionalized. The borderline between analysable and transparent is fuzzy because individual speakers/analysts may differ on the extent to which, for instance, *filth* or *dearth* belong in either of the classes. The opposite of 'transparent' is 'opaque', and both terms are gradable in this usage.

Most textbook analyses of the patterns in English word-formation are based on transparent words. For example, Bauer et al. (2013: 196) provide a discussion of nominalizing *-al* (*arrival, denial, rehearsal*) despite saying that it is "minimally productive" and despite citing only one word which might suggest that it is actually productive and despite the fact that other authors (e.g. Dixon 2014: 345) claim that it is not productive. It produces (or used to produce) words that are transparent, however. Quirk et al. (1972: 1001) discuss the verbalizing suffix *-en* (*deaden, ripen, widen*), where the form and meaning are transparent, despite the fact that *-en* is probably no longer productive (Plag 1999: 218), the most recent widely accepted formation being the decidedly jokey *embiggen* from *The Simpsons*. Examples could be found in many other sources. It is not clear whether this is ever an overt policy in such books, but it makes sense in terms of students who wish to analyse words they come across: if a word is not analysable, it will not be clear that it is meaningful to look for elements in the word (think of *lady*); if it is not transparent (e.g. *tootle* listed by Marchand 1969), finding elements will not help the analysis much. The place where handbooks might look at analysable but not transparent words is where the relevant pattern is transparent in some instances and not in others. For example, the suffix *-th* might be discussed because of words like *warmth* and despite words like *dearth*.

But if this solution is a good practical one, it is less clear that it is a sound theoretical one. Parallels in syntax are hard to come by, but we would not write a rule of current English syntax which allows a preposition to be coordinated with an adjective (*in and pretty*) just because we have the expression *by and large* (historically this had a different analysis but it is difficult to justify it in current usage: *by and large* is lexicalized). If something is lexicalized, it can no longer be used in the creation of new forms (for one reason or another – a change of meaning in an element, a change in the patterns that the grammar accepts, and so on). Theoretically, a stronger position is that the current rules or patterns are only those which are still productive. In this position, there is no rule of *-th* suffixation (and thus no *-th* suffix) because it is not productive. Similarly, we can ignore the pattern illustrated by *spoilsport* and *dreadnought* because that particular compound pattern is no longer part of English morphology.

If we accept this position, it brings with it some immediate benefits. The most obvious one is that the scope of English word-formation shrinks considerably. We no longer need to worry about whether *-sion*, *-tion*, *-ion* are variants of the same underlying element (allomorphs), and if so what conditions their distribution, because the only productive nominalization marker from the set is *-ation* and the others are lexicalized. By the same token, we do not have to worry about the morphophonological rule which gives us the alternation found in *collide* and *collision*, because if the word *collision* is lexicalized we cannot generate it in the current state of the language, and, therefore, we do not have to worry about its phonology if that phonological form arises purely in connection with some lexicalized morphological process.

Another benefit is that such a principle draws a line between synchronic morphology and etymology: morphology deals with what is possible in the current state of the language, while etymology deals with the history of words and how they came to have their various meanings. Etymological information may have little to do with the current meaning of the word, as when the English word *nice* has a Latin etymon meaning 'ignorant'. On the other hand, the etymology may make clear precisely how the current meaning of an extant word, but one no longer governed by current morphological patterns or rules, came to be. For example, etymologically speaking, we can recognize an old *-er* suffix in words like *chatter* and *stammer* which indicates repeated action.

At the same time, there are some costs. The most obvious of these can be seen in the status of a word like *collision*. The straightforward way to deal with such words would be simply to list them in the lexicon. This would then seem to imply that *collide* and *collision* are not linked, and that, in fact, there is enormous redundancy in the lexicon because the meaning embedded in related words has to be specified more than once. If we want to link them, we have to have recourse to some separate mechanism, something like the via rules of Natural Generative Phonology (Hooper 1976) or the redundancy rules of Jackendoff (1975), which is not the same as the normal rules of morphology and phonology. To some extent, we may be able to shrug this off; we already have forms in the lexicon with redundant semantics – forms like *dog/canine*, *horse/equine*, *tree/arboreal* (*canine* must repeat the semantic information associated with *dog*, even though there is no formal link). But not all scholars will be willing to accept such a large increase in memorized material at the expense of so much computed material, even if we know that speakers often have dual access to apparently morphologically complex words, both by whole-word access and through computation of meaning from form (Stemberger and MacWhinney 1986, Vannest et al. 2005).

For the sake of the argument, let us assume that we accept the position that only productive processes can be part of morphology. However much it may sound like a reasonable hypothesis, it strikes a number of practical problems.

Where does the morphologist get data on the productivity of processes? Although the *Oxford English Dictionary* (*OED*) makes some attempt at covering all of English, no other English dictionary gets close. Even the *OED* has problems. One of these is that it does not usually list words for which it does not have evidence of repeated use in the community. While a large number of low-frequency forms created with a particular morphological process is usually seen as primary evidence of the productivity of that process (Bauer 2001: 150), the *OED*'s methodology inevitably hides some of the relevant evidence.

For this reason, as well as others, many linguists use corpora, preferably large ones, as sources of data. Corpora allow rare examples of relevant formations to be found, but bring with them their own problems. One problem is the nature of the examples uncovered. Of course, they tend to be a random sample of possible formations, but it is frequently unclear whether the words formed are genuine usages of word-formation as language use, or whether they illustrate deliberate jokes on the part of the writer – puns, deliberate references to other words or expressions, indicators, in fictional texts, of a character's ignorance or status. In principle, we might think, this is unlikely to be a problem: the value of corpus data is to find patterns, including patterns that the researcher was not aware of, rather than to find rare examples of unlikely formations. To a large extent, this is true, but in cases of marginal productivity, whether a particular morphological process is used at all may be important.

We can consider a genuine example. Bauer et al. (2013) use large corpora to find data on which to base their description. When it comes to negative prefixes, they find surprising data. The overuse of *un-*, as the most productive negative prefix, is expected, as we can already find it in widespread usages such as *untypical* (partly replacing an earlier *atypical*) or *undeterminable* for *indeterminable*. But the discovery of many instances where *in-* appears to replace *un-* is unexpected: forms such as *inbearable, inbelievable, inintelligent, incertainty*. Even less expected are cases where the orthographic allomorphy of *in-* is not observed, with examples like *inbalance, inperfections, inprecision, inprescribable* (Bauer et al. 2013: 361). Here the corpus examples seem to indicate

2 Background to the Study of Word-Formation

productivity of the *in-* prefix, where previous authors had claimed it to be non-productive, but they also appear to show the breakdown of the expected allomorphy. The breakdown of the allomorphy could be because English often has a morphophonemic writing system, and one place where this shows in the writing of <unkind> rather than *<ungkind> (although [ŋ] was an allophone of /n/ at the time when the spelling was established); we also usually find <enmesh> rather than <emmesh>, which would follow the expected form if a following bilabial automatically gives rise to [m]. Note, moreover, that what was found in the corpus was not a single form, but a series of forms, sufficient to look like evidence of something new. However, one factor casts doubt on all of this: on a typewriter keyboard <m> is adjacent to <n> and <u> is adjacent to <i> – this suggests that any of these forms could easily be typographical errors caused by the nature of the technology. Since we cannot know, the status of the corpus data is thrown into doubt. This is an extreme example, but does indicate that we have to be careful with apparently clear corpus examples.

In a wider sense, whatever our source of data, it may not be clear just what indicates productivity. Consider the following examples.

> I have not got the true egocentricity of the true artist in blonde-ishment. (Jane Duncan. 1959. *My Friend Muriel*. London: Macmillan, p. 131)

> "they can wipe up any spilth". *Spilth* was a word coined by Russell, or so they believed. How the language had managed without it, they couldn't imagine. (Rebecca Tope. 2018. *The Stavely Suspect*. London: Allison and Busby, p. 206)

> the apparent safety of the now ubiquitous rideshare was just that – an apparency. (Elizabeth Breck. 2020. *Anonymous*. New York: Crooked Lane, p. 21)

> the place seemed poorer than he'd expected, since state capitals were usually stuffed with well-paid bureaucrats. Maybe, he thought, Delaware didn't well-pay its bureaucrats. (John Sandford. 2020. *Masked Prey*. New York: Putnam, p. 183)

I would suggest that none of these is evidence of productivity. Duncan's *blonde-ishment* might be a Scotticism, but rather it seems to have been formed on *blandishment*, as a joke, and *-ment* is usually added to verbs rather than adjectives. *Spilth*, perhaps based on *filth*, does fit the pattern of *-th* formations, but this is a very isolated example of the use of the suffix. *Apparency* fits all the patterns, and is listed in Marr (2008) as archaic. Bauer et al. (2013: 197) list some unfamiliar examples of *-cy* (most of them are either established or have final *-cy* instead of the expected *-ce*, where the two alternate without motivation), but there is little evidence of productivity rather than rarity. *Well-pay* as a back-formation from *well-paid* is not a typical pattern of back-formation, although other verbs are created by back-formation from bases including a past participle.

Cannon (1987) provides an analysis of the items in a set of dictionaries of new words that appeared in the 1970s and 1980s, looking at the macro-patterns of innovation that are registered in such works. Unfortunately, this particular genre of dictionary seems to have gone into decline since then, so that equivalent studies based on later data are not possible, although the *OED* can be searched for words which are first attested in or after a particular year. Despite many criticisms that can be made about Cannon's interpretation of his sources, his results are of interest.

Given what has been said here about word-formation, we might expect Cannon to have found most of the new words are compounds, then instances of prefixation and suffixation with established affixes, then a mixed set of clippings, blends, back-formations and neoclassical compounds, perhaps with a handful of instances of reduplication.

But this is not what Cannon finds, as is shown by his summary (Cannon 1987: 279). He does find that compounds are the most frequent type of formation: 29.5 per cent of the words investigated, most of which are nouns. Prefixations and suffixations provide only 21.6 per cent of the formations. Given that number, the proportion of shortenings (including abbreviations, acronyms, back-formations and blends) at 18 per cent seems much higher than might be expected, 14.4 per cent of new meanings for existing forms (very often figurative extensions, such as *lifer* extended from a prisoner to someone serving in the army) also seems high and so does 7.5 per cent of borrowings – a category that word-formation specialists ignore, though it is familiar to lexicographers and lexicologists. In comparison, only 4.1 per cent of the words were instances of conversion, which seems low. Even if the figures cannot be completely trusted (*Spaceship Earth* is cited as an abbreviation of the title of a book *Operating Manual for Spaceship Earth*), the proportions given by Cannon raise questions about the way in which vocabulary is increased, and suggest that word-formation is less important than morphologists tend to think.

Another way to approach the same question of the extent to which word-formation is important in English, is to consider the most frequently encountered words of English. The first 10,000 most frequent words in the British National Corpus (Davies 2004–) were considered. The first thousand, the third thousand, the fifth thousand, the seventh thousand and the ninth thousand were analysed. The number of clearly prefixed words, the number of clearly suffixed words and the number of compounds were counted (if more than one formation-type was present, the external one in the word was counted). Also counted, but in a separate category, were the number of words that might be considered morphologically simplex, the number of words that are morphologically complex, but in French (*government*), Latin (*introduce*) or Greek (*epiglottis*), and the number of direct loans from other languages which might be considered morphologically simplex in English, whatever their origins. Instances of abbreviations and inflected forms were noted, but are not reported here, because there were relatively few. These numbers must be taken with a large pinch of salt, since borderline cases abound and a different count could come up with different answers: for example, words like *output* were considered to be compounds, not instances of prefixation; words like *preponderance* were considered to be instances of suffixation rather than learned morphology. Nevertheless, they should give a first approximation to a view of the sources of new words. First, the number of examples of English word-formation are considered. Although the numbers in each cell are presented as number of attestations, adding a decimal point allows them to be read as percentages since each is a count out of 1,000. The numbers involved are of interest, as well as the way they change depending on the frequency of the words in use.

	1–1,000	2,001–3,000	4,001–5,000	6,001–7,000	8,001–9,000	Total/5,000
Compounds	9	25	38	56	55	183
Prefixes	32	31	63	63	93	282
Suffixes	70	138	116	154	110	588
Total	111	194	217	273	258	1,053

Overall, around 25 per cent of words are morphologically complex, with more in the less frequent words. This contrasts with the number of words which are simplex, either because they are monomorphic or because they are loans which cannot be analysed in English.

	1–1,000	2,001–3,000	4,001–5,000	6,001–7,000	8,001–9,000	Tota/5,000
Simplex	661	551	432	338	273	2,255
Loans	10	47	97	137	180	471
Total	671	606	529	475	453	2,726

This leaves the words that are complex in one of the major donor languages for English. Although most of these come directly from the donor languages, some have been formed in later usage within English (consider *telephone* which was not a word needed by the Greeks!).

	1–1,000	2,001–3,000	4,001–5,000	6,001–7,000	8,001–9,000	Total/5,000
Learned morphology	182	218	211	201	251	1,063

This means that learned morphology is just as important in numerical terms for speakers and learners of English as native morphology. The learned morphology is not necessarily as informative as the English morphology, for example, *induce* 'lead in' will take a lot more explanation than *inlay* will require, and to cover all learned morphology will require information from at least three languages (Greek, Latin and French – for example, *antagonize*, *educate* and *department*, respectively), some languages being used more in some domains than in others. Nevertheless, the importance of this aspect of English word-formation should not be underestimated.

We can also ask what formations count as word-formation. For instance, does expletive insertion as in *absobloodylutely* and *kangafuckingroo* count as word-formation? It has been treated as such by, for example, Aronoff (1976) and Bauer (1983), and it has the potential to throw light on the way in which words can be constructed, but as a case of what is more widely known as marginal morphology (Dressler 2000) or expressive morphology (Zwicky and Pullum 1987) its status as a part of word-formation is in question. In fact, despite these labels, even its status as morphology might be questioned: is *kangafuckingroo* simply a syntactic alternative to *fucking kangaroo*, or is it genuinely morphological? The spelling as it has been used here might suggest a single word (and therefore morphology), but it is often hyphenated, just like *this-person-is-a-jerk attitude* (Bauer et al. 2013) which does not necessarily imply that *person* is not a word in that expression. In a different way, we might query the status of initialisms such as *CID* 'Criminal Investigation Department', *FBI* 'Federal Bureau of Investigation', *imho* 'in my humble opinion', *lol* 'laugh out loud', *SAS* 'Special Air Service', *YHA* 'Youth Hostels Association'. Each of these represents some kind of syntactic string, though users may not always be aware of what the individual letters stand for. They are word-like in that they are fixed expressions for a given content, sentence-like in that their meaning can be unpacked into a syntactic unit, and like neither in that they are spelled out as individual letters. It may also be relevant to consider whether an initialism is a word when it is synonymous with a syntactic phrase.

We can also ask about constructions which may span or cross the divide between word-formation and syntax. The obvious relevant formations here are phrasal verbs. In English, these are typically treated as syntactic constructions, while in German apparently comparable constructions are treated as morphological constructions. In both cases the direct object can interrupt the verb + particle (something that seems typical of syntactic constructions):

> I call my girlfriend up every day.
> Ich rufe meine Freundin jeden Tag an ['I call my girlfriend every day up']

In German, though, the infinitive form of the verb is *anrufen* (a single word) while in English the infinitive is *call up* (a sequence of two orthographic words). This seems to make the distinction; but if we do not think of words as orthographic units, we might argue for a parallel treatment between the English and the German constructions.

2.6 Are There Rules of Word-Formation?

The question of whether there are rules of word-formation can be answered either way if we define our terms appropriately. For example, if we ask whether *gutcat* is a compound of English, we might answer that it is not, because it is a rule of English compounds that the superordinate terms must appear on the right, so the word must be *catgut* (either that, or the word must mean something else). In saying so, we assume that we are dealing with a rule, and so rules exist. On the other hand, if we ask whether *Congolese* is a good word of English, we might answer that although it is used, it does not seem to follow any rule of English because the <l> is inexplicable. At this point we must assume that the creation of words is not (or is not always) constrained by rules.

At a more general level, we might ask whether word-formation operates in a rule-governed way, just like syntax. (The "just like syntax" part of this might be cheating a little, since it is not entirely clear that syntactic rules always work in the way that we expect linguistic rules to operate.) This is a much bigger question, and correspondingly more difficult to answer. It will be discussed at various points in this book. But it assumes that grammatical structures are created by a series of rules which are always available and cannot be circumscribed by the presence of individual words, sounds or word-parts, and that there is freedom to insert words into the grammatical structures thus created. That is, if we have a sentence like

>   I have to see a man about a dog.

it must also be possible to have a grammatically equally good sentence of the form

>   My uncle's father has to mutter a tower about this shilling.

Trained linguists may have no problem with this (though naive speakers probably will), but when it comes to parallel discussions about the availability of words, intuitions (even among linguists) differ, and it is harder to reach a consensus. It is not clear whether we can discard the metaphor of a rule in word-formation, or whether we have to modify our understanding of what a rule means in word-formation in some principled way. If we want to replace the notion of a rule, then we have to replace it with something, and we do not have anything that is as widely understood in the linguistic community or as theoretically well developed as the rule.

2.7   Are the Elements of Words Meaningful?

At first sight, the question of whether word elements are meaningful has a self-evident answer. If we take a word like *cats*, we can split it into two elements, of which the first means 'cat' and the second means 'more than one', and *cats* means 'more than one cat'. If we take a word like *bookshelf*, it means 'a shelf for books' and the meanings of *book* and *shelf* are involved in that overall meaning – though if we are careful not to cheat, we might ask why it is not *books-shelf* since it is for more than one book, and how we know it is for books and not, say, made out of books, like *metal shelf*.

But those who have seen the TV series *The Wire* may recall that a *lake trout* is a sea-fish (not a fresh-water fish) and is not a kind of trout. As one of the characters in the series comments: "No lake, no trout". Such examples are commoner than we might think.

> *buttercup* is not a hyponym of *cup*; *foxglove* is not a hyponym of *glove*; *glowworm* is not a hyponym of *worm*; *hedge sparrow* is not a hyponym of *sparrow*; *sea wolf* is not a hyponym of *wolf*; *starfish* is not a hyponym of *fish*

> *butterfly* has little if anything to do with butter; *catgut* does not come from a cat; a *cherry birch* has nothing to do with cherries; *dogwood* does not appear to have anything to do with dogs; a *wheatear* ('bird sp.') has nothing to do with wheat (its name seems to be a corruption of an earlier form of 'white arse')

> a *howler* 'very funny joke' does not howl; a *reefer* 'marijuana cigarette' (no longer current) does not reef; a *sleeper* on a railway track does not sleep

> "What I don't get", she was saying, "is where they get off calling this Long Island Iced Tea. There must be half a dozen different kinds of booze in it, but is there any tea at all?"
> "You're asking the wrong person."
> "No tea", she decided. (Lawrence Block. 2000. *Hit List*. London: Orion, p. 138)

> I collected Martin's car for the slow slog to Freddie's place, wondering for the ten thousandth time why they call it 'rush hour' when you can't move faster than a crawl. (Sarah Paretsky. 2013. *Critical Mass*. New York: Putnam, p. 278)

> "He deadheaded to Rome for two days and is now back in London'
> 'Deadheaded?" Gershwin asked.
> "Taking a flight but not working it." (J.A. Kerley. 2014. *The Memory Killer*. London: HarperCollins, p. 35)

> And now I come to think of it, I haven't a dashed clue what an eave is either. And how do you drop them? (Alexis Hall. 2022. *A Lady for a Duke*. London: Piatkus, p. 213, with reference to *to eavesdrop*)

The first set of words above are typically classed as exocentric compounds, but bahuvrihi compounds like *redhead* ('one who has a red head – by virtue of having red hair') have not been included in this list. That is, there are several ways in which compounds might not denote a hyponym of their head element, which often makes it look as though the elements of words are not meaningful.

Another source of apparently meaningless elements in English word-formation is unique morphs. Unique morphs are morphs that occur in only one place in the linguistic system. *Vim* used to be one such, occurring only in *vim and vigour*, though modern usage allows it rather wider usage, *kith* is another, appearing only in *kith and kin*.

> They cheered and drank, knocking it back with vim. (Karen Swan. 2020. *The Hidden Beach*. London: Macmillan, p. 107)

When unique morphs are elements in words it is typically because what was once a recognizable element has, due to phonetic change or dialectal variation, become unrecognizable, and has lost its meaning as an independent unit. A classic example is *cran* in *cranberry*. *Cran* is etymologically a variant of *crane* (the bird), though the meaning link is now lost, despite the closely related spelling. Many linguists call unique morphs 'cranberry morphs' because of this example, although other berry names might have provided better examples: *bilberry* and *whortleberry* (dialectal names for the same plant and its fruit) now contain unique morphs, and the link between *whortleberry* and *hurtle* and *hurt* is completely lost. *Whort*, like *rasp* in *raspberry*, was once the name of the fruit, without any *berry* element. Other examples are provided by *cobweb, fenugreek, lukewarm* and *dishevelled*. The *cob* element in *cobweb*, also found in *attercop* (now familiar from the fiction of J.R.R. Tolkien), is related to German *Kopf* 'head'. With the berry names in particular, what the unique morph does is distinguish one kind of berry from another. In this regard, such elements are no different from the *goose* in *gooseberry* (which has nothing to do with geese) and the *locust* in *locustberry* (which does not appear to have anything to do with locusts): they are simply names which allow contrasting types to be named. A *cranberry*, on this reading, is just something we can call a *berry* which is not a *strawberry, raspberry, gooseberry* and so on. Finally, note the prefix in *midwife*, which is not related etymologically to *mid* from *middle*, but to the German preposition *mit*, Danish and Swedish *med*, 'with'. The problem here is common enough that some mechanism or set of mechanisms is required to account for such instances, even if they are relevant only in a minority of words overall.

2.8 Many of the Fundamental Principles of Word-Formation Do Not Function

Bauer et al. (2013: 635–9) draw attention to the fact that many of the principles which have been suggested as providing overall constraints in word-formation do not work as they are supposed to, or at least, do not work all the time. In some cases, it is a matter of just what the constraint is supposed to do, or a matter of how the constraint (or its field of application) is to be defined, in other cases, the proposed rule appears not to hold true. Some of these will be discussed in later chapters, such as blocking (see Chapter 5) and the right-hand head rule (see Chapter 13). Some can be discussed here briefly.

Botha (1984: 137) proposes the no-phrase constraint, phrased as "Lexical rules do not apply to syntactic phrases to form morphologically complex words". It has been pointed out by many that the name of this constraint appears to disprove the constraint, as do many phrasal compounds such as *There is a sort of Oh-what-a-wicked-world-this-is-and-how-I-wish-I-could-do-something-to-make-it-better-and-nobler expression about Montmorency* (Jerome K. Jerome, *Three Men in a Boat*, 1889). However, if such expressions are taken not to involve lexical rules or not to create morphologically complex words it might be that the constraint holds. The constraint certainly needs to be clarified.

Lieber (1981: 173) provides the repeated morph constraint, phrased as "No word formation process ... can apply to its own output". This blocks sequences of identical affixes, such as we might find in *doer-upperer, mini-mini-dress, re-reread, sub-subcontractor*. We would also need to ask whether having a compound as an element within another compound counts as a process applying to its own output. At the same time, the constraint is not without merit, since the exceptions are rare, and are usually pragmatically predictable. Again, greater clarification is required.

Aronoff (1976: 48) provides the unitary base hypothesis, namely that "A W[ord] F[ormation] R[ule] will never operate on either this or that" the bases it can operate on are "always unique". Presumably a unique base type could be, for instance, a base which is either a noun or an adjective, since noun and adjective share the feature [+N] in Chomsky's (1970) classification of word classes, and it could be, for example, a noun denoting a human being. Just what is included and what is excluded as a possible unitary description may not be entirely clear. However, the prefix *un-* in English can attach to verbs (*undo*), to adjectives (*unkind*) and to nouns (*unperson*), and this would seem to be excluded.

Corresponding, in some ways, to the unitary base hypothesis, we also have the unitary output hypothesis (Scalise 1984: 137) which "does not allow a particular phonological form to be considered a single affix if it produces outputs with different category labels or different semantics". That is, the suffix *-er* that is used in *smaller* cannot be the same suffix as the *-er* that produces *defender* because the *-er* in *smaller* creates adjectives, the *-er* that produces *defender* creates nouns, and the meanings in the two cases are different. As far as this goes, it seems very reasonable: we have to say we have two homophonous affixes $-er^1$ and $-er^2$, which attach to different bases and have different meanings. But now consider the cases with *un-* cited above. They do not produce categories, they just fail to change categories, but the *un-* in *undo* creates a verb with a reversative meaning, the *un-* in *unkind* carries a negative meaning and the *un-* in *unperson* creates a meaning which denies the suitability of the label used as a base (Bauer et al. 2013: 364–6). Are these differences sufficient for the constraint to be called into force and for us to say that we must have three different prefixes? And if not (which is the usual position taken by scholars) why not? Or, if we consider the suffix *-er* in *defender*, that in *diner* ('place where one can eat') or that in *scratcher* ('type of lottery ticket'), do the different meanings of 'agent', 'location' and 'patient' mean that we should say that we have three suffixes here (and if not, why not)? Finally consider the English prefix *a-* in words such as *alike* and *askew*. Most of these words (though not all) can be adjectives (*The twins are very alike*, *Her hat was askew*) or adverbs (*Treat all your children alike*, *The picture hung askew*). Does that mean that we should say that we have a^1- creating adjectives and a^2- creating adverbs or not? All these examples show that matters are not necessarily simple.

There may also be other criteria which can be useful in determining whether homophonous forms are a single affix or not (Bauer 2003: 146–52): whether they show the same allomorphy, whether they are both/all available, whether they potentiate the same subsequent affixation, and so on.

Aronoff (1976: 21) also introduces the word-based hypothesis, requiring that "A new word is formed by applying a regular rule to a single already existing word". Again, this may be a definition of regular word-formation processes, or it could be intended as a constraint on how word-formation operates. If the latter, it probably fails, for instance with blends which, at the time Aronoff was writing, were considered to be irredeemably irregular but have now been found to have a great deal of regularity in their formation (see e.g. Lappe 2007). If it is a definition, it excludes some things which others might wish to include under word-formation (see Bauer 1980).

Beard (e.g. 1995) proposes a separation constraint, that is that the phonological part of word-formation (e.g. affixation) should be kept separate from the semantic part of word-formation. Such a position allows generalizations over the semantics of nominalizations, for example, without having to restate them separately for *-ation*, *-ure*, *-ment* and so on. I suspect that this has not gained greater adherence because there is no generally accepted principle to allow its implementation. However, Bauer (2019b) distinguishes between formal paradigms and functional paradigms, which allows a similar consideration from a different point of view.

The surprise with all these proposed principles/constraints/hypotheses is not that there are so many of them, nor that they require further specification or even replacement. The surprise is that there is not more discussion of them in the literature, at least defending them as default expectations in word-formation, and considering how they relate to what the linguist is supposed to do with those parts of lexical creativity that they exclude.

2.9 Is Word-Formation Necessarily Morphological?

The general view of morphology is that it divides into three major areas: compounding, derivation and inflection. These are the three main ways of creating new words (in one sense or another), and morphology is distinguished from syntax because it deals with the internal structure of words rather than with the ordering of words in sentences. Of these three branches, word-formation is seen as a cover term for compounding and derivation, while inflection is seen as more syntactic, in the sense that it marks the function of words within the sentence. All of this, of course, can be questioned (see Section 2.4 on the division between inflection and derivation, for instance). One of the reasons why it might be questioned is that there are borderline issues between the three areas mentioned here. Sometimes the borderline issues are concerned with diachronic change. For instance, the derivational suffix *-dom* in *kingdom* stems historically from a word corresponding to modern *doom* so that a compound has become a derivative, and the same is true of the suffix *-ric* in *bishopric*, which is etymologically related to the German word *Reich* 'empire'. The other way round, the increasing modern use of *ism* as a word in its own right implies that words like *eclecticism*, usually seen as derivatives, could now be seen as compounds. For the borderline between inflection and derivation, there is dispute in the literature as to whether the *-ly* that creates adverbs like *thinly*, *wisely* is inflectional or derivational (or, indeed, whether the question has been misleadingly formulated).

More generally, though, there are many things which might count as new words which are not created by processes that are normally thought of as morphological. These include acronyms like *scuba* (from *Self-Contained Underwater Breathing Apparatus*) and *laser* (from *Light Amplification by Stimulated Emission of Radiation*), blends like *spork* (from *spoon + fork*) and *Chunnel* (from *Channel + tunnel*) – and for some authorities these two examples illustrate different phenomena – and clipping as in *phone* (from *telephone*), *photo* (from *photograph*) and *flu* (from *influenza*). Bauer (2019a) presents an argument for seeing all these types, and others, as being part of word-formation, but such a position is very controversial.

We also find things which might be considered words or might be considered pieces of syntax. If *artist in residence* is a piece of syntax (even that is an open question), then can *lady-in-waiting* be a word, or must it also be a syntactic construction, and what about *Middleton-in-Teesdale*? Such questions extend to a much wider range of multiword expressions from *How are you doing?* and *So it goes* to *Rain cats and dogs*.

Finally, we should consider figures of speech. When people started using the form *crown* to mean not a head ornament but the government, a new way of speaking was inaugurated. We might argue as to whether the two meanings of *crown* are a matter of polysemy or homonymy, but *crown* can now be used with verbs like *decide* as well as with expressions such as *is made of*. Is this word-formation? The most general interpretation is that it is not, but lexicographers list new meanings alongside new forms when looking at lexical innovation.

Such questions can be resolved by stipulation, but it would be preferable to have some motivated position for including or excluding the various types and circumscribing the area of word-formation (see Chapter 7).

2.10 Unpredictability

Wherever we look in word-formation, it seems that there is a great deal of unpredictability. Rules work well in describing some of the formations we wish to term instances of word-formation, but not all. In some cases, the meaning of elements is directly relevant to the meaning of the formed word, but again not in all. Some constraints seem to work well much of the time, but not all of the time. A *dishwasher* can be a person or a machine, but a *car washer* does not seem to be institutionalized as either. Even if we are familiar with individual letters from a word being used to make a new word (if it is, then, a new word), the expression *on the QT* (from *on the quiet* and meaning 'secretly') is an unusual type of formation. At every stage, we have to ask whether the unexpected is just the way that word-formation works or whether it means that certain formations cannot really be considered as a part of word-formation; we have to ask whether the unpredictable formation should be ignored or taken to be part of the range of constructions that word-formation deals with; we have to ask whether our ways of building such material into a grammar have to be flexible enough to allow for the diversity we find. The more we examine the detail, the more the apparently odd turns out to be more predictable that we thought (see Lappe 2007 for an excellent case in point). So there may be reasons for attempting to extend our field of study beyond the blandly regular. But at some point we seem to hit the irredeemably unpredictable, and we have to decide what to do with that when we meet it.

2.11 Conclusion

What counts as word-formation is controversial, how word-formation is to be described is controversial, whether word-formation exists in a different module of the grammar from syntax is controversial, and how data is to be collected to prove productivity is controversial. The inevitable outcome is that anything that is done to describe word-formation will be controversial in some way. Most of the questions that have been raised here are matters of choice for the researcher, which should ideally be clarified (justified to the extent that is possible) as a preliminary to work in the field. The only place where I think that a decision is really central to the topic, is that I believe that the distinction between word-formation and etymology should be drawn on the boundaries of productivity, even though such a position brings with it serious problems of determining what is productive, particularly in borderline cases.

Challenge

Make a case either supporting the division made here between synchronic morphology and etymology or rejecting it. If you reject the difference in the way that it is sketched here, how do morphology and etymology fit into your view of how we should model word-formation? Do you have an alternative way of delimiting synchronic morphology (or, if not, what kinds of argument might be used to support such a position)?

References

Aikhenvald, Alexandra Y., R.M.W. Dixon & Nathan M. White. (2020). The essence of 'word'. In Alexandra Y. Aikhenvald, R.M.W. Dixon & Nathan M. White (eds.), *Phonological Word and Grammatical Word*. Oxford: Oxford University Press, 1–24.
Anderson, Stephen R. (1992). *A-morphous Morphology*. Cambridge: Cambridge University Press.
Aronoff, Mark. (1976). *Word Formation in Generative Grammar*. Cambridge, MA: MIT Press.
Baker, Anne & Kees Hengeveld. (2012). *Linguistics*. Malden, MA: Wiley.
Bauer, Laurie. (1980). In the beginning was the word. *Te Reo* 23, 73–80.
    (1983). *English Word-Formation*. Cambridge: Cambridge University Press.
    (2000). Word. In G. Booij, C. Lehmann & J. Mugdan (eds.), *Morphology: An International Handbook of Inflection and Word-Formation*. Berlin: de Gruyter, 247–57.
    (2001). *Morphological Productivity*. Cambridge: Cambridge University Press.
    (2003). *Introducing Linguistic Morphology*. 2nd ed. Edinburgh: Edinburgh University Press.
    (2019a). *Rethinking Morphology*. Edinburgh: Edinburgh University Press.
    (2019b). Notions of paradigm and their value in word-formation. *Word Structure* 12, 153–75.
Bauer, Laurie & Winifred Bauer. (2012). The inflection–derivation divide in Māori and its implications. *Te Reo* 55, 3–24.
Bauer, Laurie, Rochelle Lieber & Ingo Plag. (2013). *The Oxford Reference Guide to English Morphology*. Oxford: Oxford University Press.

Beard, Robert. (1995). *Lexeme-Morpheme Base Morphology*. Albany: State University of New York Press.
Booij, Geert. (1996). Inherent versus contextual morphology inflection and the split morphology hypothesis. *Yearbook of Morphology 1995*, 1–16.
Botha, Rudolf P. (1984). *Morphological Mechanisms*. Oxford: Pergamon.
Bybee, Joan. (2023). What is usage-based linguistics? In Manuel Díaz-Campos & Sonia Balasch (eds.), *The Handbook of Usage-Based Linguistics*. Hoboken, NJ: Wiley, 9–29.
Cannon, Garland. (1987). *Historical Change and English Word-Formation*. New York: Lang.
Davies, Mark. (2004–). *British National Corpus* (from Oxford University Press). Available online at www.english-corpora.org/bnc/.
Dixon, R.M.W. (2014). *Making New Words*. Oxford: Oxford University Press.
Dixon, R.M.W. & Alexandra Y. Aikhenvald. (2002). Word: A typological framework. In Robert M.W. Dixon & Alexandra Y. Aikhenvald (eds.), *Word: A Cross-Linguistic Typology*. Cambridge: Cambridge University Press, 1–40.
Dressler, Wolfgang U. (2000). Extragrammatical vs. marginal morphology. In Ursula Doleschal & Anna M. Thornton (eds.), *Extragrammatical and Marginal Morphology*. Munich: Lincom, 1–10.
Firth, J.R. ([1930] 1965). Speech. In *The Tongues of Men and Speech*. Oxford: Oxford University Press, 139–211.
Halle, Morris & Alec Marantz. (1993). Distributed morphology and the pieces of inflection. In Kenneth Hale & Samuel J. Keyser (eds.), *View from Building 20*, Cambridge, MA: MIT Press, 111–76.
Hippisley, Andrew. (2015). The word as a universal category. In John R. Taylor (ed.), *The Oxford Handbook of the Word*. Oxford: Oxford University Press, 246–69.
Hooper, Joan B. (1976). *An Introduction to Natural Generative Phonology*. New York: Academic Press.
Jackendoff, Ray. (1975). Morphological and semantic regularities in the lexicon. *Language* 51, 639–71.
Lappe, Sabine. (2007). *English Prosodic Morphology*. Dordrecht: Springer.
Lieber, Rochelle. (1981). *On the Organization of the Lexicon*. Bloomington: Indiana University Linguistics Club.
  (2022). *Introducing Morphology*. 3rd ed. Cambridge: Cambridge University Press.
Marchand, Hans. (1969). *The Categories and Types of Present-Day English Word-Formation*. 2nd ed. Munich: Beck.
Marr, Vivian (ed.). (2008). *The Chambers Dictionary*. 11th ed. Edinburgh: Chambers Harrap.
OED. Oxford English Dictionary [online]. oed.com.
Perlmutter, David M. (1988). The split morphology hypothesis: Evidence from Yiddish. In Michael Hammond & Michael Noonan (eds.), *Theoretical Morphology: Approaches in Modern Linguistics*. San Diego: Academic, 79–100.
Plag, Ingo. (1999). *Morphological Productivity*. Berlin: Mouton de Gruyter.
Plank, Frans. (1994). Inflection and derivation. In Ron E. Asher (ed.), *The Encyclopedia of Language and Linguistics*. Oxford: Pergamon, 1671–8.

Quirk, Randolph, Sidney Greenbaum, Geoffrey Leech & Jan Svartvik. (1972). *A Grammar of Contemporary English*. London: Longman.
Scalise, Sergio. (1984). *Generative Morphology*. Dordrecht: Foris.
Stemberger, Joseph & Brian MacWhinney. (1986). Frequency and the lexical storage of regularly inflected forms. *Memory & Cognition* 14, 17–26.
Vannest, Jennifer, Thad A. Polk & Richard L. Lewis. (2005). Dual-route processing of complex words: New fMRI evidence from derivational suffixation. *Cognitive, Affective, & Behavioral Neuroscience* 5, 67–76.
Wray, Alison. (2015). Why are we so sure we know what a word is? In John R. Taylor (ed.), *The Oxford Handbook of the Word*. Oxford: Oxford University Press, 725–50.
Zwicky, Arnold M. & Geoffrey K. Pullum. (1987). Plain morphology and expressive morphology. *Proceedings of the Thirteenth Annual Meeting of the Berkeley Linguistics Society*, 330–4.

3 Reflections on Why We Need Word-Formation

As far as I know, there is no language that does not have word-formation. Since that implies that there is no language without words, and that there is no language which does not have specific ways of constructing words as opposed to sentences, this might seem odd. Why would all languages have words if they could use morphemes (or minimal signs, or standard formatives – whatever terminology the reader is easy with) instead? Why complicate matters? It is sometimes suggested that isolating languages do not have words (Hockett 1944: 255, cited in Dixon and Aikhenvald 2002: 3, argues that "there are no words in Chinese", although such a claim was controversial at the time and is probably even more controversial today – Dixon and Aikhenvald 2002: 32–3). Note, though, that even in a language like Chinese (Mandarin) we can have a sequence of meaningful elements like *huā mù* 'flower tree' which means 'vegetation', something that we would probably call a 'word'. In other languages, things which have some of the features we think of as belonging to words look rather more like syntactic structures to those who are mostly familiar with Indo-European languages, as in the following example, where the decimal point divides the meaningful elements of the whole from each other.

>*West Greenlandic*
>puu·ssa·qar·ti·nngil·ara
>
>bag·future·have·causative·negative·1SG.3SG.indicative
>
>'I have no bag for it'

Even more problematic is that we have no good definition of a word, so that it is hard to determine precisely how we recognize words when we meet them (Bauer 2000, Dixon and Aikhenvald 2002, Hippisley 2015).

In some places, it looks as though we might be able to function quite well without word-formation.

>you can't arrest them on cop-ly intuition? (Robert B. Parker. 2003. *Stone Cold*. London: Murray, p. 229)

>Judges hate to issue them on cop intuition. (same volume, p. 240)

In the first example, *cop-ly* is a case of word-formation (it creates an adjective from a noun using a suffix). In the second example, we find the noun used unchanged. In this example, we might argue that we have, despite that, used word-formation, because *cop intuition* is a new compound, but we could equally argue that *cop* is just being used in attributive position as a syntactic structure, and no word-formation has taken place. Furthermore, had Parker written that something could not happen *on a cop's intuition*, the meaning would be the same, but there would be no question that we were dealing with syntax. The point, though, is not to argue about which solution is the best one in terms of style, communicative effectiveness or grammar, but to point out that even if we think that the purpose of word-formation is to do one or both of causing an old word to be seen as belonging to a new word-class (transposition) or to expand our vocabulary, we could invent a syntax which would do that without having to make appeal to word-formation as a separate part of the grammar. A similar conclusion is suggested by the next example.

>A utilitarian concrete-and-glass building. (Matthew Palmer. 2015. *Secrets of State*. New York: Putnam, p. 40)

Concrete-and-glass is a syntactic structure, while *concrete-glass* could have been used as a clear piece of word-formation, or even *conglass*.

When we start looking, there are plenty of places where we have an apparently syntactic alternative to a process of word-formation. This is particularly noticeable with compounds, where there are several syntactic constructions which, in some cases, can cover the same content as a compound. This is most clearly the case when the two expressions exist and are synonymous or nearly synonymous or are closely parallel. We find examples where an adjective is used to modify a noun or where a genitive is used with a noun. Neoclassical formations can also be used in similar places, but then the compound looks to be the more syntactic of the two patterns.

Adjective

atom bomb	atomic bomb
car mechanic	automotive engineer
cow pox	bovine encephalitis
dog-tooth (only in metaphorical contexts)	canine tooth
home office	domestic economy

Genitive

cowlick	cow's lick
lady-smock	lady's smock
milk thistle	lady's thistle

Neoclassical compound

dictionary-making	lexicography
life sciences	biology
woman-hating	misogyny

3 Why We Need Word-Formation

The fundamental principle underlying all of this is one that is usually known as Zipf's law. Zipf actually has several laws, and the one in question here is the law of abbreviation (Zipf [1949] 1965: 38), formulated as "the length of a word tends to bear an inverse relationship to its relative frequency", that is long words tend to be rare, short words tend to be common. If we look away from the apparent circularity of Zipf's use of the term 'word' here, and say something like 'meaning-bearing construct', we can see that words are likely to be more frequent than syntactic paraphrases, and are thus better suited to being relatively short, if they are used in a repetitive manner. Of course, not all words are likely to be used in a repetitive manner, and then length per se does not matter.

> William James. He was the groundsman, handyman, if-there's-any-sort-of-difficulty-ask-William-and-he'll-fix-it-for-you person about the place. (Laurence Meynell. 1978. *Papersnake*. London: Macmillan, p. 10)

Words can be made shorter than typical syntactic phrases in several ways:

- restrict the amount of modification that is possible;
- compress the syntax by omitting redundant material;
- have processes for making words create (in most cases) shorter strings than those which create syntactic structures.

Typically, established compounds do not allow independent modification of the elements. That is, if we take *blackbird* to be a compound, we cannot have **rather blackbird* or **black omnivorous bird* if we are to retain the meaning of 'blackbird'. For many, this is part of the definition of a compound. This comes down to the difference between naming and describing, where word-formation provides a name for an entity, action or quality and syntax describes it. Words, of course, can enter into syntactic descriptions, so that *an unusually speckled blackbird* is a grammatically appropriate form which does not break the spirit of the restriction.

We find compression in the omission of grammatical words such as articles and prepositions, for example in the difference between *a book-cover* (word-formation) and *the cover of a book* (syntax). The use of figurative expressions can also provide compression, since, for example, *lollipop man* omits a lot of detail in comparison with *man helping children cross the road who has a stick with a road signal on it that looks like a lollipop*. Similarly, so-called synthetic (or verbal-nexus, or secondary) compounds like *bus-driver* omit prepositions and articles in comparison with syntactic paraphrases such as *the driver of the bus*.

The use of affixes and not just words not only makes the output shorter, but also binds the elements together more tightly because affixes cannot typically stand alone. We also find that a process such as clipping is available to make longer words shorter when they become more frequently used, as in *flu* for *influenza*, *phone* for *telephone*, *telly* for *television*. Acronyms perform similar function for longer names (e.g. for names of governmental bodies).

All of this is a matter of tendencies rather than a matter of absolutes. *Green belt* looks, superficially at least, like a piece of syntax, even though it is the name of an entity rather than or as much as a description of it. At the same time, it does not allow modification of the adjective if the meaning is to be retained: *greener belt* or *rather green belt* are possible if describing an article of clothing, but not if talking about the green belt round a town. *Find the lady* looks like syntax, but is the name for a card game, beloved of mountebanks, in which people bet on which of three inverted playing cards is the queen.

Words recur more often than phrases do, so words need to be, other things being equal, shorter than phrases. Processes used for making words can be used to make long words, just as syntactic constructions can be adopted as labels, so there is not a hard-and-fast dividing line. Nevertheless, word-formation processes are typically aimed at making more compact expressions than syntactic processes. Because of the requirements placed on words, those processes are often different from those used in syntax, and because of the ubiquity of words or word-like constructions, word-formation patterns are common, even if they are not the only way of forming new words.

Challenge

Genitives have multiple functions in English, as well as in other languages. The genitive in *the women's magazine* seems to function more like the modifier in a compound and less like a possessive marker than the genitive in *the women's experience*. Can you find criteria for distinguishing between the two? Do you think the two differ in syntactic structure? Do you think that the type in *the women's magazine* represents a type of compound? Why (not)? Are there other functions of the genitive? Does the genitive function the same way in any other language with which you are familiar?

References

Bauer, Laurie. (2000). Word. In G. Booij, C. Lehmann & J. Mugdan (eds.), *Morphology: An International Handbook of Inflection and Word-Formation.* Berlin: de Gruyter, 247–57.

Dixon, Robert M.W. & Alexandra Y. Aikhenvald. (2002). Word: A typological framework. In Robert M.W. Dixon & Alexandra Y. Aikhenvald (eds.), *Word: A Cross-Linguistic Typology.* Cambridge: Cambridge University Press, 1–40.

Hippisley, Andrew. (2015). The word as a universal category. In John R. Taylor (ed.), *The Oxford Handbook of the Word.* Oxford: Oxford University Press, 246–69.

Hockett, Charles F. (1944). Review of *Linguistic Interludes* and *Morphology: The Descriptive Analysis of Words* by E.A. Nida. *Language* 20, 252–5.

Zipf, George K. ([1949] 1965). *The Psycho-Biology of Language.* Cambridge MA: MIT Press.

4 Reflections on the Recognition of Novelty in Words

Van Santen (1992: 63–74) points out that if we believe that morphological processes can be productive, we must be able to recognize existing words in order to see the productivity. Following Corbin (1987), many authorities distinguish between two meanings of productivity: a process is available if it can be used, and profitable to the extent that it is actually used. Van Santen (1992: 72; my translation) says that "Productivity is manifested in the space between the existing and the impossible". This would seem to imply that speakers can recognize individual words which they know and are aware of words which are new in their experience.

Although there is clearly some truth to this – as will be shown just below – it seems unlikely that it is true across the board. The places where it seems to fail are those where the relevant process is particularly productive (profitable). Consider the suffix *-ing*. Although I know that I have heard the form *revolting* (both as a part of a finite verb group and as an adjective), and I know that because I have heard jokes which play on the possible ambiguity of expressions such as *Sire, the peasants are revolting,* I would be in doubt as to whether or not I had heard the word *misreporting*, although I feel rather more secure in saying that *misreporting* as an adjective is not familiar. *Consortable* is listed in Lehnert (1971), but not in Marr (2008), even though Marr (2008) lists *consort* as a transitive verb, which means that *consortable* ought to be possible. It does not seem familiar, but I cannot be sure that I have not met it previously. Lehnert (1971) also lists *composable, disposable, opposable, proposable, supposable, transposable.* Of these, I recognize *disposable* and *opposable*, I find *composable* and *proposable* to be unfamiliar, and I am in doubt as to the status of *supposable* and *transposable.* These are personal reactions; others will react differently. The point is, though, that individuals may not be able to draw a firm line between the item-familiar (Meys 1975) and the new. This was also the experience I had when asking people questions about the words discussed in Section 15.6. People found whether or not they were familiar with a given word a reasonable question to be asked, and in most cases had no problem in providing an answer. In some cases, though, it proved difficult to decide.

The situation is so normal that in occurs frequently in fiction. There, it is not the familiarity to which attention is drawn, but the instances where the word mentioned is not familiar. There are a number of stock reactions, and a number of stock ways of posing the question as to the word's status. Examples are given below.

> She ... "commonized" her accent, adopting the singsong tones of Birmingham. (M.C. Beaton. 2004. *Deadly Dance*. New York: St Martin's Minotaur, p. 157)

> and Devereux making fun of his juniority. Was there such word? If not, there ought to be. (Carola Dunn. 2007. *The Bloody Tower*. New York: St Martin's Minotaur, p. 32)

> "imagining your consternation", Leo said.
> "I am indeed consterned", I said, not caring that it wasn't a word. (Jack Frederickson. 2013. *The Dead Caller from Chicago*. New York: Minotaur, p. 305)

> They're probably wondering where I'm going so they can roadblock me up ahead. (Is roadblock a verb? It should be.) (James Patterson and David Ellis. 2013. *Mistress*. New York: Little and Brown, p. 377)

> "He was a bit Gothy himself."
> "I'm not sure that Gothy is a word, actually." (Stephen Leather. 2014. *Lastnight*. London: Hodder & Stoughton, p. 205)

> "We have been hard at work unraveling the unravel-able."
> "That's not a word." (Clive Custler with Grant Blackwood. 2010. *Lost Empire*. London: Michael Joseph, p. 88)

> Was he being politically incorrect by giving her a pass on the basis of her height? Was he being ... well, he wasn't sure the word existed, but was he being a sizeist? A heightist? (Lawrence Block. 2013. *Hit Me*. New York: Mulholland, p. 32)

> "He was a great believer in free spiritism among young people",
> "Free spiritism?" Campion snapped. "That's not even a word, let alone a philosophy." (Mike Ripley and Margery Allingham. 2014. *Mr Campion's Farewell*. London: Severn House large print, p. 229)

> "'Selective patriation'? What in God's name does that mean?" The prime minister looked from one to the other until his gaze settled on Derek Farmer. "Is it even a word?"
> "If it wasn't a word before, it is now, Geoff", said Farmer. (Andy McNab. 2015. *State of Emergency*. London: Bantam, p. 68)

> "He must have behaved in a most unvicarish fashion."
> "Is 'unvicarish' a word?"
> "I suppose not", Susan said. (Eloisa James. 2017. *Seven Minutes in Heaven*. New York: Avon, p. 16)

4 Recognition of Novelty in Words

> I came by my Francophilism, to invent a word, honestly. (Harlan Coben. 2017. *Don't Let Go*. New York: Dutton, p. 51)

> "You look like a person who relishes solitude", I said. "I pride myself on my ability to spot a fellow Churchyardian. Forgive me if I'm wrong."
> "There's no such word as 'Churchyardian'", Collier said.
> "There is now", I told him. "I've just made it up." (Alan Bradley. 2019. *The Golden Tresses of the Dead*. London: Orion, p. 159)

It does not matter that some of the coinages here are probably intended to be jocular, the important thing here is that they are thought worthy of comment. Some words are simply accepted, some are accepted but acknowledged to be new and of these some are seen as fulfilling a legitimate need. The coinage is seen as an invention, not a proper or real word, in some cases as invalid because new, or as perfectly good word once it has been coined. What these examples have in common – though there are many that do not show this feature – is that they are overtly recognized as being innovative.

The everyday experience of such instances is the claim that something is not a word in Scrabble or other word-games. The proof of something being a word, in this sense, is that it is found in the dictionary that is being used for reference. Given that dictionaries differ wildly in the number of words they list, this claim is more a claim about the familiarity of a word than it is about its actual existence in the language (whatever that means). For example, *elect(or)ess* is listed in Marr (2008) but not in Thompson (1995). It does indicate that speakers are aware of words which they expect to find (or not to find) in a dictionary, and thus what is known and what is new.

More often than not, however, new words in texts pass unremarked upon and unglossed (Renouf and Bauer 2001). We cannot assume that this means they are not noticed, but it may mean that they are intended as jokes or that their meaning is considered to be so self-explanatory in context that no special comment is required.

In short, van Santen's observation is supported by the data, although there is a fuzzy area where speakers are insecure, and that insecurity seems to be precisely with words coined by the most productive processes. This might be seen as a confirmation of Aronoff's (e.g. Anshen and Aronoff 1997) position that the most productive uses of the most productive morphological processes are not listed. But even that requires some moderation. Productive processes can give rise to item-familiar words (we know words like *driver*, *killer*, *lover* formed by the very productive affix *-er*), but because of the productivity of such processes, we cannot store all the possible outputs, and we do not know whether they are familiar or not.

Challenge

Choose half-a-dozen words which are at least four syllables long at random from a dictionary or vocabulary list. Check the relative frequencies of the words. Think of a way to check whether people find these words familiar or not (you might want to check what they know about each word – collocations, meanings, domain of usage). How far does frequency correlate with familiarity? What other factors are relevant? If your words are morphologically complex, how far do your consultants deduce meanings of unfamiliar words from the meanings of bases and affixes?

References

Anshen, Frank & Mark Aronoff. (1997). Morphology in real time. *Yearbook of Morphology 1996*, 9–12.
Corbin, Danielle. (1987). *Morphologie dérivationelle et structuration du lexique*, 2 vols. Tübingen: Niemeyer.
Lehnert, Martin. (1971). *Reverse Dictionary of Present-Day English*. Leipzig: VEB.
Marr, Vivian (ed.). (2008). *The Chambers Dictionary*. 11th ed. Edinburgh: Chambers Harrap.
Meys, W.J. (1975). *Compound Adjectives in English and the Ideal Speaker-Listener*. Amsterdam: North Holland.
Renouf, Antoinette & Laurie Bauer. (2001). Contextual clues to word-meaning. *International Journal of Corpus Linguistics* 5, 231–58.
Santen, Ariane J. van. (1992). Produktiviteit in Taal en Taalgebruik. Unpublished doctoral dissertation, University of Leiden.
Thompson, Della (ed.). (1995). *The Concise Oxford Dictionary*. 9th ed. Oxford: Oxford University Press.

5 Reflections on Blocking and Competition

It makes such good sense that speakers of languages should abhor absolute synonyms that it almost seems churlish to question the notion that a new complex word should never mean precisely the same as an existing word. Given that *transmission* is an automatically available (see Chapter 4 for the term) nominalization from *transmit*, if we have *transmittal* it must have some specialized meaning that speakers wish to distinguish from the sense of *transmission*. On some occasions, the difference will be a matter of style or collocation or regional dialect rather than strictly a matter of sense, but the general idea that absolute synonyms are not found seems to be a well-established principle.

Aronoff (1976) terms this 'blocking', and the term has become established, even though Aronoff (2023: 52) admits that it is not a particularly good term for the phenomenon, which does have other names, such as 'pre-emption by synonymy' (Clark and Clark 1979) and 'the rule of the occupied slot' (*Regel der besetzten Stelle*, Burgschmidt 1977: 43). Aronoff (1976: 43) defines blocking as the

non-occurrence of one form due to the simple existence of another

and this seems to imply that the synonym need not arise from the same base (as in the *transmit* case), but can be more general so that, to use a widely cited example (Bolinger 1975: 109), the existence of *thief* blocks the use of *stealer* with the same meaning.

We can distinguish several types of blocking, which have sometimes been treated separately in the literature.
1 Inflectional blocking: the presence of an irregular inflectional form blocks the application of a regular inflectional form to the same base. This has been argued to be an instance of the Elsewhere Condition, and alternatively has been argued to be a result of Level Ordering. Some scholars seem to retain the term 'blocking' only for derivational morphology, thus excluding such cases, which might then be seen to be instances of suppletion.
2 Individual blocking or token blocking (Rainer 1988): the presence of one lexical item blocks the coinage or institutionalization of one other in a non-systematic

manner. The *thief* example above might illustrate this, or the lack of a derived verb from *full* because of the existence of *fill*. Aronoff (2023: 52) talks about lexical blocking here, which he sees as the classic case of blocking.

3 Domain blocking or type blocking (Rainer 1988): the coinage of some new lexeme is blocked by an overall constraint on the usage of a particular morphological process. For example, the creation of verbs in *-en* on the basis of adjectives is blocked where the adjective base does not end in an obstruent, so that *bluen, *greenen, *souren are not possible (the process is probably not available any longer, which might then be seen as the absolute blocking of any more forms on this particular pattern).

In Chapter 29 several examples are given of blocking failing to apply to inflectional forms. The question there is whether the places where blocking fails can be systematized in some way, but as far as English is concerned there does not seem to be any absolute rule – or if there is, it is yet to be spelled out fully. More generally, the phenomenon is known as 'overabundance' (Thornton, e.g. 2011), and is much more widespread in a range of languages than was realized in the 1980s. What we can say here is that inflectional blocking does not work as well as was once believed.

We can also find cases where individual blocking fails. A simple example is *orientate*, which has virtually replaced an earlier *orient* (in either case, a verbalization of the noun *orient*). In this case there is an intermediate step: *orientation* could be the nominalization of the verb *orient* or of the verb *orientate* and *orientate* probably arose through back-formation from *orientation*. A separate case that seems to have worked the other way round is *compute*, replacing an earlier *computate*. Again, the nominalization *computation* is ambiguous, but this time, the shorter verb appears to have triumphed. A verb in *-ate* may also explain why *exacerbation* is now used in place of an earlier *exacerbescence*. *Regardless* does not appear to have prevented the rise of *irregardless*. *Disfranchise* has been replaced by *disenfranchise*. As with many pairs of nominalizations from the same base, *commission* and *commitment* are usually used with different meanings, although both have a range of meanings. But dictionary definitions (e.g. Marr 2008) give both of them the meaning 'act of committing', which suggests that there is at least overlap between them. Blocking would seem to presuppose that there should not be overlapping.

The coexistence of *approval* and *approbation* is probably due to the different style levels of the two words, *approbation* being far more formal, and this leads to different collocations, so that *approval rating* is found but not *approbation rating*. At an earlier stage, *approbation* and *proof* competed for the same place, but are now semantically different.

There are numerous words which do not share a base and yet appear to share at least some senses. Among others, we can think of *abbreviate* and *shorten*, *aggravate* and *exacerbate*, *surrender* and *relinquish*. Others are relatively easy

to find in any thesaurus. Some of these differ in style level, and they often have different collocations. Yet you can both surrender and relinquish territory to an enemy. Environmental conditions can exacerbate or aggravate an illness, and someone's intervention can aggravate or exacerbate a situation.

Although Stratton (2023) does not focus on the existence of synonymy per se, by considering changing patterns of synonymy for words meaning 'man' in the history of English, he illustrates a societal need for synonymy and shows that synonyms can differ by text-type, as well as gaining differing shades of meaning, and in some cases disappearing, over longer periods.

Bauer et al. (2013: 636) comment that many synonymous derived forms are found in corpora. Some of their examples could well be the result of memory lapses under the pressure of seeking words, which gives the appearance of leading to new coinages which, however, are often not institutionalized (*omitment*, for instance, in the place of the lexicalized *omission*), but others like *educationist* and *educationalist* are listed in dictionaries as synonyms, and the difference may be more a matter of fashion than of differing sense. This seems to contradict the view from Bauer (2003: 81) that it is institutionalization that is blocked rather than coinage.

We also find instances where affixes in competition appear to vary in the speech of the community or of individuals without affecting the meanings. Forms ending in *-ance/-ence* and *-ancy/-ency* and forms ending in *-ic* and *-ical* provide multiple examples (even if there are examples where the endings are used to create distinct meanings). *Residence* and *residency* may mean different things, but *complacence* and *complacency*, *luxuriance* and *luxuriancy*, *persistence* and *persistency* are synonymous pairs. *Economic* and *economical* may differ in meaning, but *episodic* and *episodical*, *logarithmic* and *logarithmical*, *philologic* and *philological*, *strategic* and *strategical* can all be synonymous (Marr 2008). In many other cases (for both patterns) only one of the pair is in general use or is in general use among professionals in the relevant area. For instance, most linguists at the present time use *phonetic, phonological, morphological, semantic* and *syntactic*, but non-linguists may vary in their usage.

Some authorities (e.g. Di Sciullo and Williams 1987) suggest that *intelligenter* is blocked by *more intelligent*, thus allowing syntactic constructions to block morphological ones. There are various problems here, even if we agree that *intelligenter* is unlikely to be used. The first is that we can argue that *more intelligent* is periphrastic morphology rather than syntax (if there is a genuine distinction to be drawn here), so that it is just morphology blocking morphology. The second is that trisyllabic adjectives (and longer) do occur with *-er* from time to time, although apart from *curiouser* and forms like *unhappier* they do not usually become established, so that it is difficult to say that *intelligenter* is actually not possible; we also occasionally find disyllabic adjectives which usually reject *-er* being used with it.

You're already rich and famous ... and you're going to be richer and famouser. (Lawrence Block. 2003. *Small Town*. London: Orion, p. 335)

It's getting mysteriouser. (Jeffery Deaver. 2003. *The Vanished Man*. London: Hodder & Stoughton, p. 46)

I've been up for three hours, nervouser than a nun at a penguin shoot. (John Sandford. 2017. *Golden Prey*. New York: Putnam, p. 19)

"A substantial sum?"
"The substantialler the better." (Grace Burrowes. 2017. *Too Scot to Handle*. New York: Forever, p. 156)

Finally, some of the people who claim that *intelligenter* is blocked also claim that *more smart* is blocked by *smarter*, where the blocking goes in the other direction. Actually, most monosyllabic adjectives can occur with *more* (for some that is the only option: consider *right*). At least one website presents the argument that *smarter* and *more smart* are not synonymous (https://allthediffer ences.com/difference-between-more-smart-and-smarter/) and avoids the issue in that way. But we can also find *more smart* as a straightforward comparative,

in a decade from now, the human capital will have grown enormously, with the same amount of people, just much more smart than they were before. (www.accenture.com/nl-en/blogs/insights/the-smart-workforce-amplifying-human-capital-by-making-the-s martest-people-even-smarter accessed 8 July 2023)

The whole subject is fraught; blocking sometimes seems to work, but sometimes it does not. When it does not, some of the reasons for its failure are easy to explain, but, again, they are not always easy to explain. Some claims about blocking are wrong, some of them may be considered to be tendencies rather than fixed patterns of behaviour, but without more detailed analysis, we probably have to conclude that blocking does not automatically apply. Plag (2003: 63–8) suggests that more frequent forms are more likely to block competitors than less frequent forms. While this makes sense, some of the examples above suggest that even that rule does not always work. Certainly, such a rule could explain how the form *orient* should end up being blocked by a new form *orientate* after the event once *orientate* has become common, but it cannot explain why the older, and at the time more frequent, form should not block the innovative form. If this solution is to be turned into a theoretical principle, a more subtle picture of just what is going on needs to be worked out.

Where different words with potentially the same meaning are created from the same base, we talk of competition. Blocking, other things being equal, should then lead to the prevention of competition. To the extent that this is not what happens (as with *-ence/-ancy* examples cited above) it is another sign that blocking has failed. Another example is the coexistence of both *rigidify* and *rigidize* or *rigidity* and *rigidness* (Marr 2008). Even then, we have to ask

5 Blocking and Competition

what it means for either of two (or more) processes to coexist. Do both forms have to be institutionalized? Do both processes have to be equally usable in every instance? Do the two have to be completely synonymous, or is it sufficient for them to have overlapping meanings? Do they have to have the same connotations, so are *meaningless* and *meaning-free* in competition if the latter implies that it is a good thing to have no meaning? Are *childish* and *childlike* equally usable if the former implies that resembling a child is bad because of immaturity, while *childlike* implies that it is good because of the implied innocence? And do the same implications have to hold in every case, so that *summerlike* and *summerish* have to differ in the same way (at some level) as *childlike* and *childish*?

Some of these questions are answerable in principle, others may not be. If we take it that the meaning associated with words becomes more specific as the words are used more in the community (see Section 10.4), then we can say that meaning that is accrued through this process is not part of the competition but is developed after the competition has applied (or has failed to apply). On the other hand, one of the ways that competition can be valuable to the community (as we have seen with several examples including *transmission* and *transmittal*) is that it allows distinctive meanings to be shown by different forms, even when the same base seems to be central to creating a relevant word. This might have to be considered a different use of competition. The difference is one between competition where two processes can apply, and which is used is random and does not lead to a semantic distinction, and competition where a competing form is used precisely because a semantic difference is required.

However, the situation that holds with *-ic* and *-ical*, with *-ence* and *-ency* seems to give rise to a paradox. We can see that the two or more suffixes come into English from borrowings which are motivated either in the donor language or by coming from a different route from a common etymon, and we can thus see that this gives rise to some words in English with one alternative and some with another. But the reduplication of effort has to be redundant, so why is one pattern not then removed in favour of the more frequent pattern, removing the redundancy, as seems to be happening with the loss of *orient*, albeit slowly? The answer would seem to be that the individual words become item-familiar in English – at least once they reach an appropriate level of frequency or familiarity – and that individual frequency maintains the form against challengers from other patterns. But that gives precedence to the individual word over the pattern. Yet the whole notion of productivity gives precedence to the pattern over the individual word. This seems to mean that we can account for token blocking if we consider single words, but type blocking only if we consider productivity, which involves patterns (or rules). If that is true, either token blocking and type blocking are two entirely distinct phenomena, or the two approaches conflict with each other. Token-blocking, in principle, cannot occur with productivity, because there is no pattern or rule which allows the blocked words to be coined. Type blocking cannot occur if precedence is given to the individual words, because each case has to be considered *sui generis* and cannot be explained by an overall rule or pattern. However we choose to proceed, we should avoid giving conflicting phenomena the same label.

We can get a different view of competition if we look at matters from an onomasiological point of view (Štekauer 2005, Grzega 2009) where the speaker seeks a word to fill a gap in their vocabulary rather than seeking a new word which is compatible with but extends the rules or patterns. In this view, presumably, almost anything can be in competition with anything else. English has multiple expressions to mean 'no longer alive', including *at rest* (a prepositional phrase), *deceased* (a past participle), *stone dead* (a compound), *dead as a doornail* (an idiomatic phrase) and dozens of others, including many figurative usages, circumlocutions, fixed syntactic phrases and so on. Even though these are not all of an equivalent style level, they make the point that this particular slot in our vocabularies can be filled by many forms. Not only is there choice in the pattern of word-formation that is used (when one is used), there is choice in the particular lexeme that is used to head the chosen expression or from which to derive the expression. Notably, there are alternatives to the use of word-formation, and if we look at lists of near synonyms in a thesaurus, we might consider that word-formation is a minor way of filling such gaps.

I have left more questions unanswered here than I have solved. The notion of blocking seems to apply to moderate the productivity of patterns which are in competition. A more subtle analysis might conclude that the two are not related, depending on how we define competition and the boundaries of competition, and on just how we see blocking as working. It seems clear that a more restrictive view of blocking is required if it is to be really useful for scholars of word-formation.

Challenge

Find several verbs which have more than one nominalization listed in dictionaries. Find as many examples of the use of each nominalization as you can. Do the uses of the nominalizations of every verb overlap, or are the meanings distinct for each nominalization? Do your findings confirm the conclusions found in dictionaries or not?

References

Aronoff, Mark. (1976). *Word Formation in Generative Grammar*. Cambridge, MA: MIT Press.
(2023). Three ways of looking at morphological rivalry. *Word Structure* 16, 49–62.

Bauer, Laurie. (2003). *Introducing Linguistic Morphology.* 2nd ed. Edinburgh: Edinburgh University Press.
Bauer, Laurie, Rochelle Lieber & Ingo Plag. (2013). *The Oxford Reference Guide to English Morphology.* Oxford: Oxford University Press.
Bolinger, Dwight. (1975). *Aspects of Language.* 2nd ed. New York: Harper, Brace, Jovanovich.
Burgschmidt, Ernst. (1977). Strukturierung, Norm und Produktivität in der Wortbildung. In Herbert E. Brekle & Dieter Kastovsky (eds.), *Perspektiven der Wortbildungsforschungen.* Bonn: Bouvier, 39–47.
Clark, Eve V. & Herbert H. Clark. (1979). When nouns surface as verbs. *Language* 55, 767–811.
Di Sciullo, Anna Maria & Edwin Williams. (1987). *On the Definition of Word.* Cambridge, MA: MIT Press.
Grzega, Joachim. (2009). Compounding from an onomasiological perspective. In Rochelle Lieber & Pavol Štekauer (eds.), *The Oxford Handbook of Compounding.* Oxford: Oxford University Press, 217–32.
Marr, Vivian (ed.). (2008). *The Chambers Dictionary.* 11th ed. Edinburgh: Chambers Harrap.
Plag, Ingo. (2003). *Word-Formation in English.* Cambridge: Cambridge University Press.
Rainer, Franz. (1988). Towards a theory of blocking: The case of Italian and German quality nouns. *Yearbook of Morphology* 1988, 155–85.
Štekauer, Pavol. (2005). Onomasiological approach to word-formation. In Pavol Štekauer & Rochelle Lieber (eds.), *Handbook of Word-Formation.* Dordrecht: Springer, 207–32.
Stratton, James M. (2023). Where did *wer* go? Lexical variation and change in third person male adult noun referents in Old and Middle English. *Language Variation and Change* 35: 199–221.
Thornton, Anna M. (2011). Overabundance (multiple forms realizing the same cell): A non-canonical phenomenon in Italian verb morphology. In Martin Maiden, John Charles Smith, Maria Goldbach & Marc-Olivier Hinzelin (eds.), *Morphological Autonomy: Perspectives from Romance Inflectional Morphology.* Oxford: Oxford University Press, 358–81.

6 Reflections on Potential and Norm

Although morphologists have spent a lot of time discussing actual and potential words, lexicalization and productivity, there is one gap that has not been dealt with well, namely the notion of norm. The idea of the norm was introduced by Coseriu (1952) for what people actually say as opposed to all the things that it would be grammatical for them to say. A similar idea, though without the terminology, is discussed by Pawley and Syder (1983) in a rather different context.

To illustrate the point, consider how you might say goodbye to a friend to whom you are speaking English. You have many choices, depending on who you are talking to, how friendly you are, where in the world you are, how old you are and your friend is, whether you are serious or joking and so on. Such possible expressions include things like *goodbye, good day, so long, farewell, laters, see you (at Christmas), ciao* and *sayonara*. But although it would be grammatical to say *until we see each other again*, you would not say it. The equivalent of *until we see each other again* would be said in German, Italian or Russian, but in English it is not part of the norm (Bauer 2022).

When we discuss word-formation we often discuss the patterns in terms of their productivity (see Section 2.5). We know that we can create compounds of the form N + N, so we might expect that we can add the noun *muscle* to the noun *dystrophy* to give *muscle dystrophy*. While that might be a potential word of English (if we assume that blocking will not prevent it – see Chapter 5), it is not what we say, because we use an adjective to give *muscular dystrophy*. On the other hand, if we know that we can use *muscle* (and because of that, the adjective *muscular*) to mean 'strong, although without literal muscles', we might expect to be able to say *muscular car*, when the expression that is part of the norm is *muscle car*. In a similar vein, alongside *burial* we might expect *marrial (where we find *marriage*), alongside *laughter* we might expect *coughter (where we find *cough*), and alongside *adventure* we might expect *inventure (rather than the *invention* that we find). What this means is that, besides knowing what is grammatical in a language, we have to know what forms among the grammatical possibilities are actually used, just because that is the way we say it. It is not clear how we built that into a model of how word-formation works.

A fairly standard picture of how word-formation has been assumed to work for many years now runs as follows. We identify a gap in our vocabulary. To fill it, we identify a word-formation process which can fill the gap (it is not clear how that is done). The process must be productive in order to be able to fill a gap, and the word which we are attempting to coin to fill the gap is then a potential word. This implies that we must have a base or bases for creating a suitable word as well as a suitable word-formation process. Again, it is not clear how that potential base is chosen, since it may, for example, involve some figurative use of language. If the potential word is not blocked (to the extent that blocking works, see Chapter 5, and to the extent that blocking can work at the coining stage rather than at the stage of institutionalization – Bauer 2003: 81), the potential word is then taken as an actual word. That actual word may or may not become established in the community for expressing the content that we could previously not express in a word. It may, but need not, later become lexicalized, or just vanish from use.

As is suggested here, there are gaps in our understanding of the process which, whatever model of word-formation we may be using, tend to focus on the formal application of the process and the shape of the output rather than on the process of choosing between alternatives. But the focus here is how we can move from a potential word to an actual word and from there to something which is part of the norm, which are psycho-social questions rather than formal questions.

We can begin with potential words. If we accept the notion that there exists a set of bases for creating words and a set of rules/processes/patterns by which words are formed, and furthermore we accept that all that is required for a word to be formed is a suitable base and a process that can apply to that base, then the notion that there are some words which are possible but are not observed is inevitable. Indeed, for Aronoff (1976), it is the job of a generative morphology to determine just what the set of all possible words is, whether they are attested or not. Rainer (2012) divides those words into potential words and virtual words, those which are prevented from surfacing as actual words because of blocking. We have seen, though (Chapter 5), that sometimes blocking appears to fail, so that we cannot be sure just which words fit into which category if we accept that distinction. It seems safer to ignore the distinction.

At the same time, experience suggests that not all words which fit extant patterns can be formed. Some words are deemed aesthetically impossible, which may or may not prevent their coinage. Adams (1973: 2) quotes such an opinion of the word *aviation* from 1909 which clearly neither prevented its formation nor its institutionalization; on the other hand, *ignoration* (a nominalization from *ignore*) is listed in the *OED*, but is not in usage for reasons which are obscure but which might include aesthetic ones. Although we have verbs from *summer* and *winter* meaning 'to spend the summer/winter' as in *They summered in a cottage at the seaside*, there is no equivalent verb to *autumn*. But this could be a potential word, although it is not clear whether the verb in *They Apriled in a cottage by the seaside* is even a potential word. Was the attested *mouthfulness* ever a potential word before it was produced? Or *sniggeruity* (although this is clearly a joke)? Or *charismability*, whose meaning is not clear?

> I wished I'd brought my apples. All I needed was to chew on something with mouthfulness. (Ann Prospero. 2000. *Almost Night*. London: Penguin, p. 143)

> Rincewind was pretty sure horses couldn't snigger, but this one radiated an air of sniggeruity. (Terry Pratchett. 1998. *The Lost Continent*. New York: Harpertorch, p. 199)

> Kyla ... whose number of *Vanity Fair* covers alone testifies to her charismability. (Richard E. Grant. 1998. *By Design*. London: Picador, p. 92)

We appear to have several problems here: we cannot tell whether something is or is not a potential word, some words are coined which were not potential words, we have words that have parallels and yet are not coined and we cannot tell whether they were never potential words (and why) or whether they remain potential words, and with some potential words that are coined we sometimes seem to have a meaning attached to them which is not predicted to occur.

One of the most frequent sources of words which do not appear to be potential words created by processes of word-formation is the apparently random deletion of phonological material from a much longer expression which is often used in the names of chemicals and the like. Barnhart at al. (1990) give many examples of the phenomenon, including *lysostaphin* (from LYSO-dissolution+STAPHylococci+IN), *pronethalol* (from PROpyl+amiNE+meTHyl+naphthALeme+methanOL) and *ras* (from RAt+viruS). The main constraint at work here seems to be having a pronounceable output, perhaps with some material from as many of the major elements of the original as possible.

Part of the difficulty here is the question of what makes a particular expression a potential word. If we assume something like a word-formation rule, this seems to imply that anything which the set of rules permits to be an output, and which is not already a known word, is a potential word. Furthermore, it seems to imply that anything which is not permitted by the rules is not a potential word. When we have a large enough corpus to consider, however, we appear to find things that are not permitted by the rules, but which nevertheless appear. If all such cases fail to become established, there is little problem, although there may be a philosophical problem of how

6 Potential and Norm

things that are not licensed can be generated in a model that uses rules. If this is true, then *mouthfulness* is a potential word (which, in fact becomes established, as in the following example).

> It could be described as mouthfulness [... which] includes not only assisting in enhancing the intensity of the five basic tastes, but also enhancing the edge or peripheral flavours of the base flavours (www.foodnavigator.com/News/Promotional-Features/Angeotide-delivers-a-superior-mouthfulness-that-enhances-taste accessed 11 August 2023)

S*niggeruity*, in contrast, is not attested elsewhere in an internet search. Examples like *autumn* (verb) and *charismability* cited above can be found with an internet search, but are very rare. Yet *inbearable*, found by Bauer et al. (2013: 361), and surely not generally accepted because of the allomorph of *in-* before <b>, is found in an internet search, but usually, though not always, corrected to *unbearable*.

The problem with all this is that even if we prefer analogy (see Chapter 8) or paradigmatic structure to rules (or an equivalent), the same problems arise. The notion of potential word seems to be rather more slippery than we might expect.

When it comes to the notion of norm, things are even more difficult. There is a link with lexicalization, in that the more a word is used, the more likely it is to become lexicalized, and the more likely it is to be part of the norm, but some words seem to become norms in their specialist areas quite quickly, if for no other reason than that there is no alternative name available. There is a distinction, though, in that lexicalization is a matter of more or less, while being part of the norm seems to be a matter of yes or no, although the size of the community that recognizes a norm may vary considerably, and the norm may change over time. A recent expression which seems to have become part of the norm in Scotland (I am not aware of it being used more widely, but it may be) is the use of *Scooby* for 'clue'. The phrase comes from rhyming slang, with the full version being *Scooby-Doo* (a cartoon character), a name which rhymes with *clue*.

> we don't have a Scooby where she's staying. (Val McDermid. 2014. *The Skeleton Road*. London: Little, Brown, p. 145)

It may be the case that attested words are automatically assumed to be part of the norm, but that can change very quickly. In New Zealand, the Australasian word *stoush* 'disagreement, fight' is no longer recognized by young speakers, although it is still used in newspapers as a useful way of saving space. A New Zealand cartoon had a dejected-looking man saying, "I was going to shoot through, but nobody knew what it meant any more" (*shoot through* means 'to move on, to leave'). These examples indicate that the norm is partly (perhaps largely) a matter of frequent usage, part of the ebb and flow of words as any language changes. This means that it is a separate phenomenon from others typically used in word-formation, but perhaps necessary for the diachronic study of word-formation, just as for the diachronic study of all vocabulary usage.

Certainly, we should not underestimate the importance of norm on the complex words that we are likely to meet. There is a certain amount of variation between speakers, or between dialect areas and so on, but for me at least, *cooker* is an instrument and *cook* is a person, while *catcher* is a person and *catch* (on a door) is an instrument. If they happened to be the other way round, we must assume that the grammar would be just the same as it now is. I say *accountancy* but *inheritance* and not *inheritancy*. Although there has been variation in the past, most linguists today use *syntactic* but *phonological*. This may not be a matter of word-formation, but what the norm happens to be can influence the productivity of different patterns, and at that point word-formation is involved.

Challenge

Make a list of words in *-ce* or *-cy* which you (as an individual or as a group) use, including those where you use both (with the same or different meanings). Then check in a dictionary to find which member(s) of the pair are listed. Is there any reason for the discrepancies? If you look in the *Oxford English Dictionary*, do the two show different periods of use? Do rhyming bases tend to show the same pattern? Are there adjectives in *-ant* that have no corresponding *-ance* or *-ancy* form? If you had to create a corresponding noun, what would it be? Can you tell why? If you prefer, you can try the same exercise with *-ic* and *-ical*. If you try both, do you get parallel results in the two cases?

References

Adams, Valerie. (1973). *An Introduction to Modern English Word-Formation*. London: Longman.

Aronoff, Mark. (1976). *Word Formation in Generative Grammar*. Cambridge, MA: MIT Press.

Barnhart, Robert K., Sol Steinmetz & Clarence L. Barnhart. (1990). *Third Barnhart Dictionary of New English*. New York: H.W. Wilson.

Bauer, Laurie. (2003). *Introducing Linguistic Morphology*. 2nd ed. Edinburgh: Edinburgh University Press.

(2022). What you must say, what you can say and what you do not say. In Andreea S. Calude & Laurie Bauer (eds.), *Mysteries of English Grammar*. New York: Routledge, 11–20.

Bauer, Laurie, Rochelle Lieber & Ingo Plag. (2013). *The Oxford Reference Guide to English Morphology.* Oxford: Oxford University Press.
Coseriu, Eugenio. (1952). *Sistema, norm y habla.* Montevideo: Facultad de Humanidades y Ciencias, Instituto de Filología, Departamento de Lingüistica.
OED. The Oxford English Dictionary [online]. oed.com
Pawley, Andrew & Frances Hodgetts Syder. (1983). Two puzzles for linguistic theory: Nativelike selection and nativelike fluency. In Jack C. Richards & Richard W. Schmidt (eds.), *Language and Communication.* London: Routledge, 191–225.
Rainer, Franz. (2012). Morphological metaphysics: Virtual, potential, and actual words. *Word Structure* 5, 165–82.

7 Reflections on Definition by Stipulation and on Word-Classes

In an ideal world, our classes of entities would be easily classified, unambiguous and non-intersecting. We do not live in an ideal world. For instance, consider the class of mammals. If we look round the farmyard in Europe, we might conclude that mammals are creatures which give birth to live young, which feed their young on their milk, the young sucking on a nipple, and which are covered in hair. We exclude ducks and hens because they have feathers, not hair and because their young are not born live but are hatched from eggs, we exclude fish because they have scales and not hair, and so on. But if we move from Europe to Australia, we meet monotremes (the platypus and the echidna) which have hair, but which lay eggs, which feed their young from their milk, but which do not have nipples. Our criteria no longer match up, and we have to create new categories, defined in different ways. In this case, the reanalysis is possible if we divide mammals into placental mammals and monotremes. The mammals of the European farmyard may be prototypical mammals (in the sense of Rosch 1973 and Taylor 2003), but the criteria we used to define them are not, in the light of further knowledge, accurate in defining mammals as a natural kind.

If we look at citrus fruit, we may recognize an orange and a lemon, say, and may be familiar with other terms such as *grapefruit, kumquat, lime, mandarin, tangerine, tangelo* and *ugli fruit*, but we may not have any criteria that we can successfully use to distinguish between these entities. Colour is a poor guide because lemons and oranges may be green before they are ripe. Size is awkward because although a mandarin may usually be smaller than an orange, it is possible to have small oranges and large mandarins. Shape is difficult to classify. If we are telling a small child what the difference is, we may resort to definition by ostentation: this fruit in my hand is a mandarin. Even the labels we use may be misleading: in French, a lime may be called a *citron vert* 'green lemon', a *wild lime* is not a lime, and neither is a *Spanish lime*; a *grapefruit* has nothing to do with a grape.

In the case of mammals and citrus fruit, genetics can be used to keep track of the various subspecies. In linguistics, though, we have no such fallback. A linguistic category such as *sentence* has no genetic definition, it has to be defined, typically in terms of its form and its function within a linguistic

7 Definition by Stipulation and Word-Classes

system. Functional and formal criteria do not always align. This has implications for the terminology of linguistics and the way the terminology is used.

Consider the definition of the linguistic term *affix*. Bauer (2004) defines an affix as

> A type of obligatorily bound morph . . . attached to a base of a particular word-class.

This assumes that we know what a morph is, what a base is and what a word-class is, but those terms (or at least, two of them) are defined in their turn in Bauer (2004) and a definition of word-class can be found in other publications. Now consider the morph *-ish* in *greenish*. Its looks as though it may fit the definition of an affix, although we would have to know rather more to be sure: how the "particular word-class" is defined for *-ish*, for example. Now consider the following example.

> "He must have been pleased to move back here."
> Daisy wrinkles her nose. "Ish . . .". (Elly Griffiths. 2016. *The Woman in Blue*. London: Quercus, p. 242)

The question is whether *-ish* is an affix in this example. It has no base and is apparently not obligatorily bound. We now have to re-evaluate. If *-ish* is not an affix in this example, it is presumably a base. Is it a base in this example but not in *greenish*, or is it a base in both instances, in which case is *greenish* really a compound? If *-ish* is an affix in *greenish*, but not in the cited example, what is it? Some authorities like to create a new category of affixoid (e.g. Kastovsky 2009, Ralli 2020) for items which are intermediate between lexemes and affixes, which sort of fixes the problem: *-ish* is an affixoid and not an affix at all. Bauer's definition of affix just needs to be modified. But there is an alternative solution. We simply state that *-ish* is an affix wherever it arises. It is simply being quoted as a form in the cited example. If we do that, *-ish* becomes an affix not because it fits with a regular pattern of form and/or function which might define it as such, but because we have stipulated that this is the case.

Stipulation might appear in this characterization to be a very bad way to conduct a scientific description (it is, in any case, deliberately set out here to be seen as such). But it is more common in linguistics than might be thought. Consider another common definition, this time from Bauer 2017: 3 – the definition in Bauer 2004 is different):

> compounds . . . are often defined as words whose elements are words.

Now consider the expression *Many hands make light work*. Is this a compound? It is certainly an expression whose elements are words, but is it a word whose elements are words (for further discussion, see Chapter 9 and

Section 16.3)? It is fixed in the same way that word is, it does not allow elements within it to be swapped out with synonyms (or with antonyms). It tends to be learned as a single unit. It is very like a word. But does being very like a word make it a word? I would expect people to deny that *Many hands make light work* is a word, and would expect them to claim that it is a syntactic structure – perhaps a sentence. But then what about *man about town*? This appears to have a syntactic structure, too, similar to *book about linguistics* (not a sentence, but nevertheless syntactic), but this time it is easier to find people who are willing to see this as a word, along with superficially similar constructions such as *man-of-war*, *lady-in-waiting* or *mother-in-law*. Are these, then, words, and if so is *man-about-town* (and the other examples) a compound, a word whose elements are words? And if it is not, why is it not? Here it seems that stipulation may be the only way we can resolve the dilemma. We either see these things as compounds or we see them as syntactic structures, but those two solutions are generally considered incompatible (see Bauer 2025, for discussion).

As a final example, consider the notion that endocentric compounds in English are hyponyms of their right-hand element. *Street corner* denotes a kind of corner, not a kind of street. Bauer et al. (2013: 434) exclude some constructions which are not hyponyms of the right-hand element from the set of compounds, thus raising the possibility that right-headedness is part of the definition of a compound (though Bauer et al. do not advocate this position). If we were to take that position, we would be stipulating right-headedness as a requirement for a compound. We would therefore exclude from the set of compounds items such as *girl Friday*, or *endgame* (*girl Friday* denotes a type of girl, not a type of Friday; *endgame* denotes a kind of end, not a kind of game). We would then have to determine what such expressions are and what their grammatical structure is. And yet *endgame* is a word whose elements are words, so the stipulation would have the effect of circumscribing the set of compounds, presumably on the grounds that in most cases it is true that right-headedness is a prototypical feature of compounds.

As with the other examples considered here, creating new types has the inevitable effect of increasing the number of borderline cases, and thus making it harder to distinguish consistently between types and increasing the requirement for criteria to help make decisions. If our criteria are not hard and fast but are prototypes, then we simply increase the uncertainty at borderlines, because we have to determine how close to a prototype something has to come before it is accepted as being part of a relevant category, and that requires some kind of measurement of approximation (a measurement we do not have). Alternatively, we have to allow some freedom to be insecure about whether things fit into one category or another. While this has some appeal, in effect it simply throws things back on intuition and does away with the need for scientific criteria at all.

7 Definition by Stipulation and Word-Classes

One of the places where all this becomes relevant is with word-classes. Word-classes are notoriously difficult to set up and to define. All discussions of word-classes have to deal with the problems this gives rise to (see e.g. Crystal 2004, Hollmann 2020), but the picture of word-classes that seems to be dominant in studies of word-formation is simplistic and gives rise to a range of questions.

Most handbooks of word-formation talk about processes (typically, processes of affixation) which create nouns, verbs, adjectives, rather than about processes which create, say, human nouns, telic verbs and gradable adjectives. Similarly, affixes are, in general terms, said to derive adjectives from nouns or verbs from adjectives rather than adjectives from human nouns or verbs from predicative adjectives. There are, of course, exceptions, such as comments on the adjectival suffix *-ly* in English being productive only on human nouns (which may not be accurate, because it could probably be used on words denoting intelligent aliens or dwarfs/elves/fairies/gods, etc.; not only *spectatorly* but also *demonly* are attested – Bauer et al. 2013: 306). The practice is not necessarily harmful, but it does make certain presuppositions about the way in which word-classes in English work. It assumes that a word like *noun*, for example, denotes the highest level of abstraction for that category, and all other types of noun can be safely subsumed under that single label (just as *monotreme* can be safely subsumed under *mammal*, even if the denotata differ in important ways). *Monotreme* and *placental mammal* may be incompatible with each other, just as *abstract noun* and *concrete noun* may be incompatible terms, but they fit neatly into a scale of hyponymy. It must be noted, though, that a given noun can be a *count noun*, a *concrete noun* and a *human noun* at the same time, so the incompatibility does not always hold. Second, it assumes that there are a very limited number of relevant categories, that they are all incompatible with each other, and that we know what they are. That interjections are rarely mentioned in works on word-formation implies that they are not relevant to the topic, that adverbs and prepositions are sometimes mentioned implies that word cannot be both at the same time (though see Chapter 23 for some discussion). Another way of looking at this is to say that *noun* implies *not adjective*, and so on. There may also be an implication that a set of nouns and verbs or nouns and adjectives and so on is not a word-class (though note the remark by Brugmann 1891: II: 93 that "Speaking generally, no sharp distinction between substantive and adjective can be drawn in the Indo-Germanic [i.e. Indo-European] languages"). Most of this is probably controversial, possibly problematic, and not least for the study of word-formation. Moreover, most of these problems are well known.

We can begin with the word-classes of bases. We should recall here Aronoff's (1976: 48) unitary base hypothesis, namely that "A W[ord] F[ormation] R[ule] will never operate on either this or that", WFRs always operate on a unique base-type.

Now consider the suffix *-er*. It attaches most obviously to verbs, giving forms like *attacker, boaster, clinger, dancer, owner, womanizer* and hundreds of others. But *-er* is also found attached to nouns, for example, in *falconer, islander, lifer, peasouper* (Bauer et al. 2013: 217–18). Having made this observation, how should we interpret it? One interpretation is that we are not dealing with the same *-er* in the two instances. The suffix *-er^1* attaches to verbs, while *-er^2* attaches to nouns, and, presumably, we have a number of other affixes attaching to adverbs (*outsider*) and numbers (*tenner*). This saves the unitary base hypothesis, but probably goes against an intuition that the same affix is involved in all of these. While intuitions can be wrong, any semantic differences between *-er^1* and *-er^2* could be argued to be the result of the word-class of the base, rather than the result of a different affix. An alternative analysis is that the class of nouns and verbs together form a natural class which can function as the requisite unique base-type. The difficulty here is that for most authorities, from the classical grammarians to Chomsky (1970), nouns and verbs are maximally distinct word-classes, and cannot easily be seen as forming a superclass. Similarly, while we can find *counter-* attached to adjectives (*counter-intuitive*), to nouns (*counterexample*) or to verbs (*counteract*), we cannot simply say that *counter-* can attach to the set of words, because *counter-* does not attach to prepositions. While, in principle, it might be possible to see any superset of word-classes as forming separate word-classes, this seems to go against the fundamental spirit of the suggested hypothesis. A third possibility – though probably not a realistic one – would be if the nouns and verb used in the bases for *-er* nominalizations had some feature or features in common which could be seen as providing the underlying uniqueness. I am not aware of any such suggestion.

Classes of base and classes of output are also important in dealing with derivation and with conversion. I shall concentrate on conversion here, though many similar points could be made with reference to overt derivation. One of the major determinants of conversion, according to most authorities, is that conversion involves a change of word-class. That is a word which belongs to one word-class loses the features of that word-class and takes on the features of another without there being any change in form. For example, the noun *position* ceases to be a noun and becomes a verb in a sentence like *They positioned themselves to compete in Europe.* To know whether this condition is met, we have to be able to tell whether the input (in this instance, the noun) and the output (in this instance the verb) belong to different word-classes, which implies that we know what the word-classes are. In the case of *position*, the answer is taken as clear-cut, but there are other instances where that might not be the case. Two examples will be considered here, though others are potentially relevant.

7 Definition by Stipulation and Word-Classes

Consider a name like *Leigh*. In a sentence such as *Leigh walked into the room*, this is clearly acting as a name, denoting a particular individual, known to both speaker and listener. However, in a sentence like *There are three Leighs in our class*, it is less clear. *Leigh* here denotes a person who is called *Leigh*, and the fact that several can be co-present in a particular space indicates that the word no longer has unique reference. In such an instance, a word like *Leigh* is in the same paradigm as a word like *linguist*, and as such appears to be acting as a common noun (the use of a capital letter in English should not be taken as significant in this regard; the English use of capitals is often indiscriminate). The question is, if *Leigh* has shifted from being a name to being a common noun, has conversion occurred? The general answer to this question is 'no'. Although I have carefully called *Leigh* a 'name' in one of its functions, it is also often termed a 'proper noun', and if we believe that label we must say that *Leigh* has shifted from being one kind of noun to being another kind of noun, and that is not a change of word-class. But at this stage we are simply playing with terminology. If I want to term *Leigh* a 'name' and not a 'proper noun', can I then claim that conversion is involved here? That is, is what determines a word-class a random choice of label, or is there some inherent content which determines the matter. We could build an argument either way: names like *Leigh* do not (in English) form part of determiner phrases (we cannot say *the Leigh* or *this Leigh* without shifting to a common noun – although we might be less sure about *my/our/your Leigh*); alternatively, part of the definition of a noun is that it can act as a semantically crucial part of the subject of a verb, and *Leigh walked into the room* shows that Leigh fulfils this function. I do not want to solve this conundrum, merely make the point that what the word-classes are – and consequently, what conversion is – may be a matter of interpretation and argumentation rather than something which is automatically obvious.

The second example I want to deal with here is genuinely unresolved. It is the matter of how to deal with participial forms like *interesting* and *building* (and also like *reserved*, but I shall ignore that type simply to save space). On the one hand, there is a verb to *interest*, with a form *interesting* (as in *I hope that their proposal is interesting their potential backers*), on the other, *interesting* is typically an adjective (as in *That's a very interesting observation*), and *building* is typically a noun (both as in *The building is four storeys high* and *Their building a block of flats on our fence-line looks like maliciousness*). Do we, then, have conversion between verb and adjective (*interesting*) or between verb and noun (*building*)? One problem is that the *-ing* in the verbal *interesting* is usually taken to be inflectional, and inflectional forms are not usually said to occur inside conversion (at least not in English, though other languages have some such examples). So, what are the possibilities here? We can defy the usual assumptions, and see this as conversion. We can deny that it is conversion, because *interesting* and *building* are verb forms in all their occurrences. We can claim that it is conversion, but conversion between a verb and a participle, making the assumption that a participle is a different word-class from a verb (this assumption was made by classical grammarians, on the basis that participles show tense and case, while verbs show only tense and nouns only case). We can assume conversion from some other starting point (perhaps all *-ing* forms are fundamentally nominal or fundamentally adjectival). We can deny that it is conversion, because conversion does not start from an inflected form. There may be other solutions, too. The important point, of course, is that unless we know what our assumptions about the set of word-classes we are dealing with are, we cannot determine whether this is conversion or not. It would be nice to be able to say that our assumptions are well founded and properly justified. But too often they are simply accepted without being questioned, and we end up with the notion that *interesting* and *building* are verbs because the forms *interesting* and *building* are sometimes word-forms in a verbal paradigm.

These are not the only problems in word-formation that depend on an analysis of word-classes, but the same general point remains true: without a better view of what a word-class is, and how word-classes work, a view which allows us to argue about the way in which different word-classes relate to each other, we do not have a way of arguing a case on these issues, and we are left with no alternative but to stipulate a solution. A stipulated answer may be useful, but the answers would feel rather more robust if we had a better way of arriving at them. It may be that word-formation allows for a way into solving the dilemma.

Challenge

Can you argue a case in favour of names either belonging to the same word-class as nouns or being in a separate word-class from nouns?

References

Aronoff, Mark. (1976). *Word Formation in Generative Grammar.* Cambridge, MA: MIT Press.

Bauer, Laurie. (2004). *A Glossary of Morphology.* Edinburgh: Edinburgh University Press.

(2017). *Compounds and Compounding.* Cambridge: Cambridge University Press.

(2025). Fixity or why English may not have compounds. In Sara Matriciano-Mayerhofer, Johannes Schnitzer & Elisabeth Peters (eds.) (2025). *Patterns, Variants and Change: Through the Prism of morphology. Studies in Honour of Franz Rainer.* Strasbourg: Éditions de Linguistique et de Philologie.

Bauer, Laurie. Rochelle Lieber & Ingo Plag. (2013). *The Oxford Reference Guide to English Morphology.* Oxford: Oxford University Press.

Brugmann, Karl. (1891). *A Comparative Grammar of the Indo-Germanic Languages.* Trans. Robert Seymour Conway and W.H.D. Rouse. New York: Westermann.

Chomsky, Noam. (1970). Remarks on nominalization. In Roderick A. Jacobs & Peter S. Rosenbaum (eds.), *Readings in English Transformational Grammar*. Waltham, MA: Ginn, 184–221.

Crystal, David. ([1967] 2004). English word-classes. In Bas Aarts, David Denison, Evelien Keizer & Gergana Popova (eds.), *Fuzzy Grammar: A Reader*. Oxford: Oxford University Press, 191–211 [reprinted from *Lingua* 17, 24–56].

Hollmann, Willem B. (2020). Word classes. In Bas Aarts, Jill Bowie & Gergana Popova (eds.), *The Oxford Handbook of English Grammar*. Oxford; Oxford University press, 281–300.

Kastovsky, Dieter. (2009). Astronaut, astrology, astrophysics: About combining forms. classical compounds, and affixoids. In R.W. McConchie, Alpo Honkapohja & Jukka Tyrkkö (eds.), *Selected Proceedings of the 2008 Symposium on New Approaches in English Historical Lexis*. Somerville, MA: Cascadilla, 1–13.

Ralli, Angela. (2020). Affixoids. In Lívia Körtvélyessy & Pavol Štekauer (eds.), *Complex Words: Advances in Morphology*. Cambridge: Cambridge University Press, 217–37.

Rosch, Eleanor H. (1973). On the internal structure of perceptual and semantic categories. In T.E. Moore (ed.), *Cognitive Development and the Acquisition of Language*, New York: Academic Press, 111–44.

Taylor, John. (2003). *Linguistic Categorization*. 3rd ed. Oxford: Oxford University Press.

8   Reflections on Analogical Word-Formation

While there is a great deal of word-formation that can be described in terms of rules applying to bases and affixes, there are also cases of words being formed on the basis of single parallel form. Although the term 'analogy' has something of a bad press in linguistics because it has been used to cover so many things from sound patterns to syntactic changes, and because it seems to be difficult to formulate in terms of a theory of what it permits and what it does not permit, it seems impossible to ignore the notion of analogy in these cases. I use the term here without any theoretical assumptions, and certainly with no presuppositions as to how an analogy is to be formulated or annotated, which I see as being irrelevant for the discussion of the examples discussed here.

The label 'creativity' is sometimes used to denote innovation which is not rule-based, though it is sometimes used more restrictively (e.g. to denote the creation of morphologically simple forms (Bauer 2001: 63)). We might, therefore, see analogical formation as being creative rather than productive. The first example to be dealt with here seems to suggest that such a proposal is not always appropriate.

This first example to be considered, the use of *-er* and *-ee* to create contrasting roles in relation to some, usually verbal, base, is interesting because there seem to be perfectly good patterns, which can be expressed as rules, for the use of both of these suffixes. Nevertheless, corresponding nouns in *-er* and *-ee* seem to arise adjacent to each other in texts, and often with parallel unusual features. This happens so frequently that direct comparison between the two words (or sometimes between the base and the suffixed word) must be a relevant factor in the coinage. This feature of such words has been commented on in the literature on the suffix *-ee*. Examples are provided below, and some remarks on the examples follow them.

> The bellower was Harmon Crundall – and the belowee the mysterious Mrs Smith. (Joan Hess. 1986. *The Murder at the Murder at the Mimosa Inn.* New York: St Martin's, p. 41)

> The toaster is hoping the toastees will have no troubles but little babies. (Laurence Sanders. 1989. *Stolen Blessings.* Wallington, Surrey: Severn House, p. 78)

8 Analogical Word-Formation 65

Candor was dangerous to both candorer and candoree. (Dave Duncan. 1996. *Present Tense*. New York: Avon, p. 139)

"Some guys are just born to have the shit kicked out of them."
"And stomped", said the other. "Like the world is divided into stomp*ers* and stomp*ees* and he's a stomp*ee*." (Stephen Dobyns. 1998. *Saratoga Strongbox*. New York: Viking, p. 46)

Sluggers don't much like getting their ass kicked by the designated sluggee. (Robert B. Parker 1998. *Sudden Mischief*. New York: Berkley, p. 63)

Lady Bella was the seducee, never the seducer, and would never overtly flirt. (Skye Kathleen Moody. 1998. *Wildcrafters*. New York: St Martin's Press, p. 100)

It was bad enough to consider being the dumper. To be the dumpee was terrifying. (Wes Craven. 1999. *Fountain Society*. New York: Simon & Schuster, p. 18)

I thought I was the *sneaker* when I was really the *sneakee*. (Clive Cussler. 2000. *Blue Gold*. London: Simon & Schuster, p. 38)

We're lover and lovee. (Robert Littell. 2013. *A Nasty Piece of Work*. New York: St Martin's, p. 184)

"So you think he has rebounded quickly from his loss?"
"I do. I think he's a fast rebounder. And his reboundee is named Susan Baird." (David Rosenfelt. 2014. *Hounded*. New York: Minotaur, p. 172)

Note that in many cases, not even the *-er* form is established in the community: a *sneaker* is usually a shoe rather than a person, a *dumper* is usually a truck, *stomper* is not established, a *toaster* is usually a kitchen implement, and *candorer* is possible for *-er* suffixation on a nominal base, but is not item-familiar. With *lover*, the word is established with the right meaning, but the person in the reciprocal relationship is usually also a *lover*. This seems to imply that it is not simply a matter of the *-ee* form copying the *-er* form (although the greater productivity of *-er* may mean that such a pattern is frequent), there is some mutual support in the coinages. It also appears, from the examples provided above, that these paired formations are often very consciously created, which some scholars, following Schultink (1961), consider to mean that the coinage cannot be a matter of productivity. Some of the formations are also clearly intended to be jocular. While this may be perfectly compatible with the conscious nature of the formations, it does not in itself mean that they are not perfectly acceptable words.

The other examples considered here are far less systematic. In the first example, it is not entirely clear that the substitution is in English.

> In Jim Beam-o *veritas*. (Jonathan Nasaw. 2003. *Fear Itself*. New York: Simon & Schuster, p. 102)

On one level this is a Latin proverb, with a loanword embedded in it. But, of course, the proverb is used in English, even if cited in Latin, and Jim Beam (a brand of whiskey) was not available in the Latin period. But whether it is a relevant example or not, it is similar to others in that the base of an affixed word is substituted for a familiar one. Other examples follow.

> If the magic was in the ear of the behearer... then Lucy seemed ready to settle for that. (Gavin Lyall. 1993. *Spy's Honour*. London: Hodder & Stoughton, p. 310)

> "If he can philander", Susie said in an airy way, "so can I. He womanises, I man-ise." (Susan Moody 1994. *The Italian Garden*. London: Hodder & Stoughton, p. 69)

> The man is a known modelizer. (Wes Craven. 1999. *Fountain Society*. New York: Simon & Schuster, p. 42)

> and Devereux making fun of his juniority. Was there such a word? (Carola Dunn. 2007. *The Bloody Tower*. New York: St Martin's Press, p. 32)

> The Hitler Youth turn into the Hitler Oldth. (Andy McDermott. 2014. *Kingdom of Darkness*. London: Headline, p. 257)

The comments on conscious, and sometimes jocular, formations that applied to the examples with *-ee* above also apply here. Sometimes here the model on which the new word is built is not overt: with *man-ize* we know that it is based on *womanize* because it is there in the text, but *modelize*, based on the same original, is presented without guidance for the reader, who has to deduce the pattern. The same is true with *juniority*, based on *seniority*. With the case of *behearer*, the reader has to make bigger steps to fill in the meaning, particularly since the original is not *beseer*, but *to be in the ~ of the be~er* provides a more extensive pattern for the reader to use.

The same kind of pattern is found when new words are substituted in otherwise familiar compounds.

> If she's dead, is that a corpsenapping? And is that a crime? (Stuart Woods. 1991. *New York Dead*. London: HarperCollins, p. 241)

> More correctly, if less grammatically, what is produced by the home musician is an 'alongsideput'. (Stephen Davies 2003. *Themes in the Philosophy of Music*. Oxford: Oxford University Press, p. 101)

> case that met military specifications for being ruggedized, meaning it was vapor-proof and dust-proof and everything-proof. (Patricia Cornwell. 1998. *Point of Origin*. London: Warner, p. 196)

8 Analogical Word-Formation

> She's just a journeyman. Journeywoman. Is that a word? (Renee Patrick. 2016. *Design for Dying*. New York: Doherty, p. 89)

Vapor-proof may well be a productive use of the element *proof*, but *everything-proof* seems to be a wild generalization based on the previous two examples. It might be argued to be a productive use of a productive pattern, but the close parallels with the other examples suggest otherwise.

The next example is very much a one-off, based on a case of univerbation that probably would not be counted as word-formation in the usual understanding.

> You wouldn't get stars staying there, only wannabes and usetabes. (Barry Norman. 1998. *Death on Sunset*. London: Orion, p. 93)

My last examples show reanalysis of the affix, so that what was originally part of the base is reassigned to the affix. Such cases are of interest because they show speakers following an overall gestalt of what a word must look like rather than following a series of patterns or rules which focus on and manipulate bases and affixes.

> They [cows] had personalities – or cow ... cowanalities – or whatever you want to call it. (Radio New Zealand, *Saturday Morning*, 4 November 2006)

> "You a socialist?"
> "I'm a nothingalist." (Brian Freeman. 2014. *Season of Fear*. London: Quercus, p. 74)

> Jingle bells / Batman smells / Robin ran away, / The Batmobile / Has lost its wheels / Now it's a Batmosleigh. (children's rhyme)

The types of example that have been explored here may not be exhaustive, and just how much of word-formation operates on such a basis is not clear. It might be argued that most blends, neoclassical formations and derivation function on the basis of such templates rather than on the basis of minimal meaningful elements. This is the kind of model that has been espoused by Bybee (e.g. Bybee 1985) for some time. It is hard to imagine what might be viewed as appropriate evidence to support such a hypothesis as opposed to, say, a rule-based hypothesis, but the alternative, that words such as the ones discussed in this chapter and the regular patterns that are generally discussed in the handbooks should be created by totally separate mechanisms also seems to be missing something.

Challenge

The suffix *-ee* has been discussed by several linguists, and many examples can be found, as well as overt commentary, in the relevant literature. On the basis of such examples or on the basis of examples you yourself can find (but not in dictionaries, where the original patterns of usage are not usually given), collect a sample of about twenty words (more if you are working as a team) containing the suffix and the ways in which they are used in early (perhaps unique) attestations. Is formation of *-ee* words regularly a matter of analogy? Or in how many instances do you think that the words are formed independently of corresponding *-er* words or a corresponding base? How can you tell? Does this influence your view of the way in which words are formed in English? Why (not)?

References

Bauer, Laurie. (2001). *Morphological Productivity.* Cambridge: Cambridge University Press.

Bybee, Joan. (1985). *Morphology.* Amsterdam: Benjamins.

Schultink, Henk. (1961). Productiviteit als morfologisch fenomeen. *Forum der Letteren* 2, 110–25.

9 Reflections on the Nature of the Lexeme

Since word-formation is usually considered to be about the formation of words in the sense of lexemes, and since compounds are words, in the sense of lexemes, whose elements are also words (lexemes), and since we have topics discussed in word-formation texts which might not be considered to result in lexemes (for instance, are initialisms like *UN* 'United Nations' lexemes?), and the same might apply to larger units which might be thought of a syntactic (are phrasal verbs lexemes, is the expression *kick the bucket* 'die' a lexeme?) the definition of the lexeme is clearly a matter of interest in word-formation. It is often simply assumed, or given a superficial definition which does not cover all that the analyst needs to know. A definition of the lexeme as a word in the sense that *cat* and *cats* represent the same word answers only some of the potential problems.

It is perhaps worth noting that the lexeme is a modern interpretation of the grammar of the classical languages, Greek and Latin, in particular under the influence of Lyons and Matthews (see references below). In those languages, words as they occur in sentences have certain 'accidental' properties which are not essential to central notion of the word (Lyons 1968: 198). This explains the older term 'accidence' for what we now more usually call 'inflection' (the spelling is now general, though *inflexion* used to be the standard British spelling). It is accidental that in the Latin sentence *Brutus Caesarem occidit* 'Brutus killed Caesar' that *Caesarem* is marked as being in the accusative case, because it is not essential to the nature of Caesar that it should be.

Lyons rephrases this a couple of years later when he says

> [A lexeme is] a unit which is manifest in one 'form' or another in sentences, but which is itself distinct from all its forms. (Lyons 1970: 21)

That is, the lexeme is the word with all its inflections stripped away (or, probably equivalently, encompassing all of its inflected forms); this makes it an abstract form, rather than one that a listener can hear, or a speaker produce. This also implies that it is a term defined for the purposes of analysis, and, as such, it is open to varying definitions. It is perfectly possible for the lexeme to be defined in different ways by different authorities.

What is not clear in Lyons's definition given above, is whether lexemes must always be represented in inflected forms or whether an uninflected item can be classed as a lexeme. Similar problems arise with parallel definitions from other linguists:

Ein Lexem kann nur definiert werden als eine Menge von grammatischen Wörten, die denselben Stamm enthalten.

[A lexeme can only be defined as a set of grammatical words which share a stem.] (Bergenholtz and Mugdan 1979: 117, my translation)

the lexeme is:

1. A complete sign on a particular linguistic level, namely the lexicon;
2. A class of variants, namely word-forms;
3. An abstract unit of the language system. (Lipka 2002: 89)

[A lexeme is a] word seen as an abstract grammatical entity, represented concretely by one or more different inflected forms according to the grammatical context. (Carstairs-McCarthy 2002: 144)

A lexeme is the abstract unit that stands for the set of inflectional forms. (Booij 2015: 158)

Bergenholtz and Mugdan (1979: 118) clarify their position by saying that *with* and *not* are lexemes despite having only one form, Lipka (2002) implies that such words are lexemes by annotating them in small capitals. However, Lyons (1977: 452–3) avoids calling *the* a lexeme, but implies that *this* might be a lexeme on the grounds that "[*this* and *these*] might be said to be forms of THIS . . . while the definite article is invariably *the*" (I have adjusted the notation for the lexeme in this quotation).

We seem, therefore, to have two distinct meanings for the term 'lexeme'. It is not clear whether Matthews's definitions of the lexeme as a "lexical word" (Matthews 1972: 161) or "the fundamental element in the lexicon of a language" (Matthews 1991: 26) fit with Lyons's usage or not, but I suspect not. There is a distinct French tradition where there is a clear distinction, drawn in rather different terms. For Fradin (2013: 102), as translated by Boyé (2018: 20), the lexeme has the following features:

It is an abstract unit to which word-forms are related; this unit captures the variations across word-forms.

It possesses a phonological representation which gives it prosodic autonomy.

Its meaning is stable and unique.

It belongs to a category and can have argument structure.

It belongs to an open-ended set and can serve as output and input of derivational morphology.

In this, it contrasts with the 'grammeme', which includes words such as prepositions, determiners and conjunctions (whether this corresponds exactly to the English term 'grammatical word' in the sense used by Bauer et al. 2013: 10, where it contrasts with 'lexical word', is not necessarily clear). In an earlier French tradition (Martinet 1967: 16), the term 'morpheme' would have been used rather than grammeme: in either case, there is a mismatch between the French terms and what appear to be the corresponding English terms.

At this point, we have three definitions of the lexeme, which overlap in that, for example, Latin PUELLA 'girl' is a lexeme which encompasses word-forms such as *puellam* ('girl.ACC.SG'), *puellae* ('girl.NOM.PL'). A word like *incurably* (created by word-formation but having only one form) is probably a lexeme for all, words like *the* and *with*, are not lexemes for all, but are for others, and *this* may be described as a lexeme if we believe it inflects.

This still leaves many questions unanswered. The most important of these is whether English *-er* in *owner* and *-ation* in *civilization* are lexemes, on the grounds that they are listed in the lexicon and so are listemes in the terminology of Di Sciullo and Williams (1987). Inflectional affixes are clearly not lexemes, at least in modern word-based theories, since they are built up by phonological rules to create word-forms from lexemic bases without creating compounds. Derivational affixes may not be either, if we believe that the distinction between a derivative like *smoker* and a compound like *smokehouse* is that the compound is a lexeme which contains two lexemes, and the derivative is a lexeme built from the appropriate stem of a single different lexeme. Derivational suffixes are also not (or are not generally) phonologically autonomous and cannot be the output of derivational morphology (to use Fradin's terms). On the other hand, derivational affixes may have stable semantics (if not always unique semantics), are abstract units which may vary in form, and probably have to be listed, rather than built up by phonological rules in the way that inflectional affixes are in Matthews (1972) and other works with a similar philosophy. The weight of the evidence is thus that they are not lexemes, but simply calling them 'elements' (Matthews 1970: 112) or 'forms' (Lyons 1977: 452) or 'formatives' does not help solve the problem of whether they are to be classed with other types of grammatically relevant chunks or whether they are a class unto themselves. In the French tradition, they can probably be classed with the grammemes, which might provide insights. The question here is not directly linked to the question of what a lexeme is, but it arises from considering that wider puzzle.

The next question is whether a lexeme, not including compound lexemes, can contain multiple lexemes as constituents. For Lyons (1977: 23) this is possible, and items such as *kick the bucket* 'die' are 'phrasal lexemes'. Although they do not use the term, Dixon and Aikhenvald (2002: 7) approve of the general notion. Again, it is not clear whether for Lyons a phrasal lexeme has to inflect, so that *kick the bucket* can be a phrasal lexeme because we can have *kicked the bucket* while *on the take* 'dishonestly accepting bribes' does not inflect and therefore is not a phrasal lexeme. The lack of clarity thus becomes more widespread. Di Sciullo and Williams (1987: 3) link such phrases to the notion of listedness (i.e. whether the speaker/listener has to memorize the words or not) and they call listed items 'listemes'. Listemes seem to include words as a subtype; another sub-type comprises syntactic structures "The listed syntactic objects are the idioms" (Di Sciullo and Williams 1987: 5). Carstairs-McCarthy (2002: 144) appears to take a similar view, but calls the listed items 'lexical items', a term which I prefer. Whether the lexical items encompass more than just the idioms may be controversial: I would take the view that *cool as a cucumber* and *To be or not to be* are also lexical items, despite not being idiomatic, on the basis that they are memorized and thus listed. Strictly speaking, the view where syntactic lexical items, particularly at least some idioms, are lexemes and the view where lexemes are a special type of lexical item indicates another potential difference of definition, although the difference is not particularly meaningful.

The conclusion here is that although there is wide agreement about the notion of lexeme in its most central or canonical uses (e.g. when we say that *am* is a form of the lexeme BE – or, more explicitly, a word-form belonging to the inflectional paradigm of the lexeme BE), once we move away from that point of agreement we find a great deal of disagreement and thus potential misunderstanding. It is easy enough to define a series of terms so that most of the points of disagreement are made unambiguous, but it would be nice if morphologists could agree on what that series of definitions comprises. It might be useful to start from the notion that although lexemes are listed, not everything that is listed is a lexeme (though borderlines might be hard to determine); a further step, that there is a level of analysis where sentences are seen as strings of lexemes, would require rather more consensus-building. Even further, we might be able to agree that anything which inflects is a lexeme (e.g. *mothers-in-law*), even if not all lexemes inflect (e.g. *with*). Such adjustments to the definition of lexeme, though relatively minor, would help clarify the nature of a central notion in modern morphology. If these proposals were accepted, the French tradition would still be separate from the anglophone tradition.

Challenge

Can you find any benefits either to using the term 'lexeme' only for words than can inflect or to using the term 'lexeme' for words which do not inflect as well? Would those benefits also be relevant to all lexical items? Does this help you decide whether lexemes are a subtype of lexical item or whether lexical items are a subclass of lexeme? Do you consider names to be lexemes? Does this affect your preferences for the definition of the lexeme? Do you think that the nature of the lexeme changes from one language to another, depending on how inflection works in the particular language?

References

Bauer, Laurie, Rochelle Lieber & Ingo Plag. (2013). *The Oxford Reference Guide to English Morphology.* Oxford: Oxford University Press.

Bergenholtz, Henning & Joachim Mugdan. (1979). *Einführung in die Morphologie.* Stuttgart: Kohlhammer.

Booij, Geert E. (2015). The structure of words. In John R. Taylor (ed.), *The Oxford Handbook of the Word.* Oxford: Oxford University Press, 157–74.

Boyé, Gilles. (2018). Lexemes, categories and paradigms. In Olivier Bonami, Gilles Boyé, Georgette Dal, Hélène Giraudo & Fiammetta Namer (eds.), *The Lexeme in Descriptive and Theoretical Morphology.* Berlin: Language Science Press, 19–41.

Carstairs-McCarthy, Andrew. (2002). *An Introduction to English Morphology.* Edinburgh: Edinburgh University Press.

Di Sciullo, Anna Maria & Edwin Williams. (1987). *On the Definition of Word.* Cambridge, MA: MIT Press.

Dixon, R.M.W. & Alexandra Y. Aikhenvald. (2002). Word: A typological framework. In R.M.W. Dixon & Alexandra Y. Aikhenvald (eds.), *Word: A Cross-Linguistic Typology.* Cambridge: Cambridge University Press, 1–41.

Fradin, Bernard. (2013). *Nouvelles approches en morphologie.* Paris: PUF.

Lipka, Leonhard. (2002). *English Lexicology.* Tübingen: Narr.

Lyons, John. (1968). *Introduction to Theoretical Linguistics.* Cambridge: Cambridge University Press.

(1970). Introduction. In John Lyons (ed.), *New Horizons in Linguistics.* Harmondsworth: Pelican, 7–28.

(1977). *Semantics.* 2 vols. Cambridge: Cambridge University Press.

Martinet, André. (1967). *Éléments de linguistique générale.* Paris: Colin.

Matthews, P.H. (1970). Recent developments in morphology. In John Lyons (ed.), *New Horizons in Linguistics.* Harmondsworth: Pelican, 96–114.

(1972). *Inflectional Morphology.* Cambridge: Cambridge University Press.

(1991). *Morphology.* 2nd ed. Cambridge: Cambridge University Press.

Part II

Semantic Questions

10 Reflections on How Words Bear Meaning, and What This Implies for Complex Words

10.1 Introduction

Perhaps because of the notion from Chomsky (1965) that what linguists are trying to explain and model is the usage of the ideal speaker-listener, and perhaps because of the availability of standard dictionaries, linguists – and, it must be said, non-linguists, too – operate on the principle that words have definite and knowable meanings, which can be fully described. Furthermore, we tend to operate on the principle that what we use when we produce instances of language is these fully explicit meanings. The first point that I want to make here is that for a large proportion of the words we think we know, perhaps all of them, this is not strictly true, which seems to imply that we may not actually communicate as much as we think when we use words. Second, I want to look at the implication for this on the semantics of complex words. This includes looking at the way meaning in complex words is deduced in a word-based model of morphological structure.

10.2 Some Examples from Personal Experience

In this section, I provide some examples from my own recent experience to illustrate some of the types of information that must underlie what we know about words. Because I am citing my own experience, the information is personal, but not only do I believe that the scenarios will be familiar to others, if not the specific examples involved, I believe that to some extent all experience of vocabulary items is personal, and that the overlap between personal experiences provides a superordinate level of experience which we might call vocabulary of English (or any other relevant language). My own reactions are, of course, skewed to some extent in that I am a linguist with an interest in vocabulary, etymology and the like, and so have available some information which not everyone will share, but I do not believe this matters in the larger scale of things.

My first example is the word *voe*. I am aware that there is a word *voe*, which I could legitimately use in a game of Scrabble. I don't know what it means at all.

I have a form to which I can attach no meaning. Note that this is not a claim that the meaning of *voe* is undiscoverable: if it were, then, presumably, we would not want to say that *voe* was a word, like *smofle* which, as far as I am aware, is not listed anywhere as a word of English.

At the other end of the scale, I was recently looking for a word whose form escaped me (temporarily). I knew that it meant writing about saints, and knew that the implication behind the word was that in such writing only the good things about the person are reported. I knew that it was a Greek compound. I wanted to use the word figuratively for a description of a real person (and not a saint) who had been described in glowing terms in something I had read. The word, of course, was *hagiography*, but for a few minutes I had a meaning, but no form. An equally familiar experience is illustrated in a passage from Wodehouse (2012). Wodehouse writes:

> I knew something was going to happen. You know that pre-what-d'you-call-it you get sometimes? Well, I got it then.

Wodehouse's narrator knows the meaning of the word and something of the form (*premonition* starts with *pre-*, although, interestingly, this is in the spelling and not in the pronunciation), but no more.

In the song 'Me and Bobby McGee' (Kristofferson and Foster *c*.1969), the singer says that he "took [his] harpoon out of [his] dirty red bandanna". I have never (to my knowledge) heard the word *harpoon* with this meaning anywhere else. In the following line the singer says he "was blowin' sad", which suggests a wind instrument, and if it could be wrapped in a bandanna, I assume it means what I would call a *mouth organ* or *harmonica* – though other instruments would be possible. I have to deduce this from the context, just as I have to deduce, later in the song, that *Salinas* is a town in America that I happen not to be familiar with (it is in California, near Monterey). Although I could legitimately assume that *harpoon* is a malapropism or a dialect word – either American English or regionally within the USA – I actually assume that it is a slang word, and the justification for this assumption might be of some interest, though it would be difficult to deduce. At no point do I assume that *harpoon* must refer to an instrument for killing whales. This illustrates firstly that we can build up a meaning from very few clues and that it is easy to reject a meaning attached to a form when it doesn't make sense, and thus assume some kind of homonymy. That there might be homonymy does not appear to cause problems with understanding.

In the same song, the singer says that they "finally sang up every song that driver knew". Many dictionaries do not list *sing up* at all, presumably because of its low frequency, and those that do, like Courtney (1983), list it only as it parallels *speak up*. I am not aware of having come across *sing up* in the sense used in this song anywhere else. But it makes a paradigm with forms like *drink up*, *eat up*, *use up*, all of which are listed by Courtney (1983). Again, we have a novel form, but one which is part of an existing paradigm, which makes it easy to understand, and allows productive use of a construction which is not compositional.

Compare this with a word that is well established in my vocabulary, and where I have quite a lot of information: *diamond*. For the word *diamond*, I might have all the following information.

- Diamonds are hard.
- Diamonds are made of carbon.
- Diamonds are mined.
- Diamonds are used for jewellery.
- Diamonds also have industrial uses.
- Diamonds come in several colours (including blue, yellow and pink).
- Diamonds are precious because expensive.
- Diamonds can be smuggled.
- Diamonds reflect light.
- Diamonds are cut to maximize this feature.
- According to the commercial slogan, diamonds are forever.
- According to a cynical song, diamonds are a girl's best friend.
- Diamonds are used for engagement rings.
- The shape '◊' is supposed to represent a diamond, and is called a diamond.
- This shape is also used for a suit in cards.
- Diamonds in cards is a red suit.
- The nine of diamonds is supposed to be the curse of Scotland.
- Fake diamonds can be made of zircon.
- Diamond is a term used in baseball (but I'm not sure what it implies).
- Diamonds are traded in London and Antwerp.
- The size of diamonds is measured in carats.
- The best diamonds are said to be of the first water.
- *Diamond* collocates with *mine, bracelet, necklace, ring, cutting, smuggling*. If we say *She wore her diamonds*, we probably mean a necklace, and perhaps more.

This set of statements about the word *diamond* cannot be exhaustive, but provides at least a starting point. Although I have, for practical reasons, expressed this information in linguistic statements, some of the information may be held in my brain in experiential ways, for example, the hardness of diamonds. Note, though, that despite all this knowledge, I cannot necessarily recognize a diamond – a zircon or even glass could probably fool me with ease. I do not know how big a diamond would have to be to be a one-carat diamond. I am not sure of the rank of diamonds relative to other suits in the card-game bridge. There is a lot of information here, but the fact that I cannot recognize something that is called a *diamond* in the same way that I can recognize something called a *book* is of interest.

The problem here is an old one. Locke was worried about how we are to define gold, given that most of us do not have the technical knowledge to distinguish gold from other things. We can call something *gold* not because we have sufficient information to know without any doubt that it is gold, but because we are willing to believe some authority that tells us it is gold.

New Zealand children throughout the country have a consistent story about the daddy longlegs spider (*Pholcus phalangioides*). The story is that this is the most poisonous spider in the world, but fortunately its jaws are too weak (or too small) to allow it to bite humans. This is almost entirely false (the creature is a spider; there are other creatures called *daddy longlegs* in other places in the world, not all of them are spiders). The creature is not particularly poisonous and can – and does – bite humans (Sirvid n.d.). The point of this example is that speakers can have totally erroneous beliefs about the world (and about the words which we use to help conceptualize the world), and can use such errors to define words ('the most poisonous spider in the world'). The definitions that individuals use do not have to be based on scientific truth to be able to function appropriately in the world.

Weinreich ([1962] 1980: 298) reports an experiment with dictionary meanings he tried with graduate students. He took a number of near-synonymous adjectives, including *gloomy, morose, saturnine, sulky* and *sullen*, and provided the students with their dictionary definitions, asking them to match each definition with a word. "The results", he reports, "were poor". I repeated the same experiment with undergraduate students and a different dictionary some years ago, and the results were rather more promising. The value of dictionary definitions is not the point here, though. The question is: if speakers know these words and do not see them as synonyms in a particular text, what kinds of information might distinguish them? Some of the answer is in collocations: *gloomy* can collocate with *house, room, picture* (especially when used figuratively), *outlook*, as well as with words denoting people. All of these words can collocate with a noun denoting a person or a person's face. They differ in style: *saturnine* is literary, *morose* is rather formal, while *gloomy* and *sulky* are neither. *Sulky* gives me the impression of not getting what you want, possibly being rather immature, and with the possibility that the emotion is short-lived. *Sullen*, on the other hand, seems rather longer-lived. *Sulky* suggests a pout, while the others do not. There are several points to make about this example. First, but perhaps least importantly, is that writing really good definitions of words is extremely difficult – even if Weinreich's experiment may have gone beyond what we normally require of such a definition. Second, that some of the information we use to distinguish between words is not the type of information which usually gets into definitions. Third, just what we know about individual words goes beyond the material provided by a typical dictionary definition.

Everyone familiar with Lear's (1871) poem 'The Owl and the Pussy-Cat' will also be familiar with the term *runcible spoon*. *Runcible*, evidently, collocates with *spoon*. But what does it mean? Since Lear invented *runcible* as a nonsense word (and used it several times, although most famously in this poem), we might justifiably argue that it has no meaning, although it does have a collocation. Not only does this show that words can exist in the community but have no meaning, it also shows that words whose meaning we do not know can have firm collocations. At a later date, hypostatization stepped in: if we have a word, there must be a thing. *Runcible spoon* came to mean what we now call a *spork*. But Lear also had a *runcible cat*, so if *runcible spoon* means 'spork' it is not clear how the meaning of *runcible* can be equally used of a cat. If this example of knowing a collocate without knowing the real meaning seems too far-fetched, consider *aneroid*. This clearly collocates with *barometer*, but until I looked it up in a dictionary, I didn't know that *aneroid* means 'not using liquid'.

There are many words for which I know a superordinate term, but not what differentiates this particular word from other hyponyms of the superordinate. For instance, I know that *sarsaparilla*, *sassafras* and *mint julep* are drinks, but otherwise I know virtually nothing about them – not even whether they are alcoholic or not. I know that *beguine*, *galliard* and *lambada* are dances, but little more. I know that *barouche*, *brougham* and *carriole* are types of horse-drawn vehicle but would not recognize any of them specifically. I know that *bézique*, *faro* and *euchre* are card games, but do not know how to play any of them. Such imperfect knowledge of the meanings of words must be very common, and indicates that speakers do not have the perfect knowledge of their vocabulary that is presupposed by most semantic theories. Despite the fact that I know only the superordinate of each of these, I assume that they are not synonyms. In a similar way, although I know the word *hurtle*, I am surprised to find it defined in a dictionary (Marr 2008) as "to move rapidly with a clattering sound" – I only know that it means 'move rapidly' and sound does not figure in the way I understand the word. In this particular instance, it may be that the dictionary is incorrect or out of date. The following examples from the British National Corpus (BNC) (Davies 2004–) do not appear to imply noise at all, even if the majority of examples in the BNC might be argued to involve sound.

> Araminta's callous mouth and Agnes Diggory's sympathetic eyes hurtled through her mind.
> Clutching a Union Jack, three-year-old Louis hurtled into the arms of his dad.
> A stone hurtled through the air and the dogs scattered.
> the situation in East Germany could hurtle out of control.
> Now a blue-grey merlin, the smallest of the falcons, hurtles across the heath.

But whatever the majority of speakers think that *hurtle* means, and independent of the accuracy of the dictionary definition, the examples collected here indicate that we do not have a full knowledge of words we can (in some sense) understand and possibly use.

I know the word *mustelid* from media discussions of predation against birds, and know that it denotes a family of carnivorous animals, of which the weasel is, for me, the prototypical member. Apart from weasels and stoats, I do not know what animals are members of the family. That is, I know the superordinate term, but not much about its hyponyms. Until I looked this up, I thought that ferrets were probably members of the family (and they are), had not thought of martens or polecats at all, and was surprised to find that badgers are mustelids. Here I know (in some sense) the superordinate term, but do not know the full range of its hyponyms, and so have a restricted impression of the range of meaning *mustelid* might carry.

As a young child (probably under the age of 7), I was relatively regularly told that I was a *spuniachie-looking thing* (/spjuːniæxi/). I was told this by my mother, whose parents were Scottish, and by my aunt, her sister. I deduced that the word meant 'skinny, weak and feeble'. I assumed that this was just another Scottish word, but when I lived in Scotland later in my life, I could find nobody who recognized the word. I now assume that *spuniachie* was a family word, not known in any wider community. In the British *Woman's Own* for 14 November 1981, a woman from near Bristol reported that in their family *puddycovers* was used for 'gloves', and *poggolies* for 'slippers'. Words need not have a very wide distribution at all, and even family words may have quite a short lifespan. Speakers may or may not be aware of the restricted nature of such words. Words may belong to very restricted communities, and even then be transient.

What these various examples show is that our individual knowledge of the words which we recognize and use is spotty, and incomplete, occasionally even false. Furthermore, what we think words mean may or may not coincide with what we can learn from a dictionary definition, and in any case includes more than can typically be found in a dictionary definition. This is not to say that a dictionary definition is not useful (although it might mean that, even in law courts, rather less infallibility should be attributed to such definitions than is often the case), just that it is not quite what is held in the head of a speaker, especially because – though not only because – it is fully specified.

Although the examples used here are my own, the general observation is not new. Clark (2023) talks of such instances as being those where speakers and listeners gradually acquire parts of the meanings of individual words. She argues that our understanding of individual words only has to be good enough to allow for communication on one particular occasion, but that speakers typically need more information about the words used than do listeners.

10.3 Some Implications

The information that is given about *diamond* (Section 10.2) indicates that much of the information we have in our heads, both about the nature of the world and the words which we use to describe that nature, is encyclopaedic information. Although this might be a controversial claim, it is made advisedly, and a justification for the position is given in Bauer (2005), where it is pointed out that, in some cases, information which would uniquely identify a particular real-world entity is not the most useful information for a real speaker, and there may be multiple pieces of information of this kind. This standpoint is also accepted within Distributed Morphology (see Siddiqi 2019: 149 and the comment in Spencer 2019: 210). I shall not try to justify this position any further here.

Many of the examples given above also hold the implication that what speakers know about individual words can change. I could come to learn what a galliard is, either in terms of what it looks like when danced, or in terms of the music to which it is danced. I could check precisely what *voe* means. I have learned that a badger is a mustelid. Readers could have learned from what was said above that the nine of diamonds is called 'the curse of Scotland' (the reason for this name is disputed).

The example of *sullen*, *sulky*, etc. indicates that what we know about words is more than a clear-cut definition will provide: we also know about collocates, about what used to be called 'connotations' and about the stylistic implications of using one word over another. In other words, we must have more information about individual words than is usually provided in a dictionary definition (though some dictionaries do attempt to provide some of this information).

10.4 Applying This to Complex Words

If all this is true of morphologically simple words, we must assume that it will also be true of morphologically complex words. The difference is that morphologically complex words tend to make some information explicit in a way that need not be true of simple words. For example, words beginning with *un-* are usually negative (usually because this does not apply to words which beginning in *under-*, for example), words ending with *-ation* are usually nouns, words ending in *-ee* that has been attached to a verb usually denote people, and so on. Sometimes, we do not need much more information than this. If we know what *happy* means, we can work out a great deal about *unhappy*; if we know what *license* means as a verb, we can predict much about *licensee*, although not that the word is often used of someone licensed to sell alcohol.

Herein lies the problem for deducing the meaning of a complex word from its morphological form. The morphology provides a framework within which we can seek a meaning but does not fully explicate the meaning. The examples given earlier show that this is not unexpected.

Morphologically complex words differ from simple ones in that some information is provided in the word. In compounds, the given information is in the meanings we, as individuals, already hold about the elements. In *windmill* that information may be more useful than in *penknife*, because we no longer use penknives to cut quills for writing. Nonetheless, the information is given, we just have to interpret it. One part of interpreting it – and this applies equally to derivatives – is knowing which homonym or polyseme is selected for the meaning in the complex word. To understand *canonical*, we have to understand *canon* refers to a standard criterion as opposed to a body of clergymen. To understand *draftee* we have to recognize that *draft* does not have any of the meanings that appear in *bank draft*, *draftsman* (*draughtsman*), or *drafty* (*draughty*). To understand *draughtsman* and *draught horse* we have to recognize different meanings of *draught*. This loss of possibilities available for the base word is a well-known principle of the semantics of new complex words (Bauer and Valera 2015).

Some affixes carry meaning in much the same way that lexemes do. This is typically the case of prefixes in English-coined words such as *post-*, *pre-*, *re-*, some of which might be considered to be prepositions/adverbs, as in *byproduct*, *overbridge*. Some suffixes are just as explicit, though typically with a more specific meaning: suffixes such as *-fold*, *-scape*, *-teen*. Other affixes may not carry specific meaning in the same way, but may simply mark the word-class of the output. Such instances include *-al* (creating adjectives), *-ar*, *-ion*, *-ity*, *-ize*, *-ness*, *-ous*. *Parental* tells us little more than that the word is an adjective connected with the word *parent*, *stupidity* is a noun connected with being *stupid*. Some affixes do both, affixes such as *-ee*, *-ess*, *-hood*, *-less*. The elements of neoclassical formations, when they attach to English words, tend to have a density of information that is similar to that of lexemes, but as they become more used as English forms, they become less specific in their meanings: *-itis* in *Mondayitis* is not as specific as *-itis* in *appendicitis*, where it still carries its original meaning of 'inflammation'.

With affixes, as with lexemes, we have to deal with homonymy or polysemy. Adverbial *-s* in *afterwards*, *downstairs*, *indoors* has a homonymous affix in *Babs* (from *Barbara*), *Debs* (from *Debora*), *Wimblers* (from *Wimbledon*); nominal *-al* in *arrival* has a homonymous affix in adjectival *-al* in *parental*. The different readings of *-er* in *driver* (agent or instrument), *believer* (experiencer), *diner* (agent or location), *jumper* (agent or clothing) are usually treated as polysemy (although the distinction is not particularly clear in this example). There are two claims from Cognitive Linguistics about the semantics of such affixes (Panther and Thornburg 2002, Basilio 2009). The first is that affixed words have a metonymical relation to their base, the second is that the readings of polysemous affixes are in a metonymical relationship with each other. The two are clearly related. To the extent that either of these holds, and there is a great deal of evidence to support them, we may not need to specify the distinctions in linguistic structure, because they are automatically covered by cognitive processes. Nevertheless, in both the homonymy case and the polysemy case, the users of the words have to be able to determine whether the affix is appropriate and how it is being used. Some authorities (Falkum and Vicente 2015, Pustejovsky 2017) suggest that such meanings are underspecified; an alternative view is that, from a linguistic standpoint, they are overspecified when they become fixed in particular usages. That is, the linguistic structure is inherently vague, and it is usage that determines just how individual words are likely to be used.

If the meanings of complex words, at least in the sense that they are determined by a grammar, are inherently vague, then it is up to the user to decide what is a plausible reading of the word, in context, provided that it is within a permitted shell of variation. In many cases, we do not even have to know what the precise relationship is, as long as we know that there is one. It is well known that the precise relationship holding between *police* and *dog* in *police dog* may not be clear (is the dog associated with the police, is the dog trained by the police, is the dog working for the police, is the dog owned by the police and so on?). The grammar says that there is a relationship (in some sense, a defining one), and that it is likely that a *police dog* is a type of dog, and that may be all we know, or we may fill in something more precise for ourselves. This is similar to knowing that a *lambada* is a dance, but not knowing any more. Sometimes we may know that whatever the relationship is, it is the same as in another, already known word. We understand *goulash communism* on the basis of *spaghetti western*, and whatever the relationship between the elements is, we recognize it as being the same in both cases. That is, we see the analogy between the forms and use it to interpret the less familiar word (see Chapter 8).

Equally, we may recognize that elements do not have a common meaning. The *-age* that occurs in *postage* does not have the same reading as the one that occurs in *wastage*, and it may not be clear whether either of those shares a reading with *frontage*. Linguistically, what we can recognize here is a noun related to the meaning of its base. The details depend on usage, and are gradually built up in the individual, as the word becomes more familiar, and in the community as more individuals agree on the frame in which the words are used.

The implication here is that words in the community, just like words in the individual, start off with minimal specification, and gradually become more fully semantically specified. Any theory of the lexicon must allow for this process, and allow for the fact that different individual speakers will have different bits of information about each word. This seems to imply that, in the community, words may function with a range of partly defined meanings, not necessarily all compatible, which may develop into new meanings for the word and cause old meanings to vanish. In the first few months of 2023, I heard the word *exasperate* used by people in news broadcasts and radio interviews to mean 'to make worse': *This will only exasperate the situation*. I have also heard a professional broadcaster say that because of traffic jams there were a lot of *exacerbated motorists* trying to get to work. This is not the first time in the history of English that a word for 'make worse' has come to be used to mean 'annoy'; the same trajectory can be found earlier for *aggravate*. At the moment, there is apparently some confusion in the community about what both *exasperate* and *exacerbate* mean. We cannot yet tell what the outcome will be. In the meantime, the community must have dual meanings for both words, even if these have not yet got into dictionaries.

The take-away message from all of this is that linguists should not expect the fully specified dictionary meaning to be what individual members of the speech community know, and should not expect that fully specified meaning to be deducible from the form of a new complex word. Rather, the form provides only a minimal amount of information about the meaning of a word; most of the interesting detail is provided by knowledge of the real world and knowledge of the way the word is used – something that can only arise when the learner has heard the word used many times in context. It remains true that the speaker usually needs a rather more elaborated meaning of the word than the listener does, but, of course, that cannot be guaranteed in cases like *daddy longlegs*.

10.5 Derivation in Word-Based Morphology

Word-based morphology (including some forms of word-and-paradigm or a-morphous morphology) has largely been developed as a way of dealing with inflectional morphology. In word-based models, the word is the fundamental unit of analysis, and the meaning of the elements within the word is derived from the meaning of the word as whole. Either the meanings of the elements are abstracted from the words using parallel words to deduce this, or the material added to stems is constructed through a series of rules which create phonological form rather than sequences of morphological elements (Blevins 2006). In either instance, the meanings attached to the grammatical material (i.e. not to the stem) are given by the grammatical system of the language concerned. If the language has inflectional case, the number of cases and their fundamental nature is supplied by the grammar, with a limited number of potential contrasts; if the language has inflectional tense, the way of dividing time into a limited number of options is presented by the way the language is used. Learners of the language who are not linguists may not name the various possibilities, but the system is there in the language to which they are exposed. The function associated with the *-us* in Latin *lupus* 'wolf' is also associated with the function assigned to -*a* in *puella* 'girl', but with a different set of stems. The meanings provided by the language fill empty slots that the language requires to supplement the stem. That is, the meanings (which, as linguists, we might gloss as 'nominative singular' or '3rd person of the present indicative' and so on) are added to the meaning of the stem without much that is unpredictable except in idiomatic structures such as the plural of *brain* being used to mean 'intelligence'.

The meanings associated with the stems are not limited in parallel ways, as we have seen. The learner's understanding of the stem increases with exposure to the stem, in the way discussed earlier in this section. Even the meaning associated with transpositional derivation is not simply additive because, for instance, *postage* has a meaning of 'cost' which is associated directly neither with the stem nor with the nominalization (not even with having a nominalization with -*age*, which in other words such as *marriage* does not carry that meaning). In other words, the way meaning arises in derivational morphology and inflectional morphology is different enough to suggest that derivational morphology cannot be treated in the same way as inflectional morphology in a word-based model. We cannot look at a word like *carriage* and deduce which part of the meaning arises from which part of the form or present a series of rules that will produce the form required to mean 'a section of a train used for transporting passengers'. This is part of the overspecification of derived forms in comparison with what can be calculated on the basis of its formal make-up. The overspecification is clearly word-based: 'used for transporting passengers' is not an association with either *carry* or with -*age*.

Consider, then, a word like *roaster*. The meaning of the stem, *roast*, is given (though not necessarily fully known), in the same way that it would be in *roasted*. The rest of the meaning is not limited by the linguistic system, and some of it is not carried by the linguistic system: whether a roaster is a person or a utensil seems to be something that falls into that category, along with the fact that a *roaster* can be something destined to be roasted or a very hot day. These various meanings of *roaster* have in common that they all indicate an entity connected with roasting. That is the most that can be attributed to the suffix. But how does that meaning arise? If the meaning is associated purely with the word *roaster*, then any affix would be suitable, just enough to indicate that derivation occurs, and possibly to indicate the word-class of the output. That is not how English (or any other language with derivation) works. Attaching the meaning to the suffix -*er*, on the other hand, would be tantamount to having morphemes, which word-based morphology does not want. So we have an option, following Beard's work, of saying that we have a nominalization, but the form of that nominalization is, in some way, idiosyncratic and not necessarily directly linked to the form used. This seems plausible, but would need some elaboration on how it would work.

A better alternative for deducing the meaning of a derivative – though not a sufficient one – is to start from the root and find the largest section of the word for which a meaning is familiar in one's personal lexicon. The person hearing the word then has to add such meaning as is definitely provided by the remaining affixes (sometimes no more than word-class), then deduce the meaning of the word in context. Finally, relevant inflectional meaning has to be added (or, in English, where a form like *inform* may be an infinitive, an imperative, or a present-tense form for most persons of the verb, the inflectional meaning must be deduced from context). In cases where a derivative shows a meaning of the base that is not available to the base in isolation (Bauer and Valera 2015), such a process will not work, and further deduction or calculation will be required. That this process demands a distinction between inflection and derivation (and thus demands a lexeme) is not a problem in a theory that is based on the lexeme.

Challenge

Find some unfamiliar derived lexemes (this book contains many examples). What can be deduced about their meaning on the basis of their form? What parts of their meaning cannot be deduced? Contrast this with some very infrequent inflected forms of morphologically simple lexemes (word-forms like *greyest, strived*). What parts of the meaning can be deduced from the form in such cases? If you assume that the full meaning is associated with the word, how do you relate phonological form with the meaning expressed? If you assume that the meaning associated with the form is supported by the form, what elements of the meaning can you find support for? What do you conclude about what the form of a word tells you about its meaning?

References

Basilio, Margarida Maria de Paula. (2009). The role of metonymy in word formation: Brazilian Portuguese agent noun constructions. In Klaus-Uwe Panther, Linda L. Thornburg & Antonio Barcelona (eds.), *Metonymy and Metaphor in Grammar*. Amsterdam: Benjamins, 99–144.

Bauer, Laurie. (2005). The illusory distinction between lexical and encyclopedic information. In Henrik Gottlieb, Jens Erik Mogensen & Arne Zettersten (eds.), *Symposium on Lexicography XI*. Tübingen: Niemeyer, 111–15.

Bauer, Laurie & Salvador Valera. (2015). Sense inheritance in English word-formation. In Laurie Bauer, Lívia Körtvélyessy & Pavol Štekauer (eds.), *Semantics of Complex Words*. Cham: Springer, 67–84.

Blevins, James P. (2006). Word-based morphology. *Journal of Linguistics* 42, 531–73.

Chomsky, Noam. (1965). *Aspects of the Theory of Syntax*. Cambridge, MA: MIT Press.

Clark, Eve V. 2023. A gradualist view of word-meaning in language acquisition and language use. *Journal of Linguistics* 59, 737–62.

Courtney, Rosemary. (1983). *Longman Dictionary of Phrasal Verbs*. Harlow: Longman.

Davies, Mark. (2004–) *BYU–BNC* [based on the British National Corpus from Oxford University Press]. Available online at http://corpus.byu.edu/bnc/.

Falkum, Ingrid Lossius & Augustin Vicente. (2015). Polysemy: Current perspectives and approaches. *Lingua* 157, 1–16.

Kristofferson, Kris & Fred Foster. (*c*.1969). 'Me and Bobby McGee'. Sung on the album *Kristofferson* (1970), released by Monument [a version of the song sung by Janis Joplin differs in some relevant respects from the version cited here].

Lear, Edward. (1871). *Nonsense Songs, Stories, Botany, and Alphabets*. Boston: Osgood.

Marr, Vivian (ed.). (2008). *The Chambers Dictionary*. 11th ed. Edinburgh: Chambers Harrap.

Panther, Klaus-Uwe & Linda L. Thornburg (2002). The roles of metaphor and metonymy in English -er nominals. In René Dirven & Ralf Pörings (eds.), *Metaphor and Metonymy in Comparison and Contrast*. Berlin: De Gruyter Mouton, 279–322.

Pustejovsky, James. (2017). The semantics of lexical underspecification. *Folia Linguistica* 32, 323–47.

Siddiqi, Daniel. (2019). Distributed Morphology. In Jenny Audring & Francesca Masini (eds.), *The Oxford Handbook of Morphological Theory*. Oxford: Oxford University Press, 143–65.

Sirvid, Philip. (n.d.). Daddy long-legs spider (https://collections.tepapa.govt.nz/topic/9428 accessed 31 August 2021).

Spencer, Andrew. (2019). Manufacturing consent over Distributed Morphology. *Word Structure* 12, 208–59.

Weinreich, Uriel. ([1962] 1980). *On Semantics*. Edited by William Labov & Beatrice S. Weinreich. Philadelphia: University of Pennsylvania Press [originally published in *International Journal of American Linguistics* 28(2), pt. 4 (1962), 25–43].

Wodehouse, P.G. ([1919] 2012). Doing Clarence a bit of good. In *My Man Jeeves*. Project Gutenberg EBook #8164.

11 Reflections on Tautology and Redundancy

11.1 Introduction

Anyone who remembers the political situation in the 1970s will recall the Strategic Arms Limitation Talks between the USA and the USSR. *Strategic Arms Limitation Talks* being too long for the headline writers, an acronym was used instead of the full expression. But the talks were not simply referred to as *SALT*, but rather as *SALT talks*. Since the *T* in *SALT* stands for *talks*, this was, in effect, *Strategic Arms Limitation Talks talks*. This looks like a prima facie case of tautology, saying the same thing twice, classically viewed as a stylistic fault.

However, one of the words that is sometimes seen as a near-synonym of *tautology* is *redundancy*: if you say the same thing twice, one of those expressions is unnecessary or redundant. The difference is that while tautology is traditionally seen as a bad thing, redundancy may be a good thing.

All natural language contains redundancies. If we say *these things*, we have made both words plural, though it would be less redundant to mark the plurality only once. If we say *pill* and then *bill*, the two are distinguished not only by the fact that the /b/ may be slightly voiced, but by the fact that the /p/ is aspirated and uttered with greater force. Logically we should not need three ways to make the distinction. If we say *I'm coming* the *am* and the *-ing* go together to make up the continuous aspect, though the *-ing* alone would convey the message. Legal language is full of expressions like *goods and chattels*, which really mean 'goods and goods' but are intended to make sure everything possible is covered by the phrase. We know that the Arabic spelling system does not mark vowels, and *v*n *n *ngl*sh w* c*n *nd*rst*nd * wr*tt*n t*xt w*th**t v*w*l l*tt*rs (it is a lot harder if the position is not marked or if only the vowels letters are left instead of the consonants). All this means that when we hear someone speaking to us in a crowded room or another place where there is a lot of background noise, if we are listening to someone speaking over a bad phone line, or if we are slightly deaf, we can still understand speech because so much redundancy is built in. At a different level, orators and teachers find it useful to repeat key points of a message to make sure it is grasped by the audience: they may do this in slogans which simply repeat the same wording, or they may reformulate the message, but repetition, a special case of redundancy, is not necessarily a bad thing.

Two questions arise: how much duplication does word-formation create? And is it tautology or redundancy when we find it?

11.2 Acronyms and Initialisms

The kind of apparent tautology illustrated by *SALT talks* is quite common with acronyms and initialisms. Some examples are given here.

> ABS system, ATM machine, Covid virus/disease, GPS system, HIV virus, ISBN number, PIN number, RAT test, SAT test, VIN number

In most of these cases, it is the head word of the underlying phrase which is repeated, though note *Covid*, which may refer to the virus as well as the disease. This is not an absolute rule, though. An example which is often cited is *Please RSVP*, where the *SVP* stands for French *s'il vous plaît*, 'please'. The trouble with acronyms and initialisms for the user is that people tend to forget what the letters stand for, and simply use the new form as a name, without any analysis of that name. Many people do not know what *Covid* actually stands for, not even whether it refers to the disease or to the virus which causes the disease. Where the acronym or abbreviation represents foreign words, as with *RSVP*, *KGB*, *SPQR*, the lack of complete understanding is likely to be much greater. Even internet abbreviations, typically much more recent and more transparent, can be misunderstood: some people thought that *lol* meant 'lots of love' when it first came out, rather than 'laugh out loud'.

If you are not fully aware of what the letters are supposed to stand for, or if you are not sure if your interlocutor knows what they stand for, then adding some clarification can be useful, and may not actually be tautology at all in the mind of the user, because there is no sense of repetition being involved. Where the acronym or initialism is fully understood, the extra gloss can be omitted, and we can talk about *ABS*, *ATM*, *ISBN* and so on with no new head noun.

Although these examples look as though they are tautological, they probably are not for many users; they may actually be useful for some listeners, and those speakers for whom they are not necessary can easily omit them.

11.3 Tautological Compounds

Tautological compounds are those where one of the elements appears to recapitulate information provided in the other element. There is not always consensus as to what counts as a relevant example, but some probable cases are given here.

alleyway, cobblestone, cod fish, collie dog, courtyard, elm tree, flagstone, oak tree, pathway, pine tree, poodle dog, pussycat, tuna fish, widow woman

Although these all look parallel, they are not all the same. To begin with, some are in more general use than others. *Collie dog* seems more usual to me than *poodle dog*, in turn more usual than *Labrador dog* (which I have seen listed but am not familiar with). Clearly, other speakers may feel differently about these, but the fact of variation is not in question. Second, some of these contrast with a different right-hand element: *oak tree* contrasts with *oak wood*, which could be seen as an argument against the use of *tree* being tautologous. *Elmwood* and *pinewood* are also found. *Cod fish* and *tuna fish* have no corresponding contrasting element.

They differ in other ways as well. It seems that any tree name can have the element *tree* inserted after it: *beech tree, birch tree, fir tree, kauri tree, palm tree, sycamore tree*. It is not clear whether there is analogy with expressions such as *apple tree, cherry tree, pear tree* or not (though note we get *banana palm, date palm* rather than *banana tree, date tree*). Not every fish can have *fish* inserted after it, though: *herring fish, sardine fish, snapper fish, trout fish*, all sound odd to my ears, although whether they are impossible is something that would require further research. *Courtyard* seems to be like the phrases *goods and chattels, last will and testament* in the sense that *court* is French and *yard* is English, and putting the two together simply covers all the possibilities.

On the other hand, all the examples given here would mean the same if the right-hand element were omitted, and the shorter version is probably the more common. This suggests that the right-hand element is redundant in these cases. Although this is true of *widow woman* today, there used to be a term *widowman* ('widower'), so that *widow* has not always been restricted to women.

Benczes (2014: 445) argues that compounds of this type are not tautological because they are

used to dignify and upgrade concepts via the conceptual metaphor MORE OF FORM IS MORE OF CONTENT, whereby a linguistic unit that has a larger form is perceived to carry more information (that is, more content) than a single-word unit.

While I would not wish to dismiss this notion, it does raise the question of whether forms like *oak tree* are single words or word-sequences, and it also raises the question of whether adding an element like *tree* can provide information on the "dignity" of the word rather than to provide semantic information about the kind of plants involved. The lack of redundancy could also be due to other reasons, for example a requirement for emphasis, which might explain why *oak* and *oak tree* can both be used, another factor which Benczes recognizes.

11.4 Tautological Names

Tautology in names often arises through words from another language being used in the relevant expressions. Consider, for example, the *River Avon* in Stratford-upon-Avon. *Avon* is a Celtic word meaning 'river' (in modern Welsh, it is spelled *afon*), so that the *River Avon* is, technically speaking, just repeating the same content twice. There are many more examples from all over the world. Consider, for instance, Māori loans in New Zealand, which give *Lake Rotoiti* and *Mount Maunganui*. *Rotoiti* means 'little lake', *Maunganui* means 'big mountain', so that the names, if translated, give 'lake little lake' and 'mount big mount'. *The La Brea Tar Pits* in Los Angeles, when the Spanish is translated, give 'the the tar tar pits'. *Penhill*, in Yorkshire, contains another loan from Celtic and means 'hill hill'.

Since the point of these examples is presumably that speakers do not understand the non-English label, it is hard to say that these are really tautologous. *Avon* (and so on for the other examples) is just a name, and the English version is the only piece to provide information. This is no different in principle from what happens in a word like *children*. *Child* is the singular, and the plural used to be *childer* (still found in some dialects). But when *-er* stopped being used to mark plurals, a new plural was needed, and the *-en* (as in *oxen*) was added to *childer* to make it plural. Dutch still has the plural *kinderen* from *kind* 'child' where the two plurals are more clearly marked. Other double plurals in English include *bacterias*, *dices*, *phenomenas*, some of which are not viewed as standard.

11.5 Conclusion

It seems that such tautology as there appears to be in these formations is not clearly tautologous for language users, and, indeed, is often not even redundant. In terms of the norm of English (see Chapter 6), that is just the way things are done. It may be part of the phenomenon of using longer words for important things (Janda 2021), but even that is not clear.

Challenge

Look for double plurals in some large corpus. How common are they? Do they all have the same basic motivation of ensuring that the plurality is clearly marked? Do *fish*, *sheep* and *deer* get marked for plural? Why (not)? How do double comparatives and superlatives (*more prettier*, *most prettiest*) fit into the general pattern? Do we find double marking of derivational categories?

References

Benczes, Réka. (2014). Repetitions which are not repetitions: The non-redundant nature of tautological compounds. *English Language and Linguistics* 18, 431–47.

Janda, Richard D. (2021). Perturbations, practices, predictions, and postludes in a bioheuristic historical linguistics. In Richard D. Janda, Brian D. Joseph & Barbara S. Vance (eds.), *The Handbook of Historical Linguistics*, vol II. Hoboken, NJ: Wiley, 523–650.

Part III

Syntactic Questions

12 Reflections on Recursion

It is noted in Bauer (1983: 69) that in a few places in English there appears to be recursion in suffix sequences. Two patterns are given there, one involving *-ation*, *-al* and *-ize*, where any one of the suffixes can be the first in a sequence of three, as in

>   sensationalize
>   formalization
>   civilizational

and the other involves the suffixes *-ic*, *-al* and *-ist* in a similar way:

>   classicalist
>   nationalistic
>   egotistical

Both these examples give rise to problems of analysis. Is *-ation* a single suffix, the only productive affix containing the Latin *-ion* formative or is it a sequence of *-ate* and *-ion*? Is *-ical* an independent suffix, or is it a sequence of *-ic* and *-al*? And is *-istic* an independent suffix, or is it a sequence of *-ist* and *-ic*? (There is also the possibility that both patterns exist.) Merging of affix sequences into single affixes has been termed affix-telescoping (Haspelmath 1995: 3–6). Whether telescoping applies or not may not matter in the sense that any rule-based system is going to have to allow recursion in this set of affixes, and therefore allow for potential words like *sensationalization* (noted by Miller 1981: 114) as well as for words like *institutionalizationalize*, which do not occur. Ljung (1970: 13) notes that the longest suffixal string he has attested contains just four suffixes, but as we have already seen, such numbers depend on how you count some suffixes.

Sequences of two suffixes are common in English, and are dealt with in descriptive terms in Bauer et al. (2013: ch. 27) and in theoretical terms in works in Lexical Morphology and by Fabb (1988). It is worth noting that such sequences do not generally allow for recursion of the same suffix. Note, however, the construction illustrated by *breaker-upperer*, discussed in Chapter 13, the word *perfectionation*, where the *-at(e)* is arguably an independent suffix, so this is not strictly a straightforward repetition, and *fractionation*, where the same is true, and where the first *-ion* is attached to a bound root, which may be important. Note also the rather unusual example below (which might be argued to involve homonymous affixes rather than repetitions of the same affix).

> I'm only kind of Jewish. I'm Jewish-ish. (John Connolly. 2018. *The Woman in the Woods*. London: Hodder & Stoughton, p. 69)

Repetitions of the same sound-sequence are allowed, e.g. in *adulterer*, *ringing*, but even such sequences are not common.

Sequences of three suffixes are rare, anyway. Some examples are given below.

> Christianizer
> dictatorialness
> establishmentarian
> justifiableness
> musicianship
> polarization
> polarizer
> pressurizer
> provincialization
> Prussianization
> sensationalism
> truthfulness
> verbalizer

The list of types here is not exhaustive, and this list is based on established words, while nonce words may provide a wider range of types. Yet there is sufficient data here to suggest some generalizations.

The suffix *-ize* always permits subsequent suffixation with *-ation*. Since this is one of the main sources of *-ation* suffixation, this is not surprising. The same seems to be true with *-er* added to *-ize*. Again, given the productivity of *-er* suffixation on verbs, this is not surprising. Given that *-ize* can attach to words with several different suffixes, this means there is a large pool of available bases to lead to three-suffix sequences. It also suggests that *computerizer* (with recursion of *-er*) should be possible, though it mainly seems to be used as a trade name. The same is true with *containerizer*.

The same argument applies to *-ness*. This suffix attaches very freely to adjectives, and there are many adjectives that are created by adding a suffix to a noun, which may already end in a suffix, so a route to three-suffix sequences is assured. Some adjectives of Latinate origin (or suffixes in such words) prefer *-ity* to *-ness*, but *-ness* is always available as an alternative – not always a synonymous alternative – even, for instance, with *realness* alongside *reality*.

Dixon (2014: 390–1) cites some examples with four derivational suffixes in a sequence, but this seems to be seen as something plausible rather than something attested. *Nationalistically* is attested, if most often in dictionaries, but with *-istic* and *-ical* in the word, counting the affixes seems fraught. Dixon even suggests *subsidizationalistic* as having five, but this is not attested (and might be four if *-istic* is seen as a single affix).

This gives rise to a hypothesis about possible sequences of suffixes. The hypothesis is as follows:

In any sequence of two or three derivational suffixes at the end of a word, if the word is not item-familiar with all the observed suffixes, just one suffix has been added to a word which is item-familiar.

Bauer et al. (2013) list a few apparent exceptions (such as *foolageness* and *witchessery*), but these turn out not be exceptional, because *foolage* and *witchess* are in use, even if they are not particularly common. If the hypothesis holds up, then recursion of suffixes is not a genuine phenomenon. Where we think we find it, it is the result of an analysable suffix being added to a (more or less) unanalysable word, and any recursion is the result of the same affix being found in established words and available for productive use. The hypothesis does not mention sequences of four suffixes, because it assumes affix-telescoping. If any such really exist, I would guess that the same rule holds.

Dealing with prefixes is slightly more difficult in that it is not necessarily clear whether a given form is a prefix, an initial combining form from a neoclassical formation or a preposition forming the first element of a compound. Bauer et al. (2013) are quite liberal in what they accept in their lists. Even then, their examples fit with the proposed hypothesis. The jocular *psychosociopseudohistorian* (cited by Bauer 1983: 68) goes against the general pattern (although these are combining forms rather than real prefixes), but this may be part of its deliberate effect. Bauer et al. (2013: 498) give only sequences of two prefixes, though they also find *sub-sub-sub-contractor* (2013: 499), and Dixon (2014: 392–4) also finds a limit of two.

If this holds, it has important implications. First, although compounds may show different bracketings, derivations must always show left-branching for prefixes and right-branching for suffixes: [(prefix) [(prefix) [(prefix) [[[[root]]]] (suffix)] (suffix)] (suffix)]. Only when prefixes and suffixes interact do genuine ordering problems arise (Bauer et al. 2013: 501). Second, the most marginal affixes are likely to be the most productive ones, the innermost (those nearest the root) the least productive ones. Inflection has not been mentioned here, but if an inflectional affix is added – possibly leading to a sequence of four suffixes – it is (nearly) always on the righthand edge of the word, and inflection is, by definition, extremely productive.

Note that the repetition of prefixes is possible, as long as this makes pragmatic sense: *meta-meta-rule* is grammatical (Dixon 2014: 393 cites others that sound totally plausible, Bauer et al. 2013: 499–500 give some attested examples), and Bauer et al. also cite examples of synonymous or nearly synonymous prefixes being chained: *micro-minivan* and *mega-superstar*. The hypothesis given above for suffixes seems to apply here for prefixes.

> It is unlikely that any of the mega-mega-rich will be invited to that particular blow-out. (Ben Elton. 1989. *Stark*. London: Sphere, p. 13)

Stein (1977) points out that we prefer to say things like *re-write again* rather than *re-re-write*, *not unfair* rather than *un-unfair* and *rather shortish* rather than *shortishish*, which means that the need for the repetition of affixes is not great. At the same time, such limits as there are must probably be considered to be pragmatic limits rather than being determined by the structure of the grammar.

Recursion in compounds is well attested at the level of the word-class: that is long compounds made up of sequences of nouns are regularly found, for example in headlines, although they rarely become established. Even here, the length of such compounds seems to be more limited in English than in other Germanic languages. Hansen (1938: 113) comments that in Danish "newspapers have been seen to start competitions where competitors had to create the longest word" (my translation). Quite apart from finding a definition of a word in English which would support such an enterprise, the result in practical terms would probably be quite limited: six elements is very long for English.

> Louis and I sat eating chocolate-chip-cookie-dough ice-cream. (John Connolly. 2000. *Dark Hollow*. London: Hodder & Stoughton, p. 233)

Recursion of the same lexeme in a compound is rare, but not impossible, most obviously in repeated-element compounds:

> "Mine is green."
>
> "Green green? Or more like an olive green?" . . .
>
> "The salesman called it olive", he said. (Lawrence Block. 2000. *Hit List*. London: Orion, p. 118)
>
> Think me up a way to earn some blunt, would you? Not earn-earn it, but come into it proper-like. (Grace Burrowes, 2017. *Too Scot to Handle*. New York: Forever, pp. 236–7)
>
> This is just a storm-storm. But it'll be a whopper. (A.J. Finn. 2018. *The Woman in the Window*. New York: Morrow, p. 137)

These repeated-element compounds or 'identical constituent compounds' (Hohenhaus 2004) usually give rise to the meaning 'a real ~, a proper ~, a prototypical ~', but as Hohenhaus shows, not inevitably. They might be considered another type of tautologous construction (see Chapter 11), but the meaning suggests that they are not tautological. They do seem to show recursion, though.

Since a syntactic construction can be used to modify a head noun, and this is usually considered to form a compound (Bauer et al. 2013: 456–7), syntactic recursion can also be relevant in compound formation.

And there was straight extortion, too, genuine strong-arm, give-me-the-money-or-I'll-blow-your-brains-out scenarios. (Stephen Solomita. 1989. *Force of Nature*. New York: Putnam, p. 24)

Recursion is found in compounds where 'recursion' simply means that nouns can be strung together, and in derivation in the same sense that affixes can be strung together. Repetition of the same affix (or the same word in compounds) is rare, and occurs in a few relatively predictable contexts. This means that recursion of a specific element is rarer than might appear at first glance.

Challenge

What evidence can you find that might resolve the status of *-ation*, *-ical* and *-istic* in English? Do these suffixes always have the same status, or can the same sequence realize two distinct patterns of underlying elements? Does it make any difference if you consider only productive uses (e.g. if you consider only words found in newspapers or online that are not listed in some reasonably extensive dictionary)?

References

Bauer, Laurie. (1983). *English Word-Formation*. Cambridge: Cambridge University Press.
Bauer, Laurie, Rochelle Lieber & Ingo Plag. (2013). *The Oxford Reference Guide to English Morphology*. Oxford: Oxford University Press.
Dixon, R.M.W. (2014). *Making New Words*. Oxford: Oxford University Press.
Fabb, Nigel. (1988). English suffixation is constrained only by selectional restrictions. *Natural Language and Linguistic Theory* 6, 527–39.
Hansen, Aage. (1938). *Indledning til nydansk grammatik*. Århus: Aarhus Universitetsforlag.
Haspelmath, Martin. (1995). The growth of affixes in morphological reanalysis. *Yearbook of Morphology 1994*, 1–29.
Hohenhaus, Peter. (2004). Identical constituent compounding – A corpus-based study. *Folia Linguistica* 38, 297–331.
Ljung, Magnus. 1970. *English Denominal Adjectives*. Lund: Acta Universitatis Gothoburgensis.
Miller, George A. (1981). Semantic relations among words. In Morris Halle, Joan Bresnan & George A. Miller (eds.), *Linguistic Theory and Psychological Reality*. Cambridge, MA: MIT Press, 60–118.
Stein, Gabriele. (1977). The place of word-formation in linguistic description. In Herbert E. Brekle & Dieter Kastovsky (eds.), *Perspektiven der Wortbildungsforschung*. Bonn: Bouvier, 219–35.

13 Reflections on Problems with Heads in Word-Formation

Williams's (1981) right-hand-head rule, proposed to be general rule of morphological structure, continues to be very influential insofar as it relates to English. Although the right-hand-head rule, which states that the rightmost element (morpheme) in a word is the head of that word, has since been subject to a great deal of criticism (see e.g. Bauer 1990, 2019: 61–5), where compounds are concerned it has held up remarkably well, and may even be considered part of the definition of a compound in English.

The head of a compound is usually defined as being the element in the compound from which the compound-as-a-whole inherits its word-class (noun, adjective, verb), from which, other things being equal, it receives its inflectional behaviour and which is the superordinate term (sometimes called a 'hyperonym') of the compound. *Snowgoose* is a noun because *goose* is a noun, its plural is *snowgeese* because the plural of *goose* is *geese*, and *snowgoose* is hyponym of *goose*, and so *goose* is the head in *snowgoose*. Although there are many major classes of exception to these general principles (some of them dealt with elsewhere in this volume, see e.g. Chapter 29) these principles are generally taken to hold for endocentric noun and adjective compounds in English, and if verbal compounds are excluded, it is because some authorities still see verbal compounds as being rather marginal in English.

One problem with what has just been said is the inclusion of the word *endocentric*. Since *endocentric* means 'having an internal centre', where *centre* is another term for *head*, this risks becoming circular. *Endocentric* contrasts with *exocentric*, and an exocentric construction is one that does not have an internal head, and when applied to compounds (Bloomfield 1935, although the term appears to go back to Aleksandrow 1880 – see Carr 1939: xxvii), means that there is an external element which fulfils the functions of a head. That external element, however, is invisible. To take a standard example, consider the compound *redcap*. *Redcap* is not a hyponym of *cap*, and though *cap* is a noun and *redcap* is also a noun, *redcap* is not a noun by virtue of this fact, but by virtue of the fact that it denotes an entity. Just what entity it denotes depends to a large extent on the dialect you speak: it could be a railway porter (US English), it could be a military policeman (British English), it could be a goblin (Scottish English) or a bird. But like the names for other things of the same type, *redcap* is a noun. There is nothing in any of this to suggest that its plural should be anything but regular, so we gain no extra information from the fact that it is. The missing head must be something that bears a meaning such as 'person' for the first two readings, a meaning such as 'creature' for the 'goblin' reading, and 'bird' for the last reading. Just what else this presumed head contains is obscure. Because of the right-hand-head rule, we assume that it has an underlying position to the right of *redcap*, and is either deleted on the way to the surface, or is an element which never has any form, however this is to be achieved in a grammatical model. We do have a problem in that *big top* 'circus tent', presumably also an exocentric compound since it is neither a big nor a top, has no obvious meaning to attribute to the head. If the head means 'tent', then we must account for the fact (as we do with other examples) that *big top tent* is a rather odd expression. And with *redhead* 'person with red hair' (another exocentric compound of similar structure) we must account for the fact that *redhead person* is not grammatical; we would need to have *red-headed person* (Bauer 2022).

Such factors might lead us to seek a better solution for these exocentric compounds, and fortunately one is easily available in the literature (Bauer 2016, 2017b and references there). The proposal is that just as we can talk about the *crown* and mean 'the monarch, the person closely associated with the crown because of wearing it', using a figure of speech (here metonymy), so we can talk about a *redcap* and mean 'the entity that wears/possesses/has a red cap'. Metonymy, or more specifically synecdoche, is involved. If *redcap* means what it does by virtue of various figurative readings, we do not need an empty head element, just as we do not need an empty element as the head in *crown* 'monarch, government'. The right-hand-head rule must apply to the compound as it appears (so the head is *cap*), but the hyponymy rule is not relevant because the figurative interpretation makes it irrelevant, just as *crown* has to be referred to as *it* when it means the headwear, but as *he* or *she* when it means 'monarch'. Not only does this avoid having a word like *redcap* whose meaning is explained both by it being a figurative reading and by it being an exocentric compound, it also allows us to extend the right-hand-head rule for English compounds in a satisfactory way. Moreover, it may be enough to extend the notion of endocentricity so far that we can get rid of the notion of exocentricity completely (for further arguments on this, see Bauer 2016).

That is not the end of the story, though. There is another set of compounds, coordinative compounds, where this solution seems less successful. Coordinative compounds are those that are made up of two (or more) elements, each of which is on an equal footing in interpreting the compound, just as we find in syntax when words or other constructions are coordinated. Since just where the borderline of coordinative compounds runs in English is awkward (Bauer 2023, ch. 22) just a handful of relevant examples will be cited here.

They include *Alsace-Lorraine, HarperCollins, dinner-dance, historical-philosophical, bitter-sweet, cough-laugh, drink-drive*. These have problems for the notion of head. For example, while *Alsace-Lorraine* is a hyponym neither of *Alsace* nor of *Lorraine, dinner-dance* is a hyponym of both *dinner* and *dance*. Perhaps because of the existence of these two types, some scholars see coordinative compounds as having no head, and some see them as having two heads, although it is not clear just what is implied by any construction having two heads, just as it is not necessarily clear what is implied by a construction having no head (an invisible external head is only one possible interpretation of this – for extensive discussion, see Matthews 2007). In syntax, a more modern position than that of Bloomfield (1935) is that all structures are endocentric, and so all have a head. We might expect the most helpful criterion to be just what the compound-as-a-whole inherits from the individual elements. English provides us with very little information on this, though French and Spanish, for example, tend to get the gender of the compound from the left-hand element: French *taxi-camionnette* 'taxi van' gets its masculine gender from *taxi* (Arnaud 2004: 337), though we might not be sure whether *taxi van* or its French counterpart are genuinely coordinative compounds. English compound verbs, like *drink-drive*, might be expected to provide similar information, but not many of them have irregular past tenses, and with *drink-drive*, the lexeme occurs almost exclusively in the infinitive (often appearing in attributive position) or in the *-ing* form. In any case, in English any inflection has to occur on the right-hand edge of the word, whether we think this is the head or not: we could never have a form like **drinking-drive*, unless *drink-drive* was thought to be a syntactic sequence of two independent words. Most dictionaries do not list a past tense for *joy-ride*, but Collins (2006) gives *joy-rode*. Another potential example, *test-drive*, is listed in dictionaries as having the past tense *test-drove*, but it is not clear whether it should be interpreted as 'to test and to drive simultaneously' (a coordinative reading) or 'to drive by way of a test' (a subordinative reading); if it is to be glossed as 'to test by means of driving' then not only is it subordinative, but left-headed in terms of the hyponymy criterion.

One piece of information that English does allow us to consider is which element speakers feel to be the most important one in such constructions. Unfortunately, the place where we have information is in a type not listed above, and often (misleadingly) called appositional compounds, like *singer-songwriter, actor-director* and possibly *café-restaurant* in which the same entity is named by two facets of its nature. The type is very common, not only in English, but in other European languages, too, but whether these examples are compounds or not may be controversial, an alternative analysis seeing them as instances of syntactic coordination without an overt coordinating element. If we accept their compound status, though, then the compound is a hyponym of each of its elements, as we have seen with other examples above.

> to bask in the painter-writer-musician glamour of the place. (Lawrence Block. 1999. *The Burglar in the Rye*. Harpenden, Herts.: No Exit, p. 9)
>
> Stephen wasn't happy with only being a doctor, however. He was a doctor-screenwriter-producer. (Randall Hicks. 2005. *The Baby Game*. San Diego: Wordslinger, p. 32)
>
> That's a question you cannot ask a lawyer. Or even teacher-lawyers. Or even builder-teacher-lawyers. (Nury Vittachi. 2008. *Mr Wong Goes West*. Crows Nest, NSW: Allen & Unwin, p. 81)

Bauer (2010: 39) cites the example below, which seems to indicate that the speaker sees the left-hand element as being the more important in such a word.

> "I am a lawyer-musician, not a musician-lawyer", he says. "My calling is the law."

A similar implication is provided by the following.

> My best friend's a demon witch. Or it's probably a witch demon, because there's more of the witch. (Nora Roberts. 2022. *The Choice*. New York: St Martin's Press, p. 161)

This is surprising, because if only one element is the head, we would expect it to be the right-hand element in English, following the right-hand-head rule. This is obviously less clear than it might seem.

A similar problem is raised by some coordinative blends. The difference between a *tigon* and a *liger* is whether the lion is the sire or the dam: sire first, dam second. The same is true of the difference between *zorse* and *hebra*, but does not appear to apply to *labradoodle*, for example, even though *poobrador* is also attested. In those instances where the distinction is upheld, however, the two elements coordinated in the blend are not of equivalent status. Here it is not clear to me which is perceived as the more important: the dam, whose status as a parent is beyond doubt, or the sire, in line with our culture's traditional focus on the male. Another case in point is *Japlish* (and also other parallel words, though not always to the same extent) which can be a variety of Japanese with a lot of English words, or a variety of English with strong Japanese influence (Bauer 2017a: 161). Because the evidence comes from very few examples, perhaps the best we can say in all these cases is that in coordinative word-formation, the position of the head seems to vary, and not be consistently on the right. If we see these words as having two heads, we have to account for differences of interpretation, which might be harder than allowing left- or right-headed constructions.

There is also a very small number of apparent compounds which are left-headed. The two most frequently cited examples are *endgame* (which is a kind of end rather than a kind of game) and *man/girl Friday*, which is not a hyponym of *Friday*. We can dismiss these as not being compounds, but then we want to know what their structure is. They could be abbreviated forms of *end of the game* and *man/girl named Friday* (possibly *man/girl of Friday*), in which case they might be seen as compressed forms of structures such as *maid-of-honour*, but if that is the case we might expect to find more of them, and for the derivation to be clearer.

Another set of compounds also provides difficulties. These are compounds like *woman doctor*. Compounds of this type look as though they are coordinative compounds, because they can be glossed as 'a woman and a doctor' (see Chapter 22), and some authorities treat them in this way (e.g. Fabb 1998). Rather more scholars, though, right back to the Sanskrit grammarians, see such forms as being subordinative, or more specifically, attributive or ascriptive, with the first element being a gender marker. English has many compounds of this form, including *boy scout, girlfriend, gentleman-farmer, hen pheasant, manservant, nanny goat* or, with a different format, *she-wolf*.

However, while we have expressions where the gender-marker comes first, as in the examples already cited and in *baby rabbit, buck rabbit, bull-calf, bull elephant, cock lobster, cock robin, dog-fox, nanny goat, tom cat*; we also find expressions where the gender-marker (sometimes an age-marker) comes second, even though its function seems to be entirely parallel: *Arab mare, Clydesdale stallion, Hereford bull, lion cub, turkey hen, woodcock*. The order of the elements is largely predictable: a gender marker goes in front of a species name, but after the name of a breed. But this is not the whole story, since *cub* goes second (except in *cub reporter, cub scout*), and *hen* can be either first or second in position. The question of headedness here is important. Storch (1886 as cited in Carr 1939: xxviii) sees the second type here as being left-headed. If we want to say that all these are right-headed, then we have to assume that the gender is sometimes more important than the animal, while on other occasions the animal is more important than the gender, but it is not clear why this difference should be so predictable. If we want to see a difference in headedness, we need to explain why the right-hand-head rule should fail to apply in such a minor class.

A different minor-class is discussed by Bauer and Renouf (2001). This class is made up of compound adjectives whose second element is *only*: *fruit-only* (*conserve*), *oestrogen-only* (*pill*). As Bauer and Renouf point out, *oestrogen-only* is a hyponym of *oestrogen*, so that on semantic criteria it looks as though the left-hand element is the head. They also point out that if this is just a matter of a syntactic expression being used attributively, we would expect *only oestrogen*, which is the more common ordering in syntactic usage. If *oestrogen-only* is not a compound, its left-headedness might not be a problem, but in that case, we need an alternative analysis for it, and none seems to be forthcoming. Similar problems arise with words such as *sugar-free*, but the *free* here may be an affix rather than a compound element.

A different kind of problem is raised when the suffix *-er* is added to some complex verbs. To think about this, we need a little background. Carstairs-McCarthy (2002) suggests that words cannot inflect internally, so that because we can have *maids-of-honour* but not *maid-of-honours, *maid-of-honour* must be a phrase, but because we can have *mother-in-laws* (although *mothers-in-law* is also quite normal), *mother-in-law* can be seen as a single word. This notion does not seem to be particularly controversial, although it suggests that inflectional markers go on the right-hand edge of a word, rather than on the head of a word, which is often claimed (e.g. Zwicky 1985). We would expect, on the basis of this precedent, to find derivational affixes on the right-hand edge of a word, and mostly that is the case. There is one construction where this does not work, though.

> I always thought of him as a bit of a hanger-oner, if you know what I mean. (Hazel Holt. 1997. *Mrs Mallory and the Only Good Lawyer*. New York: Dutton, p. 125)

> Doris, headwaitress/receptionist at the George and Dragon, was one of the best finder-outers in the village. (Hamilton Crane. 1997. *Bonjour, Miss Seeton*. New York: Berkley, p. 27)

> A real fixer-upper [viz. a house in decay]. (Donna Andrews. 2003. *Crouching Buzzard, Leaping Loon*. New York: St Martin's Minotaur, p. 121)

> You and I are the hander-outers. (Kerry Greenwood. 2004. *Earthly Delights*. Crow's Nest, NSW: Allen & Unwin, p. 106)

> The netherworld of stardom-hanger-on-er. (Randal Hicks. 2005. *The Baby Game*. San Diego: Wordslinger, p. 19)

> I wasn't sure that she herself wasn't one of the holder-outers. (Susan Moody. 2006. *Quick off the Mark*. Sutton, Surrey: Severn House, p. 178)

> She never gave up, which was odd, because she considered herself a champion giver-upper. (Kate Kessler. 2016. *It Takes One*. New York: Redhook, p. 4)

If, for example, *give up* is a phrase (which is how these verbs are often treated in English), then we would expect *giver-up*. If *give up* is a word (which is how similar verbs are treated in German, for instance), we would expect *give-upper*. What we get in these cases is a blend of the two. The *-er* is added to the head of the phrase (or, possibly to the verb, which provides the same result), and then is added on the right-hand edge of the word, thus illustrating perfectly the halfway status of constructs like *give up*. This happens, though, at the expense of an apparent reduplication of the suffix, which is not normal behaviour. We would not expect to find a person who is looked up (either visited, or searched for) to be termed a *lookee-uppee*, though it is not clear what we could call them. Neither would we expect, even if we accept the construction type sketched above, to find, as we do in some varieties of English, a *giver-upperer*, where the third *-er* seems completely redundant.

> *The Breaker Upperers* is a New Zealand romantic-comedy film (*Wikipedia*)
>
> The classroom mixer-upper-er (www.educationalvantage.com/EDVAN/product/PR309 accessed 11 July 2023)
>
> improvised ping pong ball picker-upperer (www.reddit.com/r/mildlyinteresting/comments/ab5ufc/this_improvised_ping_pong_ball_pickerupperer_made/ accessed 11 July 2023)

Since the idea of affixes being added to the right-hand edge of words in English has been raised in this section, it is worth adding that occasionally we find examples which seem to support such a conclusion. Two such examples are given below.

> Then he called a week later and said never mind, so I never minded. (Barbara Parker. 2000. *Suspicion of Malice*. New York: Dutton, p. 65)
>
> make suring they work (Radio New Zealand, 7 p.m., 20 March 2012)

Such examples may not be part of the normal standard grammar of English, but they arise, and they contradict the common assertion that inflections are added to the head of a word (see Bauer 2017a: 29–32 for more discussion).

Overall, the right-hand-head rule, which starts out looking so persuasive, leads us into places where it creates problems and fails to give clear-cut answers. It may still operate as a canonical rule – and, indeed, we have seen some evidence that its application may actually be wider than was originally thought. We still need some way of dealing with the problem areas, though.

Challenge

Can you find any examples of English verbal coordinate compounds which must be glossed as coordinate and cannot be glossed as being subordinate? Ask the same question with regard to nouns and adjectives, though these two types are slightly easier to deal with. Do you think there are any coordinate compounds in English? Justify your position. Can you find any examples of words that look like compounds but are clearly left-headed? How can you be sure that they are both compounds and left-headed?

References

Aleksandrow, Aleksander. (1880). Litauische Studien, I. Nominalzusammensetzungen. Doctoral dissertation from the University of Dorpat (now Tartu, Estonia).

Arnaud, Pierre J.L. (2004). Problématique du nom composé. In Pierre J.L. Arnaud (ed.), *Le nom composé: données sur seize langues*. Lyon: Presses Universitaires de Lyon, 329–53.

Bauer, Laurie. (1990). Be-heading the word. *Journal of Linguistics* 26, 1–31.

(2010). Co-compounds in Germanic. *Journal of Germanic Linguistics* 22, 201–18.

(2016). Re-evaluating exocentricity in word-formation. In Daniel Siddiqi & Heidi Harley (eds.), *Morphological Metatheory*. Amsterdam: Benjamins, 461–77.

(2017a). *Compounds and Compounding*. Cambridge: Cambridge University Press.

(2017b). Metonymy and the semantics of word-formation. In Nikos Koutsoukos, Jenny Audring & Francesca Masini (eds.), *Morphological Variation: Synchrony and Diachrony*. Proceedings of the Mediterranean Morphology Meetings vol. 11, 1–13. Available at http://mmm.lis.upatras.gr/index.php/mmm/issue/view/352

(2019). *Rethinking Morphology*. Edinburgh: Edinburgh University Press.

(2022). Exocentricity yet again: A response to Nóbrega and Panagiotidis. *Word Structure* 15, 138–47.

(2023). Coordinative compounds, including dvandva. In Peter Ackema, Sabrina Bendjaballah, Eulàlia Bonet and Antonio Fábregas (eds.), *The Wiley Blackwell Companion to Morphology*. Hoboken, NJ: Wiley.

Bauer, Laurie & Antoinette Renouf. (2001). A corpus-based study of compounding in English. *Journal of English Linguistics* 29: 101–23.

Bloomfield, Leonard. (1935). *Language*. London: Allen & Unwin.

Carr, Charles T. (1939). *Nominal Compounds in Germanic*. London: Oxford University Press.

Carstairs-McCarthy, Andrew. (2002). *An Introduction to English Morphology*. Edinburgh: Edinburgh University Press.

Collins (2006). *Collins English Dictionary*. 8th ed. Glasgow: HarperCollins.

Fabb, Nigel. (1998). Compounding. In Andrew Spencer & Arnold M. Zwicky (eds.), *The Handbook of Morphology*. Oxford: Blackwell, 66–83.

Matthews, P.H. (2007). *Syntactic Relations: A Critical Survey*. Cambridge: Cambridge University Press.

Storch, Theodor. (1886). *Angelsächsische Nominalkomposita*. Strasbourg: Trübner.

Williams, Edwin. (1981). On the notions 'lexically related' and 'head of a word'. *Linguistic Inquiry* 12, 245–74.

Zwicky, Arnold M. (1985). Heads. *Journal of Linguistics* 21, 1–29.

14 Reflections on Coordination in Word-Formation

In phrases, elements of the same type can coordinate with each other quite freely. Just what 'of the same type' means may require some explanation, since the type may be a matter of word-class or of function or both: *Cars and buses are allowed in the city centre* is fine because *cars* and *buses* are both nouns and are both subjects of the verb, *The cover of the book is red and white* is fine because *red* and *white* are both adjectives and both subject complements, *All the vehicles going into the city centre are red and cars* is odd, not only because the message seems unlikely – although if we had said *are red cars* it would be equally unlikely but less grammatically weird – but because we are trying to coordinate an adjective and a noun. *Come here and sit down* is fine because we are coordinating two verb phrases, but *Come and relaxing* is odd because although *come* and *relax* are both verbs, they are not sufficiently similar for the coordination to work.

Things are not always so easy to explain. *He wore a green and yellow shirt* follows the rules, and is perfectly acceptable, *the once and future king* (a phrase from Sir Thomas Mallory, describing King Arthur) is also fine although *once* is an adverb and *future* is (superficially, at any rate) a noun, but both act as modifiers dealing with time. *Blue Danish porcelain* is fine, but *blue and Danish porcelain* is not (if it means the same thing) because we are not coordinating like with like.

But now consider the following. *She was sure she had seen blackbirds and bluebirds in the tree.* We coordinate two nouns both of which are the direct object of *see*, and all is well. *She was sure she has seen black and bluebirds in the tree.* We are apparently coordinating two adjectives both of which modify the same noun, but now there is something wrong. Yet *She was sure she had seen yellow and green leaves on the tree* is fine again. And it is perhaps not altogether clear whether *She was sure she had seen red and grey squirrels in England* is like *black and bluebirds* or like *yellow and green leaves*. *Red* and *grey* in this sentence are both classifying adjectives (*red squirrel* and *grey squirrel* are both types of squirrel while *yellow and green leaves* are descriptive adjectives but do not create classes of leaf). One solution to the problem is that modifiers to a noun head can be coordinated (provided they are suitably alike) in a syntactic construction (a phrase), but not in a compound (Payne and Huddleston 2002: 448–9). Moreover, the same is true of the head nouns in such a construction: we can have *black cars and buses* (syntactic construction) but not *blackberries and birds* (at least not if the *black* also modifies the *birds*). We can find many examples which seem to support such an explanation: we do not get **They are building a new motor and railway*, **Tear and raindrops were running down her face*, **I've got a tooth and headache*. But it turns out that it is difficult to be sure, and that speakers do not agree. Payne and Huddleston classify *ice-cream* as a compound using this criterion, claiming that you cannot have *ice-lollies and creams*, but Bauer (2014) cites examples such as the following:

> Living on the broken dreams of ice lollies and creams (www.melodramatic .com/node/70347?page=1 accessed 12 January 2011)

> Far too many ice-lollies and creams had been consumed but we were all happy little campers (http://yacf.co.uk/forum/index.php?topic=33253.120 accessed 16 January 2011)

> These nine months were filled with dripping ice lollies and creams, spilt soft drinks and lost maltesers (http://keeptrackkyle.blogspot.com/2006/07/tidy ing-up.html accessed 16 January 2011)

Payne and Huddleston (2002: 450) admit that the line between compounds and phrases is blurred, but see the fundamental distinction as vital and the failure of the coordination criterion in some places as a price worth paying. We could also claim that *ice-cream* is a compound for some speakers and a phrase for others.

If we look at what happens in German, we find that the coordination is rather less problematic in what are clearly compounds (some examples from Wiese 1996: 70–1, Fleischer and Bartz 2007: 92). Dutch seems to resemble German, and the Dutch facts are discussed by Booij (1985), but are omitted here to save space.

German example	*Gloss*	*Comment*
Hals- und Beinbruch	neck and leg.breakage	equivalent to English break a leg
Mast- und Schotbruch	mast and sheet.breakage	the seafaring equivalent
Frühlings- und Herbsttage	spring and autumn days	
Hol- und Bringedienst	fetch and carry.service	
Ostersonntag oder -montag	Easter Sunday or Monday	

The phenomenon has a specific name in German, apparently from Grimm, 'decomposition' (Erben 1975: 30). But German scholars look at the phenomenon from a different angle. Since *Hals- und Beinbruch* (and equivalently for the other examples) must come from *Halsbruch und Beinbruch* ('neck.breakage and leg. breakage'), they see this not as coordination but as deletion of a repeated element. The claim is not that the German tradition necessarily transfers to English; that is a dangerous assumption to make – see Chapter 26. What is interesting is that there is a completely different way of looking at the situation, which might make it easier to understand.

One of the benefits of the German solution is that it generalizes beyond compounds to other types of word-formation, specifically affixation. In both English and German, it is sometimes possible to coordinate prefixes. The English examples below come from Di Sciullo and Williams (1987: 105–6) and Bauer et al. (2013: 434), the German examples come from Wiese (1996: 70).

> pre- and post-test methodology
> pro- or anti-feminist
> mini or micro engines
> super and supra national
> Über- oder unterbau 'super- or substructure'
> pro- und antiamerikanisch 'pro- and anti-American'

In both English and German, we can find coordinated bases using the same suffix, but this is not generally available.

> child- and home-less
> business and family-wise
> sugar- and fat-free
> mütter- und väterlich   mother- and father.ly
> Brüder- oder   little brother or sister (where the suffix -*chen* is
>   Schwesterchen   translated as 'little')
> *Komponist- und   female composer and teacher (the suffix -*in* means
>   Lehrerin   'female')
> *damp- and stoutish

Booij (1985) and Wiese (1996) point out that where affixes can take part in this process in Dutch and German, the deleted element must be a phonological word. This is compatible with the view expressed by Di Sciullo and Williams (1987: 105), who say of prefixes that are allowed to stand "these prefixes have achieved a tentative status as a kind of free form". This tentative status is a status as a phonological word. Wiese (1996: 70) points out that in German there is some variability in what speakers allow in such deletion, and that not only is further research required, but that it is clear that the deletion is not confined to places where coordination is involved. Since English has not been considered from this point of view, and since examples of the phenomenon are rare in English, the comments hold to an even greater extent.

If the phonological form is relevant in English, too, this explains why we can have *pre- and post-war* but not, say, **dis- and re-colour*, why *sugar- and fat-free* is fine, but **damp- and stoutish* is not. But there are other things going on.

The first is that we cannot leave a bound root standing alone or delete it.

> *re- and insist
>
> *persist and vade, *superpose and sede (note that *super* is a phonological word)

14 Coordination in Word-Formation

The exception is if the bound root is a neoclassical element used as a prefix to an English word.

socio- and psycho-linguistics

We do not appear to be able to do this if there is an entire neoclassical formation involved or if the neoclassical element is a suffix.

*neur(o)- and psychology

*music- and icon-ology

In English, suffixes must not only be phonological words, but apparently have to have the form of words, so, as pointed out by Di Sciullo and Williams, we cannot have

*educate and rehabilitation

(meaning 'education and rehabilitation') any more than we can have

*compact and completeness

where -*ness* is not a phonological word. *Child-* and *home-less* (given above) seems to imply a full vowel in *less*, since /ləs/ would not be a phonological word.

There are many possible patterns for coordination in a 3-term compound, and often at least two interpretations of the patterns. We ignore constructions such as *art galleries and museums, head, shoulders, knees and toes, lake view and balcony*, where the coordination involves two or more independent phrases with no interaction. Some of the examples here are taken from the British National Corpus (Davies 2004–). Impossible combinations must, of course, be made up, and the reader may disagree with the asterisks.

	Bracketing	*Internally bracketed items act independently*	*Externally bracketed item treats the internal items as a unit*
1	[[A B] and C]	data collection and analysis fruit trees and bushes gas exploration and production ?ice-creams and lollies sunrise and set	
2a	[A [B and C]]	city shops and sights Christmas cards and trees	copper pots and pans
2b		anti-Christian and Jewish	anti-rules and regulations
3a	[A and [B C]]	air- and ground-search *black and bluebirds black and whiteheads earth and moonquakes ?fire and candle-light ?foot or basketball	

114   Part III Syntactic Questions

		*ginger and shortbread	
		*guide and cookbooks	
		horse or camelhair	
		in- and out-flow	
		landlord and tenant act	
		sesame or rape oil	
		*tooth and headache	
		*swim and sportswear	
		road and rail crossings	
		water- and weatherproof	
3b		pre- and post-operative	
		pro- and anti-British	
4a	[[A and B] C]	health and safety standards	life and death decisions
		oak and ash trees	cease and desist order
			food and drug administration
			husband and wife team
			salt and pepper moustache
			steak and kidney pie
4b		salt and sugar free	

The rows labelled (b) show examples with affixes, the other rows show compounds or potential compounds. Since one of the claims about such examples is that they distinguish between compounds and phrases, I do not want to make strong claims about the accuracy of those claims: readers must decide whether it is always the case that the acceptable sequences are phrases, and the unacceptable ones are compounds. They must also determine to what extent blank cells can be filled with acceptable or unacceptable examples. On the basis of the examples given above, it seems that the unacceptable examples represent a very small section of the possible patterns (given that even unacceptable examples have to make sense for the test to be a fair one: *sesame and motor oil* might not be acceptable, but that is because a coordination of the two seems unlikely; *foot and handball* may be better than *foot and basketball* because of the parallel between *hand* and *foot*).

As a final point, consider the prefixes which seem to be able to coordinate. We have seen that there may be a restriction to prefixes which are phonological words, so that *a-, be-, en-, for-, in-* 'negative' and so on may be excluded by this proviso. But the pairs that seem perfectly possible include

mini- and maxi-
mini- and micro-
mono- and poly-
pre- and post-
pro- and anti-
super- and supra-

14 Coordination in Word-Formation 113

Those that do not appear to be possible (or are rare), include

ante- and post-	Ante- and Postpartum (M. Hoedemaker, D. Prange and Y. Gundelach. 2009. Body condition change ante- and postpartum, health and reproductive performance in German Holstein cows. *Reprod Dom Anim* 44, 167–73)
endo- and exo-	*endo-skeleton and exo-skeleton* seems to be the more common usage
sub- and super-	*subscript and superscript* is used rather than *sub- and super-script*
pseudo- and quasi-	*pseudo- and quasi-isometrics* (www.sportsmith.co/articles/pseudo-isometrics/ accessed 28 February 2024)

Not only are there very few, the majority of these are antonymic (only *pseudo-* and *quasi-* and *mini-* and *micro-* might be considered quasi-synonymic). Examples such as *up-* and *down-* may involve compounds rather than prefixes, it is often difficult to tell. The restriction to prefixes which are opposites excludes most prefix pairs, and, for example, rules out all negative prefixes from occurring in this construction.

The whole question of coordination within compounds and derivatives is more complex than is generally acknowledged. Not only do intuitions differ about the data, but the number of factors involved makes it difficult to work out precisely what is going on. Parallels with languages like Dutch and German do not appear to work completely, and Smith (2000) claims that the situation in German has been oversimplified anyway. One of the factors he feels needs to be included is parallel forms of modification. Part of the problem for the linguist trying to describe this area is that relevant data is hard to find, with negative data impossible to find. However, since coordination is possible within derivatives, albeit rare in English, it seems unlikely that it can be used to define a compound.

Challenge

The examples presented above as instances of different bracketing patterns are incomplete and subject to challenge, since different people might not agree on what is or is not possible in English, and will certainly disagree as to what is a compound in English. Do you agree with the asterisks that are given? How far can you extend the data set, especially with reference to the blank cells? If you wanted to test the various hypotheses on coordination, or look for further restrictions on coordination, how would you find relevant data? In particular, to what extent can relevant data be found via automated searches?

References

Bauer, Laurie. (2014). Grammaticality, acceptability, possible words and large corpora. *Morphology* 24, 83–103.
Bauer, Laurie, Rochelle Lieber & Ingo Plag. (2013). *The Oxford Reference Guide to English Morphology*. Oxford: Oxford University Press.
Booij, Geert E. (1985). Coordination reduction in complex words: A case for prosodic phonology. In Harry van der Hulst & Norval Smith (eds.), *Advances in Non-Linear Phonology*. Dordrecht: Foris, 143–60.
Davies, Mark. (2004–). British National Corpus (from Oxford University Press). Available online at www.english-corpora.org/bnc/
Di Sciullo, Anna Maria & Edwin Williams. (1987). *On the Definition of Word*. Cambridge, MA: MIT Press.
Erben, Johannes. (1975). *Einführung in die deutsche Wortbildungslehre*. Berlin: Schmidt.
Fleischer, Wolfgang & Irmhild Barz. (2007). *Wortbildung der deutschen Gegenwartssprache*. 3. unveränderte Auflage. Tübingen: Niemeyer.
Payne, John & Rodney Huddleston. (2002). Nouns and noun phrases. In Rodney Huddleston and Geoffrey K. Pullum (eds.), *The Cambridge Grammar of the English Language*. Cambridge: Cambridge University Press, 323–524.
Smith, George. (2000). Word remnants and coordination. In Rolf Thieroff, Matthias Tamrat, Nanna Fuhrhop & Oliver Teuber (eds.), *Deutsche Grammatik in Theorie und Praxis*. Tübingen: Niemeyer, 57–68.
Wiese, Richard. (1996). *The Phonology of German*. Oxford: Oxford University Press.

Part IV

Interfaces

15 Reflections on the Interface between Word-Formation and Phonology
Morphophonemics

15.1 Introduction

It is well-known that various morphophonemic alternations arise under word-formation in English, and these were of particular importance in the theory of Lexical Phonology and Morphology (sometimes called Level Ordered Morphology though 'stratum' is preferred to 'level' here, see Allen 1978, Kiparsky 1982, Mohanan 1986, McMahon 1994, Bauer 2003a: 166–95). While the simplistic versions of Lexical Phonology that introduced the theory in the 1970s and 1980s have been shown to be incorrect in their predictions in several ways, the morphophonemic alternations themselves have rarely been challenged. For example, the phonemic alternation found in morphologically defined environments such as *adhere* (with /r/) and *adhesive* (with /s/ or /z/, depending on the speaker) is recognized as a bona fide phonological phenomenon. In this chapter, five case studies are considered briefly, suggesting that, if lexicalization is taken seriously, the range of morphophonemic patterns is much smaller than is generally allowed for, but also that some of the alternations may not be related to phonology at all.

15.2 Sequences of Stop Consonants

In the middle of words, English allows sequences of non-identical stop consonants (including nasals as stop consonants) in which the second consonant is voiced, with various constraints. We find the patterns illustrated below.

gm agma, paradigmatic
gn lignite, signify
mb amber, umbrella
mn amnesia, amnesty
nd conduce, endure, handful, pander
ŋg bungalow, finger, linger

Such clusters are not found word-finally (except for /nd/), and neither are they found in some other environments, specified in terms of structural features of the relevant words. In standard morphophonological descriptions of English, we can thus find statements (often formulated as a rule) that

Stop + voiced stop clusters not including /d/ are simplified by deletion of the plosive element (or if there is no plosive, one of the nasals) at the end of a word and in some other definable environments.

We will return to the other definable environments, but they include before the suffix *-ing*, so that *singing* (in standard British English, though not in all varieties) is /sɪŋɪŋ/ and not */sɪŋgɪŋ/. This looks like a straightforward morphophonemic rule, where the common meaning is reflected in the spelling, which can be considered morphophonemic in this regard, and whose limited use makes it easy to get oversight of the process.

With the aid of a reverse dictionary, ninety-eight words of English ending in the relevant written sequences of consonants (<nd> was not included) were discovered. Then Marr (2008) was used to find related words in which these sequences were followed by a vowel, except that a following <le> was permitted and sometimes /r/. This option was chosen as the only places where it is possible to have the sequences of consonants pronounced. Instances where extra words included a case which was already listed (e.g. *designable* and *designability*) were not counted twice. Following *-ing* and comparative *-er*, superlative *-est* were ignored because they are usually seen as inflectional. When those cases where no relevant words were found in Marr (2008) were removed, sixty-two base words remained, with 130 related words where the consonant sequence was followed by a relevant segment. Pronunciations, when not given in Marr (2008), were also checked in other reference works, though not all were listed (e.g. *womby* related to *womb*, a Shakespearian usage).

The first thing to notice is that the rule as stated above is shown to be incorrect. Contrary to the predictions of the rule, some words are listed with two-consonant pronunciations in standard reference works. *Iamb* and *dithyramb* can both be found listed with the consonant sequence pronounced at the end of the word. *Limn* is often given as having /mn/ before *-ing*. Although *iamb* and *dithyramb* are both borrowed from Greek, other Greek words on the list, such as *paradigm*, do not share this possibility, so that etymology does not appear to be a decisive factor here.

We have to ask what general result we might expect. It could be that Germanic affixes behave differently from learned ones, with the proviso that occasionally the etymology does not entirely reflect current linguistic patterning. In light of the large literature on Lexical Phonology and Morphology or Stratal Morphology, it could be that individual affixes, independent of their origin, show their own consistent behaviour with regard to the sequence

15 Word-Formation and Phonology   121

simplification. The least expected result would be for individual affixes to behave in an unpredictable manner.

The behaviour of the adjective-forming *-y* (e.g. *clingy*) and the noun-forming *-y* (e.g. *thingy*) both behave as expected. The rule applies before both on every occasion, so that there is only one consonant pronounced.

The suffix *-ity* (n = 3, e.g. *benignity*) behaves consistently in the other way: the rule never applies before it, so that both consonants are pronounced.

Between them, these two examples are consistent with either the etymological hypothesis or the Stratal hypothesis.

The suffix *-le* (if we can count it as an English suffix) has a two-consonant pronunciation before it, and the suffix *-ism* has a single consonant pronunciation before it, but neither has many examples (*tangle* and *dongle* are possibly not real derivatives, *twangle* is rare; the only relevant example of *-ism* in my data set is *foreignism*). But to the extent that they can be accepted, they suggest that the strict etymological hypothesis is wrong.

More interesting are those suffixes which behave inconsistently.

-er usually has only one consonant before it, but *limner* can have two.

-ic usually has both consonants pronounced before it, but *tombic* can have no /b/.

-ish usually has only one consonant before it, but *youngish* can have two.

-ist usually has two consonants pronounced before it, but *columnist* can have no /n/.

-ous would normally be expected to have two consonants before it, as in *fungous* (although that has truncation), but *wrongous* may have no /g/.

These might be explained as errors – although that is a dangerous line to take, given that these pronunciations are widespread enough to make it into reference works – or, more obviously, as being individually lexicalized cases. They could be treated as coming from a different dialect, but there is no evidence of consistent behaviour. But if they are lexicalized, we have reason for surprise because most of these words are rare, and we would expect rare words to follow the rules if there are rules.

We also find a lot of words where what follows our presumed consonant sequences can scarcely be interpreted as an English affix. *Bombard, clangour, gangrel, hymnody, phlegmon, rhombos, rhombus* illustrate some of the range of forms found. In these instances, as might be expected, the words are treated as if they do not have affixes, and both consonants are pronounced. Note, however, *columel* 'a small column', where even the orthography does not include an <n>, and *clangour* which some people – like me – pronounce with no /g/. All of these must count as lexicalized forms because they cannot be produced in the current state of the language, and that makes the morphophonemics irrelevant, since their forms must be listed.

This example shows the value of a concept of lexicalization and taking the current patterns of word-formation as being the productive patterns and not all those forms which happen to be analysable. However, that is not the end of the story.

Many people don't like the word *wronger*. They will say that if you want to compare *wrong*, you have to say *more wrong*: *Both of these things are wrong, but the first is more wrong than the second*. Similarly, they will prefer *more right* to *righter*, something that descriptive grammars support.

However, even speakers that say they don't like the word *wronger* will pronounce it /rɒŋə/. The pronunciation /rɒŋgə/ is clearly wronger than the pronunciation /rɒŋə/. This is odd, because if we consider the other words which seem to belong to the same pattern, *long* and *strong*, they have a /g/ in the pronunciation when they are in the comparative form: /lɒŋgə/, /strɒŋgə/. *Younger* works the same way, and the superlatives follow suit. We would expect the high-frequency words to influence the form of the low-frequency word, and for all of these adjectives to behave the same way, but they do not.

On the other hand, the comparative of *numb* is *number* /nʌmə/ (not homophonous with *number* 'numeral'). We can again appeal to lexicalization. But for adherents of Lexical Phonology, there is at least a puzzle here, when inflection behaves like Stratum 1 affixation instead of like Stratum 2 affixation, and where inflection, often defined by its regularity, behaves just as irregularly as derivation does.

15.3   Velar Softening

English spelling has a rule, with some minor exceptions, that <c> before <e>, <i> or <y> is pronounced /s/, but before <a>, <o>, <u>, a consonant or a word-boundary is pronounced /k/. The rule applies where no morphological intervention occurs, and is illustrated by words like *fence, cite, cycle, call, colour, cucumber, crash* or *tic*. However, when this rule applies over morphological boundaries it has the effect of changing a word-final /k/ to a word-medial /s/ before an affix boundary. In some instances, the following <i> acts as a diacritic, further changing the /s/ to a /ʃ/, as in *magician, special* and so on. This morphophonemic rule has been given the name of 'velar softening' (Chomsky and Halle 1968), which can be used here.

We should note that velar softening is not really a phonological rule; it is an orthographic rule, based on Romance traditions of spelling. Not all final /k/ sounds are affected, only those which are spelled <c> (never those spelled <ck> or <k> or <ch>). Words like *monarchist* (*monarchic, monarchism*, etc.) do not show velar softening, *adhocism* (perhaps not widely used) shows no softening, retaining /k/, as does *arced*, and neither do words like *zincify* (also spelled <zinkify, zinckify>, *zinciferous* and other related forms. In fact, this is a rule which applies only if the input ends in -*ic*, and probably (even if not strictly a case of English word-formation, but a borrowing), the suffix -*ic*. But beyond that, velar softening does not apply before all affixes beginning with the relevant vowel letters. If we were to invent *electricish* or *academicy* they would have /k/ at the end of *electric* and *academic* rather than /s/ (see *rheumaticky* in Marr 2008). So the rule of velar softening (or this version of the rule, based on the letter <c>), to the extent that it is a phonological rule at all, has to be specified as follows:

/k/ in the suffix -*ic* is replaced by /s/ before the affixes -*ian*, -*ity*, -*ist*, -*ism*, -*ize*, -*ify*.

It is not entirely clear whether these sequences are productive or not. Bauer et al. (2013) cite examples containing these sequences, but very few of their examples are clearly new. There is also some doubt as to whether the rule of velar softening is available to speakers at all: when Ohala (1974) asked consultants to produce unfamiliar (because invented) words ending in such sequences, velar softening was not consistently applied, and even when it was applied, it is not clear whether it was applied as a morphophonemic rule or as a rule of orthography. The suffix -*ic*, though, "shows some productivity" (Bauer et al. 2013: 303), so we might expect the affix sequences to be available, if not common, and velar softening thus also to show some productivity.

This example shows just how difficult it can be to determine whether a given pattern is lexicalized or not, whether it is a morphological pattern or a morphophonological pattern. But it is also a warning not to assume too easily that observable patterns over familiar vocabulary are necessarily productive.

15.4 Degemination

Degemination is the simplification of a sequence of two adjacent identical phonemes to a single phoneme. There are no instances of geminate consonants and no geminate vowels internal to a morph in English (Bauer 2003b). For example, a word like *missel* has only a single /s/ in the pronunciation, and the <ss> is simply an indication that the preceding vowel is short. Over boundaries between an affix and a base, however, gemination is found. For example

misspell has geminate /ss/
posttonic has geminate /tt/
unnamed has geminate /nn/
embalmment has geminate /mm/
palely has geminate /ll/

Upton et al. (2001) indicate that British and American English may differ in some of these words, with fewer geminates in American English, but I am using

British pronunciations as the basis for my discussion. In all of these instances, a consonant on the margin of an affix is identical to a consonant on the abutting margin of the base. Since both consonants can be motivated from the form of the relevant element in other contexts, the geminate is expected, and what is not necessarily expected is degemination in such positions, that is the deletion of one of the identical consonants. Degemination can be heard, for example, in *fully* (whose elements are *full* and *-ly*, but English orthography does not allow a spelling with three identical consonants). The question, therefore, is when does degemination occur.

Retention of the geminate seems to be the general pattern with prefixes, which are often more word-like than suffixes. This seems to be true with both consonants and vowels, though geminate vowels are extremely rare, perhaps restricted to *co-own(er(ship))*, although there seems to be no principled reasons why others should not exist. However, there are exceptions. Some examples showing degemination, not always to the exclusion of retained gemination, are given below. Most of the words cited also have morphologically related words, which are relevant (e.g. *connote*, *dissatisfy*).

> connotation
>
> dissatisfaction, dissemble, dissever, dissimilarity, dissoluble, dissymmetry
>
> granddad, granddaughter
>
> illegal, illegible, illegitimate, illiberal, illicit, illiterate, illogical
>
> immaterial, immature, immeasurable, immemorial, immiscible, immobile
>
> innocuous, innumerable, innumerate, innutritious

From the point of view of a Stratal theory of morphology, this looks as though it may be easily explicable. The prefix *grand-* (if it is a prefix and not a compound element) loses its final /d/ before any consonant (*grandchild*, *grandmother*) and all the other examples illustrate Stratum I prefixes. However, things are not quite that simple. Not all Stratum I prefixes allow degemination. *Sub-* (which must be on Stratum I because it is stressed in *subplot* and *subsequent*) does not permit degemination in *subbreed*, *subbranch*. Also, more importantly, *dis-* shows variable degemination, so that degemination is not automatically related to Stratum I. There are ways round these problems in various models of Stratal Morphology, but they weaken the predictions of the theories.

Suffixes are harder to deal with. Although there are relatively many suffixes in English, very few provide relevant data. These main ones are *-ly* (adverbial and adjectival), and, potentially, *-ness*. With *-ly,* a geminate is typically retained after a stressed syllable, but degemination occurs after an unstressed syllable; with *-ness*, a geminate is typically retained (but far less in American English). Some examples with *-ly* from three pronunciation dictionaries are presented below.

15 Word-Formation and Phonology

Word	Jones et al. (2003)		Upton et al. (2001)		Wells (1990)	
	+Gemin	−Gemin	+Gemin	−Gemin	+Gemin	−Gemin
dully	✓		✓	✓	✓	✓
foully	✓		✓		✓	
really		✓		✓		✓
shrilly		✓	✓	✓	✓	
severally		✓		✓		✓
wholly	✓		✓		✓	✓

Degemination seems to be a result of high frequency, but with some varieties more susceptible to it than others, but there is not absolute agreement as to when it occurs, even in the same variety.

Here, then, we have a morphophonemic process whose application is not entirely predictable, which is influenced by frequency and by the individual affixes (possibly the individual lexemes) involved. That means that it is quite difficult to explain just what the process is, and even more difficult to predict the outcome. The phonological process can be easily described, but not when it will apply. Something which looks simple, is actually more complex than appears at first sight.

15.5 Alternations before -*ian*

There is one apparently morphophonemic rule which is clearly productive, even though it affects relatively few forms. It is brought about by suffixation of adjective-forming -*ian*, usually considered a variant of the -*an* suffix or having an -*i*- extender (Bauer et al. 2013: 181). Since the use of the extender is unpredictable in general, but is usual in this construction (note *Elizabethan* as an exception), -*ian* is treated here as a separate suffix.

The suffix -*ian* is attached to proper nouns to make adjectives. Typically, the vowel immediately before the suffix is stressed and long (*Christian* provides an exception, probably because of the two consonants following the stressed vowel, as with *Egyptian*). Some examples are given below. The suffix is transcribed as disyllabic /iən/ here (as in Wells 1990, Jones et al. 2003), which accounts for the main stress pattern on the antepenult, though this is sometimes reduced to monosyllabic /jən/.

Amazon/Amazonian /æməzəʊniən/
Aristotle/Aristotelian /ærɪstəti:liən/
Babylon/Babylonian /bæbɪləʊniən/
Bacon/Baconian /beɪkəʊniən/
Caesar/Caesarian /si:zeəriən/

Devon/Devonian	/dɪvəʊnɪən/
Handel/Handelian	/hændiːlɪən/
Johnson/Johnsonian	/dʒɒnsəʊnɪən/ (and other names ending in *-son*)
Lilliput/Lilliputian	/lɪlɪpjuːʃən/
Venus/Venusian	/vɪnjuːzɪən/
Venice/Venetian	/vɪniːʃən/

I have omitted a lot of examples where the facts of the case may be obscured by other factors, for example where the base word ends in <ia> (*Patagonia/Patagonian*) or some phonological material is deleted (*Olympus/Olympian*) or some unpredictable consonant change has occurred (*Troy/Trojan* < earlier *Troian*), for example, but that should not affect the general pattern. Because the pattern is productive, the list cannot be finite.

If we look at the above examples in terms of the alternating vowel sounds, we find the following patterns:

ə	alternates with	əʊ
ə	alternates with	iː
ɒ	alternates with	əʊ
ə	alternates with	eə
ʌ	alternates with	juː
ə	alternates with	juː
ɪ	alternates with	iː

If we take the point of view that /ə/ is the neutralization in unstressed syllables of (nearly) all the other vowels, then we might have to replace the /ə/s in the above with the relevant underlying vowel to see a pattern. This gives problems with many of the words listed such as *Amazon*, *Aristotle*, *Bacon*, *Caesar* where, precisely in the base forms illustrated here, there is no independent evidence as to what the underlying vowel might be. In words ending in *-son* we might presume that we have an underlying /ʌ/. We then have /ʌ/ and /ɒ/ alternating with /əʊ/ in apparently the same environment, and /əʊ/ and /juː/ both alternating with /ʌ/ in apparently the same environment.

However, if instead of looking for alternating vowel sounds, we look at the vowel letters, things become clearer. What we have is the long vowel in the environment before *-ian* which corresponds to the short vowel that is written in the base word. The only trouble with this solution is that it goes against all that we usually assume about the nature of orthography: specifically, the usual assumption is that orthography derives from the spoken language, not vice versa. So this is a surprising, and perhaps disturbing, finding.

It is, however, supported by some further examples. Words which end in <f> and <w> have an *-ian* form which contains /v/ (written <v>) in the corresponding position. There are few relevant forms, but the patterns appear to be productive to the extent that this is a relevant consideration.

15 Word-Formation and Phonology

Aronoff/Aronovian	/ærənəʊviən/
Harrow/Harrovian	/hærəʊviən/
Marlowe/Marlovian	/mɑːləʊviən/
Shaw/Shavian	/ʃeɪviən/
Skiddaw/Skiddavian	/skɪdeɪviən/
Snow/Snovian	/snəʊviən/

Since the /f/ and the /w/ do not share phonetic qualities, and the <w> is not even pronounced as a consonant in these examples, and the stressed vowel in *Shavian* can best be explained in orthographic terms, such examples seem to strengthen the case that the basis of this word-formation pattern is orthographic rather than phonological.

15.6 Participial *-ed* before Other Suffixes

The allomorphy of past tense and past participial *-ed* is familiar from many textbooks. The variant /ɪd/ is heard following /t/ or /d/, otherwise the pronunciation is determined by the voicing of the segment immediately preceding the suffix. We find the variants illustrated in *wanted* /wɒntɪd/, *watched* /wɒtʃt/, *loved* /lʌvd/. In a small number of words, this patterning breaks down when the participle is used adjectivally. We say /blesɪd/ rather than /blest/ for *blessed* (or we used to in attributive position), we say /lɜːnɪd/ rather than /lɜːnd/ for *learned* (*learnt* does not seem to be used attributively of a person) and /bɪlʌvɪd/ rather than /bɪlʌvd/ for *beloved*. We could add *naked* and *sacred*, although these are no longer felt to be participles, and *naked* probably never was one, from the etymological point of view. This seems to be part of retaining old participial forms in adjectival use that is also illustrated by *drunken*, *new-mown*, *shaven* and the like. We could treat these forms as belonging to different lexemes from the base verb (as long as our model allows for lexemes). This might help explain why we can have *an aged man* (/eɪdʒɪd/) but would have to have *an aged piece of beef* (/eɪdʒd/) (Quirk et al. 1972: 246).

Participles acting as adjectives can, when it makes sense, also be turned into manner adverbials by the addition of *-ly* and into nouns by the addition of *-ness*. When the verb ends in /t/ or /d/ these have no option but to take the /ɪd/ allomorph of *-ed*: *admittedly, animatedly, belatedly, contentedness, disappointedly, excitedly, excitedness*, and so on. Equally, those adjectives where the <ed> is pronounced /ɪd/ even when it would not be the regular form, keep that pronunciation when there is a subsequent derivation: *blessedly, learnedness*.

But where the /ɪd/ allomorph is not automatically required by the phonology of the adjacent consonants or the phonological make-up of the adjective, things are less clear. *Fixedly* and *markedness* have the /ɪd/ pronunciation, even though their phonology does not seem to require it, *determinedly* and *tiredness* do not.

Some specification of just what the relevant *-ed* suffix is does little to clarify matters. The *-ed* that has been discussed so far is added to verbs. There is another, homophonous *-ed* which is added to nouns, and these nouns may become elements in compounds, so that we find *bearded*, *red-handed* (with /ɪd/ because of the preceding /d/), *good-humoured*, *good-natured* (which have /d/ rather than /ɪd/). It is not automatically obvious that the two types of *-ed* will function in the same way (though we might expect them to, if they belong to the same morpheme – Aronoff 1994). Fowler (1965 sv -edly) treats them all as the same, but he also treats those that have /ɪd/ as a function of the /t/ or /d/ preceding the /ɪd/ in the same way as those where the /ɪd/ is less obviously justified. I shall ignore the denominal *-ed*, though I think it behaves in much the same way as the deverbal one.

We also need to ask whether a prefix on the adjective makes any difference: is *reserved* any different from *unreserved*, *ordered* any different from *disordered*? The main difference does not appear to be phonological, but perhaps a matter of norm (see Chapter 6): the prefixed forms are more regularly used as adjectives. It should also be noted that many dictionaries do not give pronunciations for relevant forms – either because they are assumed to be obvious, or to save space, or both – and in some cases do not list them at all. Intuition is not the best data to use in instances like this, but may be what is available.

Jespersen ([1942] 1961: 29) thinks he has the answer. The /ɪd/, he suggests, "forms a connecting link (syllable) between stem and ending, but it is not required when the stem ends in an unstressed syllable". Certainly, many of the instances where the /ɪd/ arises are found where the verb has final stress: *allegedly, ashamedly/-ness, assuredly, cussedly/-ness, markedly/-ness, supposedly*. Equally, there are instances where the verb does not have final stress, and the /ɪd/ is missing: *bewilderedly, determinedly, hurriedly, impoverishedly*. But Jespersen himself does not know which class *ashamedly* fits into, and Jones et al. (2003) give *preparedly* /prɪpeədli/ but *preparedness* /prɪpeərɪdnɪs/. Also *tiredly* and *tiredness* have no /ɪd/ although they are on a monosyllabic (and thus stressed) base.

Fowler (1965) has a different solution. Although his terminology is not the same as mine, he would say that the pronunciation with /ɪd/ is lexicalized: we use the /ɪd/ pronunciation only when we know that the word requires one (from previous experience of the individual word). For Burchfield (1996), completely rewriting Fowler's article, this cannot be true because some unfamiliar words nevertheless get given the /ɪd/ pronunciation; in other words, the rule is productive.

I would support Burchfield in this view, but there are problems. What is the productive rule (Burchfield admits that he doesn't know)? Do all speakers share the same view of what the rule is? *Reservedly* (listed by Jones with /ɪd/) could get that pronunciation because of *unreservedly*, or the two could independently be following the same rule. Burchfield cites *admiredly, depressedly, harassedly, labouredly, scatteredly* and *veiledly* from the *OED* (none mentioned by Jones et al. 2003). From *Wikipedia* (https://en.wiktionary.org/wiki/Category:English_terms_suffixed_with_-ly accessed 7 June 2023) we can add *abashedly, allowedly, authorizedly, barbedly, bedraggledly, belabouredly, bemusedly, blurredly* and dozens of others. Burchfield says that for him, some of this list would have /ɪd/, but doesn't tell us which ones. Even a small-scale survey suggests that not everyone agrees on all of these, so there is the possibility that there is an ongoing change affecting these cases, which makes the rule even harder to discern. The change is probably a loss of the /ɪd/ pronunciation, which is, in any case, a remnant of a much older pronunciation of such forms. But if there are unfamiliar forms which speakers pronounce with the /ɪd/ pronunciation, then the problem remains. Again, a small-scale survey suggests that speakers use both pronunciations in words they claim not to know, and that final stress in the base is not a determining factor for which pronunciation is produced.

The bigger question that this example raises is whether we can talk of rules in a situation where the productivity of a given pattern is fading. What we seem to find is conflicting usages based on principles which are not clear, varying from speaker to speaker and even within the usage of a single speaker. This means that it is not even straightforward to talk in terms of lexicalization of individual examples, although that may be part of a solution.

15.7 Conclusion

Morphophonemic rules often apply in unpredictable ways, and some of them are not even morphophonemic, because the variation is based on the orthography rather than on phonemic alternations. This leads to a grammar which is hard to write or hard to apply. Just how the speaker knows when a given rule applies is not clear, but it seems to be based on experience of the relevant formatives or lexemes, rather than on formulating a rule.

Challenge

There is alternation between the phonemes /s/ and /ʃ/, and correspondingly between /z/ and /ʒ/, in a number of related words in English, such as *substance* and *substantial, confuse* and *confusion, space* and *spacious*. Find a representative set of related pairs using dictionaries, reverse dictionaries, phonology books, pronunciation guides and any other sources available to you. Can you always tell what the relevant pairs are? How would you want to treat such pairs in a linguistic description of present-day English? What benefits would you gain from your way of treating such pairs as opposed to other potential ways of dealing with them? What might be the major disadvantages of your proposed way of dealing with the pairs?

References

Allen, Margaret R. (1978). Morphological Investigations. PhD dissertation, University of Connecticut.
Aronoff, Mark. (1994). *Morphology by Itself*. Cambridge, MA: MIT Press.
Bauer, Laurie (2003a). *Introducing Linguistic Morphology*. 2nd ed. Edinburgh: Edinburgh University Press.
 (2003b). The phonotactics of some English morphology. In Henrik Galberg Jacobsen, Dorthe Bleses, Thomas O. Madsen & Pia Thomsen (eds.), *Take Danish – for Instance: Linguistic Studies in Honour of Hans Basbøll*. Odense: University Press of Southern Denmark, 1–8.
Bauer, Laurie, Rochelle Lieber & Ingo Plag. (2013). *The Oxford Reference Guide to English Morphology*. Oxford: Oxford University Press.
Burchfield, R.W. (1996). *The New Fowler's Modern English Usage*. 3rd ed. Oxford: Oxford University Press.
Chomsky, Noam & Morris Halle. (1968). *The Sound Pattern of English*. New York: Harper & Row.
Fowler, H.W. (1965). *Modern English Usage*. Second edition revised by Sir Ernest Gowers. Oxford: Oxford University Press.
Jespersen, Otto. ([1942] 1961). *A Modern English Grammar on Historical Principles. Part VI: Morphology*. London: Allen & Unwin/Copenhagen: Munksgaard.
Jones, Daniel, Peter Roach, James Hartman & Jane Setter. (2003). *Cambridge English Pronouncing Dictionary*. 16th ed. Cambridge: Cambridge University Press.
Kiparsky, Paul. (1982). Lexical morphology and phonology. In-Seok Yang (ed.), *Linguistics in the Morning Calm*. Seoul: Hanshin; 3–91.
McMahon, A[pril] M.S. (1994). Lexical phonology and morphology. In R.E. Asher (ed.), *The Encyclopedia of Language and Linguistics Vol. 4*. Oxford: Pergamon, 2155–60.
Marr, Vivian (ed.). (2008). *The Chambers Dictionary*. 11th ed. Edinburgh: Chambers Harrap.
Mohanan, Karuvannur Puthanveetil. (1986). *The Theory of Lexical Phonology*. Dordrecht: Reidel.
OED. The Oxford English Dictionary [online]. oed.com
Ohala, John. (1974). Experimental historical phonology. In John Anderson & Charles Jones (eds.), *Historical Linguistics II*. Amsterdam: North Holland, 353–87.
Quirk, Randolph, Sidney Greenbaum, Geoffrey Leech & Jan Svartvik. (1972). *A Grammar of Contemporary English*. London: Longman.
Upton, Clive, William A. Kretzschmar Jr & Rafal Konopka. (2001). *The Oxford Dictionary of Pronunciation for Current English*. Oxford: Oxford University Press.
Wells, J[ohn] C. (1990). *Longman Pronunciation Dictionary*. Harlow: Longman.

16 Reflections on the Interface between Word-Formation and Syntax

Syntactic structures arise in word-formation as apparent bases, and although some scholars have suggested strict limitations on such usage, it appears to be extremely free in modern usage. Examples of relevant formations will be given here, and two questions will be dealt with: what is the output of the formation? And how is its use limited in word-formation (if at all)?

There are two, apparently distinct, patterns of such usage: syntactic structures arise as complex modifiers in what are usually taken to be compounds, and syntactic constructions are found as the bases in affixation. The two will be dealt with individually before generalizations are sought.

16.1 Syntactic Bases in Affixation

Some examples of the phenomena are listed here, ordered by the suffix used, with an adjectival example first.

> trying to sound completely don't-care-ish. (Judy Astley. 2013. *In the Summer Time*. London: Bantam, p. 62)

> Very much a tooth-for-toother was our Tris. (Susan Moody. 2016. *Quick off the Mark*. Sutton, Surrey: Severn House, p. 169)

> "Free spiritism?" Campion snapped. "That's not even a word, let alone a philosophy." (Mike Ripley and Margery Allingham. 2014. *Mr Campion's Farewell*. London: Severn House Large Print, p. 229)

> born of the boundless can-doism of the immediate post-war. (Harry Stein. 1995. *The Magic Bullet*. New York: Delacorte, p. 14)

> He's such an I'm-right-ist. (attested in conversation, 1996)

> Managing-a-tight-budget-itis. (Judith Cutler. 1999. *Dying by Degrees*. London: Headline, p. 170)

> uppityness and snotty-nosed finer-than-thou-ness. (Trevanian, 1998. *Incident at Twenty-Mile*. New York: St Martin's, p. 201)

> the that's-the-way-it-is-ness (Louisa Luna. 2020. *The Janes*. Melbourne: The Texts company, p. 62)

> his familiar, blank expression, his irritating look of not-really-there-ness. (Paula Hawkins. 2017. *Into the Water*. London: Doubleday, p. 150)
>
> Rankin watched it go, saying several un-bright-spring-day things under his breath. (Gavin Lyall. 1999. *Honourable Intentions*. London: Hodder & Stoughton, p. 82)
>
> Lattice windows give it a story-book appearance, while inside it's even still more once-upon-a-timeyfied. (Jerome K. Jerome. [1889] 1968. *Three Men in a Boat*. Harmondsworth: Penguin, p. 173)

Most of the examples cited above, as well as most of those cited by Bauer et al. (2013) suggest that the phrase used in the base must be a familiar one, or if not particularly familiar, a direct quotation, and some scholars have suggested this as a restriction. It seems likely that this is an epiphenomenon of needing the word to be of a reasonable length, since most such examples use a phrase made up of two or three words. Despite this, there are examples which show that the unfamiliar is also possible. Bauer et al. (2013) cite the following:

> does nothingness, metal-lumpish, post-Connery-as-Bond, pre-Redford-and-Hoffman, senior-skier-hood

One factor that does appear to be relevant is the productivity of the affix. It seems as if it is the most productive affixes which are found in such constructions.

16.2 Phrases as Modifiers

This situation is very common, particularly, though not exclusively, when the phrase modifies a noun. Some examples are given below.

> William James. He was the groundsmen, handyman, if-there's-any-sort-of-difficulty-ask-William-and-he'll-fix-it-for-you person about the place. (Laurence Meynell. 1978. *Papersnake*. London: Macmillan, p. 10)
>
> Natalia wasn't sure – not committed-for-the-rest-of-her-life sure – that's what she did want. (Brian Freemantle. 1996. *Charlie's Chance*. Bath: Chivers Large Print, p. 279)
>
> She was dressed all in black – not a scruffy, Camden, it-doesn't-show-the-stains and-hides-my-fat-black, [hyphenation as in the original] but a designer-label it-allows-me-to-express-my-elegant-simplicity sort of black. (Lauren Henderson. 1996. *Too Many Blondes*. London: Hodder & Stoughton, p. 151)
>
> that infuriating I-know-I've-been-bad-but-I'd-probably-do-it -again grin. (Barbara Seranella. 1999. *No Offence Intended*. London: Hale, p. 13)
>
> The theory has been dubbed the "Did He Fall (on purpose)? Theory". (Robert Rankin. 2003. *The Hollow Chocolate Bunnies of the Apocalypse*. London: Gollancz, p. 56)

our fear-of-terrorist-atrocity society. (Dick Francis. 2006. *Under Orders*. London: Joseph, p. 87)

Eric's Aunt I-told-you-she-was-wrong-for-you Lena. (Patricia Smiley. 2005. *Cover Your Assets*. New York: Mysterious Press, p. 65)

As in scream-out-loud, best-sex-I've-ever-had good? (Maggie Sefton. 2013. *Poisoned Politics*. Detroit: Thorndike, p. 264)

Assuming that the examples here represent the same phenomenon as the use of syntax in the base of derivatives, which seems reasonable, though it may not be open to proof, the requirement of familiarity or direct citation seems to be completely disproved. While the example from Smiley might be a rather lengthy instance of direct quotation, the examples from Meynell and Henderson seem unlikely to be quotations or familiar expressions.

The major question these examples raise is the nature of the output. Is *scream-out-loud good* (to use one of the shortest examples here) a compound, or is *scream-out-loud* simply a word (which may or may not clearly belong to a word-class) which is inserted into a syntactic structure (the two need not be incompatible). One piece of evidence, of dubious reliability, is the spelling. Except in the case flagged above, which may be considered a typographical error, the usual spelling convention for these constructions is for the syntactic construction to be hyphenated (presumably to indicate its unity), but for that construction not to be linked by a hyphen to the head of the phrase. This seems to imply that the syntactic construction is considered to be a word, but that the head is not part of the same word. In English, this could be a reflection of the stress, since such expressions are stressed on the head of the phrase. But it is notable that parallel compounds in other Germanic languages bind the head together with the syntactic phrase into a compound. Consider the examples below (Bauer 1978: 186) which illustrate the difference.

Swedish

hon hade komochtagmigomdukanminen på sig

She had come-and-catch-me-if-you-can-look.the on her

'She was wearing her come-and-get-me-if-you can-look'

Danish

hvorfor-skal-man-op-om-morgenen-stemme

Why-must-one-up-in-morning.the-voice

'Why-do-I-have-to-get-up-in-the-morning voice'

This contrasts with what happens in French, where compounds are not signalled by orthography in the same way, and the syntactic construction is not linked to the head of the entire expression.

French

son côté m'as-tu-vu

3SG.POSS side me-have-you-seen

'his/her have-you-seen-me side'

16.3 Discussion

The first point to note is that syntactic phrases can act as words even if they are not involved in further word-formation, although it is not obvious whether this makes them lexemes (see Chapter 9). The main difference between these word-like objects and the syntactic constructions we have been looking at is that many of those cited above are not frequent enough to become item-familiar, and that those items which do become item-familiar can last long enough for their grammar to become outdated, as with *forget-me-not* (as opposed to **don't-forget-me*), apparently borrowed into several languages from Old French. Established examples are nonetheless rather rare.

> attorney general, by and large, farewell, go-between, man-at-arms (from earlier *man-of-arms*), wannabe

New such expressions are, however, possible.

> What was he? Her ex? Her erstwhile lover? Her lover-in-abeyance? (Val McDermid. 2006. *The Grave Tattoo*. London: HarperCollins, p. 5)

These examples raise the question of whether the use of hyphens is significant or not. It might well be that any multi-word expression (MWE), hyphenated or not, is a relevant example. This might include any or all of the examples below.

> all things considered, as warm as toast, bed and breakfast, bite the bullet, an eye for an eye, a piece of cake [= 'easy'], put up with, rich pickings, under the weather

In fact, it might not even be necessary that multiple orthographic words are involved. Perhaps *deceased* in the example below is a syntactic expression which has been used as a word with the genitive marking part of the structure of the surrounding sentence. Alternative analyses are, of course, possible, too.

> I'm handing you a batch of email correspondence between my client and various members of the deceaseds' families. (M.R. Hall. 2012. *The Flight*. London: Mantle, p. 237)

If this is the case, then we have a mode of word-formation which is simply a matter of syntax. Formal models of word-formation would probably need to build in a loop from the syntax back to the morphology to allow for this, but easier ways of dealing with the descriptive problem might be possible. If the relevant new words are simply syntactic constituents rank-shifted to be words, then these words can act just like other words in being able to take affixes and to be used as modifiers to rather more canonical words. Syntactic rules might have to be expanded slightly to allow this new kind of word to act in this way with adjectives and verbs (which is why the comment was made above that these new words might not belong to a word-class), but that would not mean a major disruption to syntactic patterns.

However, this argument does not hold up easily. It fails to hold up because most of these postulated words cannot act as syntactic heads. In this, they differ from the MWEs mentioned above, which can act as syntactic heads. However conjoined nouns are dealt with in the syntax, *bed and breakfast* can be dealt with in the same way; *bite the bullet* acts syntactically just like any verb phrase, and like any other verb phrase, for example, confers sentencehood on the construction of which it is a part: *I bit the bullet and presented my apologies*. On the other hand, *I told you she was wrong for you* cannot be a noun, verb, adjective or adverb – it can only be a sentence unless it is used in attributive position. We can find, though, occasional exceptions.

> not in this atmosphere of "we've-all-come-out-here-to-enjoy-ourselves-let's-get-on-with-it". (Agatha Christie. 1964. *A Caribbean Mystery*. Leicester: Ulverscroft (large print), p. 81)

> indulge your carnal appetite in exchange for a little looking-the-other-way. (Gerald Hammond. 2004. *Dead Letters*. London: Allison & Busby, p. 87)

> The chief was a has-been, big-city detective, (Sandra Brown. 2005. *Chill Factor*. Waterville, Maine: Thorndike large print edition, p. 10)

> I don't need a tagalong. (Iris Johansen and Roy Johansen. 2014. *Sight Unseen*. New York: St Martin's, p. 53)

Even these examples might be considered not to contain a new word (despite the hyphens). Alternatively, we can modify the constraint (as do Bauer et al. 2013: 490) and limit it to ruling out phrases as heads in compounds.

Furthermore, it appears that such expressions need not be syntactic constituents. Bauer et al. (2013: 457) comment that "determiner phrases seem not to be allowed". As stated, this must be wrong in the light of examples such as *no-phrase constraint* (Botha 1984: 137) or *no-frills airline*, but it contains some truth since **her the-fear-of-terrorist-atrocity society* is not possible. Just what the real constraint might be is not easy to see, though, since Bauer et al. (2013: 457) cite *this-person-is-a-jerk attitude*, which could easily be preceded by an article or a possessive pronoun. It may only be *a(n)* and *the* which are ruled out in initial position in the phrasal element, but even that seems dubious in the light of the following examples from COCA (Davies 2008–).

> The His Dark Materials books by Philip Pullman
>
> poems have appeared in the His Rib and Got Poetry anthologies as well as in various literary journals
>
> the North American leg of his the Thrill of It All Tour
>
> he'd published his The Principles of Psychology three years earlier
>
> Orson Welles (1915–1985) adapted War of the Worlds for his The Mercury Theatre on the Air series
>
> His The New York Times Best Seller

Bauer et al. (2013: 457, see also Bauer 1978) also comment that the syntax need not be a constituent, citing *thumbs-up sign*, and later (2013: 488) they also give as an example *tortoise-and-hare syndrome*, where ordinary syntax would probably demand articles (*the syndrome recalling the tortoise and the hare*).

However we interpret this or try to model it, we have to know just what structures are included and what are not. Is this, for instance, the same structure as gives us compounds before suffixes, as in the following examples?

> asshole-ishness explains a lot of things these days. (Dallas Murphy. 1992. *Lush Life*. New York: Pocket Books, p. 158)
>
> He ... could be described as either muscular or couch-potato-esque. (Sarah Andrews. 2002. *Fault Line*. New York: St Martin's, p. 52)
>
> It was all very Girl-Guide-ish. (Vivienne Plumb. 2003. *Secret City*. Auckland: Cape Catley, p. 178)
>
> It's too science-fiction-y. (Nury Vittachi. 2008. *Mr Wong Goes West*. Crows Nest, NSW: Allen & Unwin, p. 183)

Do the following examples count as instances of the same type, or are they (or some of them) of a different type?

> black-robed attorneys, go-fast stripes, no-go area, red-light district, three-syllable word

Plag (2003: 221–2) deals with some of these, but it has to be acknowledged that the borderline between things that might be compounds and things that are not, or between words and syntactic structures, is very fuzzy in this area. In the case of *three-syllable word*, for instance, there is no plural marking on *syllable*, which is typical of what happens in compounds, yet *three-syllable French word*, where the expression is interrupted by another adjective, makes the whole thing look more like a piece of syntax than like a word.

Just what is going on here remains obscure, but it does look as though the use of syntactic phrases inside complex expressions is more a matter of word-formation than simply a matter of syntax, and subject to slightly more restrictive rules than plain syntax.

Challenge

The most constrained set of syntactic expressions seems to be those that can occur as the base in further derivation. Find further examples (Bauer et al. 2013 give some found in COCA, for instance), and see what the constraints are. Are the constraints related to those on derivation on adverbial bases discussed in Chapter 23?

References

Bauer, Laurie. (1978). *The Grammar of Nominal Compounding*. Odense: Odense University Press.
Bauer, Laurie, Rochelle Lieber & Ingo Plag. (2013). *The Oxford Reference Guide to English Morphology*. Oxford: Oxford University Press.
Botha, Rudolf P. (1984). *Morphological Mechanisms*. Oxford: Pergamon.
Davies, Mark. (2008–). The Corpus of Contemporary American English (COCA). Available online at www.english-corpora.org/coca/
Plag, Ingo. (2003). *Word-Formation in English*. Cambridge: Cambridge University Press.

17 Reflections on the Interface between Word-Formation and Phonetics

Sound symbolism, the use of the sounds of language to represent or reflect the world in different ways, is a topic that has fascinated linguists and philosophers for millennia (see Hinton et al. 1994, Feist 2013, Benczes 2019 among hundreds of others). Most of the phenomena that are discussed under this title, though, do not have anything directly to do with word-formation. For example, the use of onomatopoeia in representing animal sounds (*cuckoo, oink, miaow*) but also in far less direct reflections of natural sound (*flutter, grate, twitter*) have become ordinary words, with form made up of phonemes, whose form varies with language change: would *squeak* feel like such a good representation of an un-oiled gate or a mouse in its Middle English form of [skwɛːk]? They are also extremely culture-bound: pigs may say *oink* in Greek as well as in English, but they do not say that in Swedish or Dutch. But if this is word-formation, it is a word-formation of a very different kind from that which gives us *inexpressibility*. Similarly, it appears that many languages have a close front vowel in words for things that are close and an opener and/or back vowel for things that are far away (as in English *here* and *there, near* and *far*). Lengthening the stressed vowel in *enormous* may make it clear to one's interlocutor that the entity described is particularly big. But none of these things are matters of word-formation. Since this book is about word-formation, the relevant factors here are those where word-formation seems to be related to the sounds used, and there are far fewer such instances. Two will be of particular interest here: phonaesthemes and diminutive marking, and rhyme will be briefly considered.

17.1 Phonaesthemes

One of the obvious places where word-formation may interface with phonetics is in phonaesthemes. Phonaesthemes are sequences of sounds that, while not being morphemes, nevertheless carry some, typically vague, meaning relevant for the word in which they appear. For example, the sequence /ʌmp/ is often thought to provide some meaning referring to a dull sound, as in *bump* (although there are not particularly many relevant words) or something awkward, as in *frump* and *slump*. Similarly, the sequence /sl/ is often thought to indicate slipperiness to some extent, as in *slide, slime, slip, slither, slope* (see Adams 2001: 126–7). Bergen (2004) finds that such patterns are used by speakers to link words together, and in that sense are real to speakers of English, and Bauer (2019) suggests that there is some point in seeing them as part of word-formation, though under the heading of 'resonances' rather than as 'morphemes'.

One phonaestheme often cited for English is the one with the sequence /gl/. The oddity of this sequence is that it is associated with two distinct meanings, one of them to do with light, often faint or reflected light (*glimmer, glisten*), while the other meaning is to do with dullness, depressedness or lack of transparency (*gloaming, gloop, glum*). To see the value of phonaesthemes, words beginning with /gl/ in English were investigated.

Marr (2008) provides a list of 129 words beginning with /gl/, with many derivatives which are ignored here. This list was then compared with a frequency list from COCA (Davies 2008–), and only words from the most frequent 10,000 words of English were retained. This left a list of just thirty words, which were likely to be familiar to all competent speakers of English (the list could have been extended beyond the 10,000-word mark, but any cut-off point would be arbitrary). Of these just four reflected the dullness meaning, twelve could be thought to be related to the light meaning, and the final fourteen were not obviously related to either (assignment to these semantic classes is often personal, so that other observers might find different values, but the abundance of the 'neither' category is striking). The fact that the majority of words with initial /gl/ belonged to neither pattern seems to be a problem for the notion of phonaesthemes as meaningful and useful elements in word-formation.

Yang's (2016) Tolerance Principle seems relevant here. Yang sets out parameters for how many exceptions there can be to a given pattern for it to be perceived as a 'rule', that is, something that can be used productively in the creation of new forms. Yang (2016: 67) sets up quite specific numerical expectations, and although we do not need here to examine the mathematics behind his predictions, he proposes that for a body of forms of size twenty, the maximum number of allowed exceptions is seven, if a rule is to be productive, and for fifty examples, the maximum number of exceptions is thirteen. Fourteen exceptions with twelve forms complying with one of our patterns is far too many, and the other pattern is even less compliant. This makes it sound as though the /gl/ phonaesthemes cannot be rules and cannot be productive, if Yang is right. This seems to contradict Bergen's (2004) position.

Such a conclusion, though, may be overly hasty. Bergen says that speakers use phonaesthemes to link established words, not that phonaesthemes are productive, and although Abelin (1999) talks in terms of productivity, he too looks at perceived links with constructed words. If phonaesthemes are not productive, they do not all fall within the purview of Yang's Tolerance Principle. We thus have a compromise solution available here, which offends neither Abelin (1999) and Bergen (2004) nor Yang: phonaesthemes are perceived in words, where they are discovered over sets of semantically related words that happen to contain common sound sequences, but cannot be used to create words; they are a feature of word-analysis rather than a feature of word-formation. This would explain why phonaesthemes can be ambiguous (as stressed by Feist 2013). If this is a tenable position, its implications are yet to be discovered.

17.2 Diminutives

One place where phonetics is often thought to have a place in word-formation is with diminutives (and, possibly the same thing, with hypocoristics or pet names). Jespersen (1922) is one scholar who finds, cross-linguistically, a close front vowel in words meaning 'small' or 'a short period of time'. Diminutive markers are supposed to follow this general trend (Jespersen 1922: 402). Bauer (1996) examines this claim in a cross-linguistic sample of thirty languages that have overt markers for both diminutives and augmentatives, and finds that as a linguistic universal, there is no overall trend in this direction. But he points out that there are some languages in which the proposed pattern does seem to exist. The question then becomes whether English is one of those languages.

English does not have many diminutive suffixes, and they are not used as widely as diminutive suffixes in Dutch, German, Italian or Spanish. Nevertheless, there are some relevant forms.

Suffix	*Examples*	*Sound*	*Comment*
-er:	fresher, footer, rugger, soccer	ə	Also with additional -s
-ette:	kitchenette, roomette, statuette	e	Also with other meanings
-ie:	auntie, ciggie ('cigarette'), doggie, goalie	i	Also spelled with \<y\>
-kin:	catkin, lambkin, pannikin	ɪ	Very rare
-let:	booklet, piglet, streamlet	ə	
-ling:	foundling, weakling; duckling, gosling, spiderling	ɪ	
-o:	ambo, drongo, lesbo, medico	əʊ	More common in Australia
-s:	ducks, pops, preggers	s ~ z	Alone, often in vocatives or hypocoristics
-zza	Bazza (from Barry), Mazza (from Amanda)	ə	used only in hypocoristics

If we just look at this set of suffixes, it is hard to see that close front vowels feature particularly significantly in diminutive markers in English. There are, though, a significant number of other ways of marking the small in English,

17 Word-Formation and Phonetics 141

including clipping, and the forms *hypo-*, *mini-*, *micro-*, *nano-* and possibly *-ola* (as in *aureola*) and *-een* (as in *poteen*, an Irish loan) (see Bauer et al. 2013). It could be argued that to the extent these show relevant vowel sounds, they are vowels sounds from other languages, and not particularly relevant. Alternatively, they may be borrowed precisely for their phonetic form. English does have other ways of marking diminutivization, though, illustrated in

> beddy-byes, drinky-poo, kitten, owlet, toothy-peg

This is a mixed set, and not everyone will consider them relevant. But to the extent that they are relevant, they do not add greatly to the notion that close front vowels occur in English diminutives. The one factor that does point in that direction is that of all the diminutive suffixes in English *-ie* is by far the most productive, overwhelming all other models except possibly clipping (which is iconic in a different way). In terms of token-frequency, then, close front vowels are the rule.

17.3 Rhyme in Word-Formation

There is an argument to be made that rhyme is phonetic rather than phonological. How far this argument is accepted will depend on just what is considered to be phonology, and just what is considered to be phonetics.

The argument in favour of viewing rhyme as phonetic is that phonologically distinct items can nevertheless be perceived as good rhymes. For example, *sword*, *cored* and *awed* all rhyme in Standard Southern British English, despite the fact that the /d/ in *cored* and *awed* alternates with /t/ and /ɪd/ on different bases while the /d/ in *sword* does not, and despite the fact that the <r> in *cored* represents an alternation between /r/ and Ø, while there is no /r/ pronunciation of the <r> in *sword*.

The argument against seeing rhyme as phonetic is that detailed phonetic analysis shows that *freeze* and *frees* are phonetically distinguishable (see Plag et al. 2017, Seyfarth et al. 2018). If we see these as being homophones (and therefore as rhyming) we must be operating at the phonemic level (which is phonological) rather than at the phonetic level.

For present purposes, it is not particularly important which of these positions we want to take – all that is at stake is where such material might be dealt with in this book. Treating it here is not necessarily unmotivated.

The first question we need to ask about rhyme is what its function is outside of its poetic usages, where it has functions such as making the poetry's structure more predictable and thus easier to remember and also more enjoyable for the listener. There is a huge literature on the subject, and I do not wish to get embroiled in it here. It seems likely that rhyme outside poetry draws attention to the rhyming words, perhaps linking them together in some way. Just what that attention involves is not necessarily simple. Bauer and Huddleston (2002: 1666) talk of a "trivialising effect" in compounds whose elements rhyme such as *copshop* and *gang-bang*. But any trivializing may be the result first, of the ludic element involved in rhyme and second of drawing specific attention to the words in a way which contrasts with the serious nature of the real-world referents involved. Items such as *walkie-talkie*, which may be based on reduplication rather than compounding, show the attraction of rhyme for the user, and expressions such as *hoity-toity* have only the rhyming form and no semantic content, to justify them. Rhymes are clearly fun, and because rhyme is relatively rare in ordinary usage, it is surprising. Note the standard reaction when a person produces a rhyme without having planned it: I'm a poet and I don't know it.

Alliteration and assonance have similar effects, but are even less clearly phonetic rather than phonological.

Challenge

How many words can you find that end in <ug>, like *bug*, *slug*, *smug*? Does the /ʌg/ have a meaning in some of them? If so, what is the meaning, and in how many of them is it found? Is there any external motivation for the sound to represent that particular meaning? Do speakers agree? Try the same exercise with initial /fl/ or with final /ʌf/. Do we need to distinguish between different types of phonaestheme, and if so, how?

References

Abelin, Åsa. (1999). Studies in sound symbolism. PhD dissertation, Göteborg Universitet. Acta Universitatis Gothoburgensis 17.
Adams, Valerie. (2001). *Complex Words in English*. Harlow: Longman.
Bauer, Laurie. (1996). No phonetic iconicity in evaluative morphology. *Studia Linguistica* 50, 189–206.
(2019). *Rethinking Morphology*. Edinburgh: Edinburgh University Press.
Bauer, Laurie & Rodney Huddleston. (2002). Lexical word-formation. In Rodney Huddleston & Geoffrey K. Pullum, *The Cambridge Grammar of the English Language*. Cambridge: Cambridge University Press, 1621–1721.
Bauer, Laurie, Rochelle Lieber & Ingo Plag. (2013). *The Oxford Reference Guide to English Morphology*. Oxford: Oxford University Press.
Benczes, Réka. (2019). *Rhyme over Reason: Phonological Motivation in English*. Cambridge: Cambridge University Press
Bergen, Benjamin K. (2004). The psychological reality of phonaesthemes. *Language* 80, 290–311.
Davies, Mark. (2008–). *The Corpus of Contemporary American English* (COCA). Available online at www.english-corpora.org/coca/
Feist, Jim. (2013). 'Sound symbolism' in English. *Journal of Pragmatics* 45, 104–18.

Hinton, Leanne, Johanna Nichols & John J. Ohala (eds.). (1994). *Sound Symbolism*. Cambridge: Cambridge University Press.
Jespersen, Otto. (1922). *Language: Its Nature, Development and Origin*. London: Allen & Unwin.
Marr, Vivian (ed.). (2008). *The Chambers Dictionary*. 11th edn. Edinburgh: Chambers Harrap.
Plag, Ingo, Julia Homann, & Gero Kunter. (2017). Homophony and morphology: The acoustics of word-final S in English. *Journal of Linguistics* 53, 181–216.
Seyfarth, Scott, Marc Garellek, Gwendolyn Gillingham, Farrell Ackerman, & Robert Malouf. (2018). Acoustic differences in morphologically-distinct homophones. *Language, Cognition and Neuroscience* 33, 32–49.
Yang, Charles. (2016). *The Price of Linguistic Productivity*. Cambridge, MA: MIT Press.

18 Reflections on the Interface between Word-Formation and Orthography

In Chapter 15, apparently morphophonemic rules shown in, for instance, *Shaw / Shavian* were discussed and considered to be based on spelling rather than phonology. A similar case might be made for velar softening. These are, then, instances where word-formation has an interface with orthography. In this chapter, we look for other cases of this interface.

One such case is with acronyms. Acronyms are abbreviations which are pronounced as words rather than as sequences of letters. Examples are *Aids* 'acquired immune-deficiency syndrome', *BASIC* 'Beginners' all-purpose symbolic instruction code', *NATO* 'North Atlantic Treaty Organization' and *WASP* 'white Anglo-Saxon protestant'. Apart from the variation in the way in which acronyms are spelled, sometimes using all capitals, sometimes using lower-case letters, it should be noted that there is a certain amount of laxness in what counts as an element of the base expression from which the acronym is derived: *all-purpose* is treated as providing a single letter to *BASIC* while *Anglo-Saxon* provides two letters to *WASP*. Articles are often ignored. We should also consider the emergence of the backronym, in which the appropriate surface form is chosen first, and then a suitable phrase is invented to provide those letters: *SAD* 'seasonal affective disorder' is probably a backronym, and perhaps the most famous example is the *USA PATRIOT Act* 'Uniting and Strengthening America by Providing Appropriate Tools Required to Intercept and Obstruct Terrorism', where the full version sounds far more negative and threatening than the backronym.

The link with orthography comes from the fact that acronyms are based on the letters in the base expression rather than the sounds. Once the letters are put together, they are then pronounced according to the usual grapheme-to-phoneme rules for English. Consider *BASIC* as cited above. If we look at the way in which the relevant letters are pronounced in the original, we would expect /b/, /ɔː/, /s/, /ɪ/, /k/, but we get /beɪsɪk/, where long <a> is pronounced /eɪ/ in accordance with the same rules that lead to the pronunciation of the ordinary word *basic*. Similarly, if PATRIOT used the phonemes represented by the letters in the supposed underlying form, we would get /pətrɪɒt/ rather than the actual /peɪtriət/. Even when the acronym does not have the form of an already

18 Word-Formation and Orthography   145

existing word, the same principles are involved. In the case of *UNICEF* 'United Nations International Children's Emergency Fund' we get /juːnɪsef/ rather than /juːnɪtʃɪf/, and with *laser* 'light amplification by stimulated emission of radiation' we get /leɪzə/ rather than /læser/ (which is phonotactically impossible).

These principles seem to hold in many places where there is shortening. Consider clipping compounds, in which the elements of the compound are clipped forms of words. *Modem* 'modulator and demodulator', pronounced /məʊdem/, following the spelling, with an open first syllable, rather than /mɒdiːm/ which we would get from following the values attached to the letters in the base form. Similar comments can be made about *fin-lit* 'financial literacy', *hi-fi* 'high fidelity', *sci-fi* 'science fiction'. *Biopic* is relevant if pronounced /baɪɒpɪk/ but not if pronounced /baɪəʊpɪk/. It is not clear whether examples like *e-mail* and *Man U* count as clipping compounds, but the single letters get the pronunciation of the name of the letter, whatever the source: we do not find */emeɪl/ for example.

Clippings that are not parts of compounds seem to be slightly more immune to this phenomenon, but even then, we find both respelling to maintain the appropriate phonemes and changed pronunciation of the original (Jamet 2009).

> Respelling: caff (< café), coke (< Coca-Cola or < cocaine), cos (< because), cuz (< cousin), delish (< delicious), indie (< independent film), mike (< microphone), natch (< naturally), Oz (< Australia), peeps (< people), ute (< utility vehicle)

> Repronouncing: merc (/mɜːk/ < mercenary /mɜːsɪnəri/), mayo (/meɪəʊ/ < mayonnaise /meɪəneɪz/), rasp (/rɑːsp/ < raspberry /rɑːzbri/), zoo (/zuː/ < zoological garden, at least for those who say /zəʊəlɒdʒɪkəl/)

> Both simultaneously: bike (< bicycle)

Note that in *fan* (/fæn/ < fanatic) the full vowel follows the spelling, because a lexical item with only the vowel /ə/ would not be possible. What Bauer and Huddleston (2002: 1636) call 'embellished clippings' have extra material at the end, but this does not seem to affect the pronunciation, except that words ending <(s)sie> seem to be pronounced with a /z/ rather than an /s/: *Aussie* (/ɒzi/ < *Australian*), *mozzie* (/mɒzi/ < *mosquito*, note the spelling reflects the new pronunciation), *possie* (/pɒzi/ < *position*). Just occasionally the embellishment allows more consonants in the base of the clipping, which must help recognizability: *lesbo* (< *lesbian*, with *lez* and *lezzie* as alternative forms – none of them necessarily flattering terms).

Blends seem to be rather more constrained by the pronunciation, but spelling is also relevant. *Musicassette* and *magicube* have /i/ rather than /ɪ/ for those speakers for whom the two vowels are not homophonous, *tigon* has a full vowel for the <o>, even though the corresponding vowel in *lion* is reduced. The meaning behind *evilution* and *medievil* (Lopez Rua 2012) can be discerned only from the spelling, as can *fauxbia* (Beliaeva, p.c.), and *funerealm* depends on the spelling to work at all. Adams (1973: 153) comments on the use of /ɪ/ rather than /iː/ in the first syllable of *skinoe* (from *ski* and *canoe*).

Back-formation occasionally shows examples where the derived form's spelling determines its pronunciation, especially with cases that end with <t> such as *contracept*, where the <t> is pronounced /ʃ/ in the complete form *contraception*. *Attrit* from *attrition* shows the same phenomenon. In this case, though, the same alternation is found in instances which are not formed by back-formation, such as *act / action* and *alternate / alternation*.

The most obvious place where orthography is involved is in the creation of words – often tradenames, and often involving drugs – where letters from a long name are put together to make a new name. An example from Barnhart et al. (1990) is *pemoline* 'a drug used to relieve depression', supposed to come from *PhEryliMino-OxazoLIdinoNE* (where the capitals indicate the letters that made it through to the name). Although it may not be true, it looks as though the drug could just as well have been called *phyzolone*. It is not clear that words like this are formed by word-formation (as opposed, say, to word-manufacture, assuming the two can be distinguished), but the influence of the spelling is clear.

More surprising than these are the instances of apparently straightforward word-formation where the spelling nevertheless has an influence. Consider the name of the educationalist *Piaget*. His name, if not pronounced in the French way, is /piæʒeɪ/. There is an adjective derived from his name, *Piagetian*. We might expect this to be pronounced /piæʒeɪən/ (which is apparently the most usual pronunciation in the USA) or perhaps /piæʒiːʃən/ (like *Venetian*), though this does not seem to occur. However, we do find (Wells 1990) /piəʒetiən/. The /t/ must arise from the spelling. We find the same phenomenon with other French names, such as *Corneille* /kɔːneɪ/ giving *Corneillian* /kɔːneɪliən/ or /kɔːniːliən/, *Flaubert* /fləʊbeə/ giving *Flaubertian* /fləʊbɜːtiən/, *Louis* /luːi/ giving *Louisiana* /luːiːziænə/. *Rabelais* giving *Rabelaisian* /ræbəleɪʒən/. It is not clear how far this effect spreads. *Pasteur*, with /æ/, gives rise to *pasteurize*, with /ɑː/, which might be an orthographic influence, but it is less clear.

What becomes clear is that word-formation is not purely a matter of creating phonological strings from phonological representations: orthographic representations are also important in creating new words.

Challenge

Find other examples of new inventions being named in the way illustrated by *pemoline* in the text. Could you generate such names by taking the full form and applying some mathematical formula to it (e.g. take the first letter, then a random letter following that, then the letter in numerical position that is the square of the second letter, then add the number of the second letter . . .). If not (and I assume that the answer is that you cannot) what constraints are there on choosing letters to make up such names? For example, what consonant clusters arise in the names? Are there always analogies with already known words?

References

Adams, Valerie. (1973). *An Introduction to Modern English Word-Formation*. London: Longman.
Barnhart, Robert K., Sol Steinmetz & Clarence L. Barnhart. (1990). *Third Barnhart Dictionary of New English*. New York: Wilson.
Bauer, Laurie & Rodney Huddleston. (2002). Lexical word-formation. In Rodney Huddleston & Geoffrey K. Pullum, *The Cambridge Grammar of the English Language*. Cambridge: Cambridge University Press, 1621–1721.
Jamet, Denis. (2009). A morphophonological approach to clipping in English: Can the study of clipping be formalized? *Lexis* 2. https://doi.org/10.4000/lexis.884
López Rúa, Paula. (2012). Beyond all reasonable transgression: Lexical blending in alternative music. In Vincent Renner, François Maniez & Pierre J.L. Arnaud (eds.), *Cross-Disciplinary Perspectives on Lexical Blending*. Berlin: De Gruyter Mouton, 23–34.
Wells, J.C. (1990). *Longman Pronunciation Dictionary*. Harlow: Longman.

19 Reflections on the Interface between Word-Formation and Borrowing

19.1 Introduction

Neoclassical word-formation creates multiple problems of description for many European languages, not least for English. The words formed by this process are generally called 'neoclassical compounds' because a word like *photograph* is not a word formed in Greek and borrowed into English – the Ancient Greeks did not have photographs. Rather, they are words made up of Greek elements (hence the element 'classical'), but they are modern (hence 'neo-'); the elements are derived from Greek words (hence 'compounds'), but they may include affixes as well – sometimes Greek affixes (such as the *-ia* in *euphoria*) and sometimes English affixes (such as the *-er* in *philosopher*). Because of this, it is probably more accurate to term the relevant words 'neoclassical formations'. What we are dealing with here is a part of the word-formation of English (and, of course, of other languages as well) whose fundamental elements have been borrowed, mainly from Greek but also from Latin, and many of the problems associated with neoclassical formations arise because of this.

19.2 Patterns of Neoclassical Formation

Canonical neoclassical formations are created from two elements each of which is borrowed from one of the classical languages. *Photograph* illustrates a word made up of Greek elements, *agriculture* one made up of Latin elements. In words found in modern usage, it is not always possible to tell whether the formation is created in English (sometimes borrowed from French or German) or is borrowed as a unit from the classical languages. *Photograph* is a recent formation, *agriculture* is borrowed from Latin (probably via French).

The rules of formation for these words are not always clear. The medial *-o-* in words of Greek origin and the *-i-* in words of Latin origin are probably best treated as a linking element, and are usually omitted when the form of the first element brings two vowels into contact with each other, as in *homonym* from *homo-* 'same' and *-onym* 'name' or *nephralgia* from *nephr-* 'kidney and *-algia* 'pain' (contrast *nephropathy* 'kidney disease' from *nephr-* + *o* + *path* + *y*). The linking element is normally deleted before Greek [h] (often termed 'rough breathing' in the literature on the Greek language) as well. These rules are not always followed by the time the word is found in English, so that *glycaemia*, *glychaemia* and *glycohaemia* are all used synonymously in English, albeit not equally frequently at the same period. Greek and Latin inflections are usually deleted in both elements, so that the Latin form of *agriculture* had a case/ number marker *-a* at the end: *agricultura*. The stress in English is typically determined over the complete formation, treated as a word without morphological boundaries.

In a less canonical pattern, a classical element is linked with an English word. *Demonology, Egyptology* and *typology* provide examples of English words linked with Greek *-ology*. Even though *type* comes from a Greek original, the meaning shown in *typology* is not the meaning it had in Greek. The *-ology* element, derived from a Greek element meaning 'word', has developed a new meaning of 'subject of study, science' in modern English. The word *hieroglyph* may provide a better model for this reason, though a less familiar one. Once a foreign element becomes familiar enough to be considered an unexceptional word, it can be treated the same way as native forms, and used in the same constructions as native words. Although words like *Egyptology* are different from words like *photograph* from an etymological point of view, in the eye of people coining new terms, they are probably much the same, or the *-ology* is seen as being an English affix. This also accounts for the phenomenon of a mixture of Latin and Greek elements occurring in the same word, as in *television*.

As was mentioned above, neoclassical elements can also contain affixes, either classical or English. In some cases, it may not be clear whether the affix is classical or whether it is English. These affixes may also attach to obligatorily bound stems that are not compounds. This means that a sequence of, say, classical element + classical element + suffix may have the structure [[classical element] [classical element + suffix]] or [[[classical element] [classical element]] [suffix]], and it is not always easy to determine which structure applies.

The English affixes (some of them with etymons from the classical languages, sometimes through French) that are used tend to be the most frequent affixes, as illustrated below.

-al exoskeletal, matriarchal, octahedral, primogenital, puerperal
-er oceanographer, philosopher
-ic chromospheric, encephalitic, haemostatic, homeopathic, matronymic, philharmonic, photostatic, plutocratic, psychogenetic, pyrotechnic
-ism demagogism, necrophilism, pentadactylism, phototropism, zoomorphism
-ist gymnosophist, homeopathist, hydrologist, oenologist, palaeobotanist

-ize   anthologize, democratize, hypnotize
-ous   androgenous, coprophagous, homophonous, phosphorous, polygenous, zygomorphous
-y   androgeny, cacophony, gastronomy, geometry, hagiolatry, historiography, homonymy, hydrocephalous, oligarchy, philanthropy, polygamy, rhinoscopy, tracheotomy

Greek affixes include

a-, an-	atypical, aneroid
endo-	endocarp
exo-	exogamy
hypo-	hypochondria
neo-	neology
poly-	polyglot
syn-, sym-	syncope, sympathy
-ia	phobia
-itis	hepatitis
-oid	anthropoid

Latin affixes include

ab-, abs-	ablative, abstruse
ad-, ac-, af- etc.	advent, accept, affluent
con-, col-, com-, cor-	conceal, collect, compact, correct
contra-	contradict
in-, im-, il-, -ir	invisible, impatient, illegible, irrelevant
inter-	intercede
pro-	produce
-ion	legion
-ix	testatrix

There are two important points to note about these affixes. The first is that it is often difficult to be sure that they should be classified as affixes rather than as compound elements. The classification in the original language may be different from the classification in modern English. This is particularly the case where the element is homophonous with an adjective, adverb, preposition or number in the original language. The second is that, especially with Latin affixes, the form may also be used as an English affix, sometimes with a different phonology or a different meaning from the original Latin. For example, Latin *ex-* in *expel*, where *ex-* means 'out' is not the same element as the *ex-* in *ex-wife*, where *ex-* means 'former'; the Latin *re-* in *refer*, although it is historically related to the English *re-* in *re-educate*, is pronounced differently (/rɪfɜː/ versus /riːedjʊkeɪt/) and is rather more transparent in meaning.

Finally, it should be noted that some of these borrowed elements can have multiple functions in English. *Mega-* looks like a neoclassical element in *megaphone*, like a prefix in *mega-deal*, and like a lexeme when it means 'excellent'.

19.3 Discussion

Borrowing from Greek and Latin (and to a lesser extent from French, although many classical words are transferred to English via French) causes problems of description in English. If we borrow *Schadenfreude* from German, we treat it as a single unanalysable unit despite the fact that it is analysable for German speakers. If we borrow *orthodox* from Greek, where it originally came from elements meaning 'right opinion' we have a cluster of related words that allow us to isolate each element: words like *orthopaedic, orthographic, orthoepy, paradox, heterodox*. The temptation is thus to treat such words as illustrating a kind of word-formation, especially as the processes are often productive (the overall pattern of compounding is productive, and compounds with particular elements may be productive). Yet the meaning of the elements or of the word as a whole may have changed over time (*orthodox* would probably be glossed as 'received opinion' rather than 'right opinion' these days), the link between *mage* and *magic* is etymological, but no longer semantic. There may be alternative expressions (e.g. *received wisdom*) which have to be distinguished from the borrowed word, often in very subtle ways. The analysis becomes awkward, and it may not be possible to treat all neoclassical forms in the same way.

Overall, the fact that so many words have been borrowed into English from the classical languages and used in formations that look more or less like classical formations means that a coherent treatment of words of this type is theoretically and practically very difficult. Borrowing of isolated words from other languages has a minimal effect on the system of English morphology. We can even borrow affixes (such as *-age* and *-ment* from French) without upsetting the general way in which word-formation operates. The swamping of English vocabulary from Greek and Latin, though, upsets the processes of word-formation by introducing new patterns which are too pervasive to be ignored, but which are often variable, difficult to analyse (depending, for instance, on when they are coined and by whom) and which show traces of the gradual assimilation of the Greek and Latin elements into English, often with formal and/or semantic changes.

Challenge

The suffix *-ia* in *mania* and *phobia* was cited in this chapter as an instance of a Greek suffix. Is it used only on Greek bases, or is it used elsewhere as well? The suffix -*ic* in *manic* and *phobic*, on the other hand, while of Greek origin (boosted by Latin usage), is usually discussed as an English suffix. Are the two really as different as this implies? How do they differ from each other, and how can they be seen as two distinct examples of the same phenomenon?

Part V

Patterns of Word-Formation in English

20   Reflections on the Limits of Conversion

20.1   Introduction

One of the places where the borderline between word-formation and syntax is least clear is in the area of conversion, and specifically its borderline with what is called 'coercion' (Pustejovsky 1995). Although I talk about syntax here, coercion is really a semantic process whereby the semantics of a particular word is adjusted in order to make sense in its syntactic/semantic/pragmatic environment. There are many examples of this phenomenon, which typically work within a word-class while conversion typically works over word-class boundaries (for discussion and more examples and for a classification, see Audring and Booij 2016).

>They seem to be very British.
>
>I began the book.
>
>The light flashed until dawn.
>
>There are three Rachels in my class.
>
>I need to read some index.

Very British makes the adjective *British* gradable, when it would be ungradable by default; *begin* usually implies an activity, while a book is an object, so that *beginning a book* has to be interpreted as reading or writing the book (at least in normal discourse; it could feasibly be interpreted as eating a book under suitable conditions); flashing is a momentary event, while *until dawn* implies continuity; *Rachel* is usually a name, but here must mean 'people called Rachel' and so be a common noun; *index* is usually a countable noun, but in context has to be read as uncountable. The difficult examples arise where it is not clear whether there is a shift of word-class or not. For example, Nagano (2018) argues that the difference between relational and qualitative adjectives should be seen as a matter of conversion rather than coercion, so that the difference seen in

>A young professional soccer player
>
>A (very) professional young soccer player

(where the differing order of *professional* with relation to the adjective *young* indicates a different class of adjective) is a matter of a shift of word-class, not a matter of coercion, despite the fact that conversion is usually taken to imply a change in major word-class (e.g. a change from noun to verb or noun to adjective without any change in form – for recent discussion, see Bauer and Valera forthcoming).

In this chapter, I look at three places where the borderline between conversion and coercion may be relevant.

20.2 Example 1: *The Rich* and Related Constructions

Payne and Huddleston (2002: 417) point out that it is possible to have what they term "fusion of internal modifier and head" with some classes of adjective and some syntactic structures. Some of their examples are given below. The importance of Payne and Huddleston's analysis in the present context is that they see this as neither conversion nor coercion.

> Henrietta likes red shirts, and I like blue.
> Henrietta likes Russian vodka, and I like Polish.
> I prefer cotton shirts to nylon.

They note that "the boundaries to what is admissible are hard to define". They include here examples like

> The rich cannot enter the kingdom of heaven.

In relation to such examples, they say that *the deceased* and *the accused* are unusual in having the potential to be singular or plural. They further note (Payne and Huddleston 2002: 418) that adjectives derived from nouns by conversion cannot participate in this structure:

> *The intellectual are not to be trusted. [my example, not theirs]

They reject (2002: 421) an analysis whereby the relevant word has a different function in modifier and head positions while retaining its fundamental category because the constructions in

> I prefer cotton shirts to nylon.
> I prefer cotton to nylon.

would not be distinguished if *nylon* were a noun in both.

There are several things to worry about here.

The first is that it is not clear whether we are dealing with the same construction in all these cases. In

> Henrietta likes red shirts, and I like blue

20 Limits of Conversion 157

we can only interpret *blue* in the light of the preceding material. If we had

>Henrietta likes red hair dye and I like blue

blue would have a different interpretation. This seems to imply that, in this instance, *blue* gains its interpretation as a function of the syntactic environment. This is different from what happens in

>The rich cannot enter the kingdom of heaven

where *the rich* must mean 'people', independent of the syntactic environment, and where a definite determiner is required, which is not the case in some of Payne and Huddleston's other examples. Payne and Huddleston cite examples with adverbial modification of *rich* in such uses to show that *rich* remains an adjective, but adjectival modification is also found, which implies that *rich* is (or has at least some features of) a noun.

>The very rich cannot enter the kingdom of heaven.

>The powerful rich cannot enter the kingdom of heaven.

It is far from clear that nouns by conversion are excluded from this construction, although when they do appear they do not have access to the range of possibilities that such adjectives usually have. Consider

>I think we the intellectual are suffering from too much thinking because we haven't gotten rid of ignorance completely (https://philosophistry.com/archives/2004/04/if-ignorance-is.html accessed 12 August 2023)

It is relatively easy to show that adjective to noun conversion like *intellectuals* and the construction illustrated by *the rich* are different constructions. One relevant question to ask, though harder to answer, is whether this means that they belong to different word-classes.

intellectuals	*the rich*
can take a range of determiners	requires the determiner *the*
can take a plural marker	cannot take a plural marker
relatively restricted productivity	relatively free productivity
freely modified by adjectives, not modified by adverbs	can be modified by adverbs or adjectives

The productivity of the construction like *the rich* is problematic. Where *the rich* gets plural agreement, it musts refer to humans (perhaps better, to rational beings), while singular agreement implies that the reference is to non-humans (except with *the accused* and *the deceased* mentioned by Payne and Huddleston 2002).

>The poor are always with us.

>The improbable we will do at once, the impossible takes a little longer.

158   Part V Patterns of Word-Formation in English

> The rich are different from us.
>
> The rich is bad for the digestion.

The adjectives that can take part in this construction are numerous, but apparently not unrestricted, as we see if we compare with what happens in other languages. For Amade and Bécaud (1967)

> L'important c'est la rose
>
> the important is the rose
>
> 'The important thing is the rose.'

And for Hans Andersen in *The Ugly Duckling* (Andersen [1835–72] 1961: 197)

> [D]et Grønne er godt for Øinene
>
> The green is good for eyes.the
>
> 'Green is good for the eyes.'

Yet these do not allow translation into English with the same construction as we see with *the rich* above. It seems that the rules for noun phrases apparently headed by adjectives are not equivalent across languages. Payne and Huddleston (2002: 417) classify these examples alongside other such as

> The French do these things differently.
>
> This is verging on the immoral.
>
> They like to swim in the nude.

They see such examples, just like the *rich* examples, as having special interpretations, and thus, presumably, in the terms of Construction Grammar, being members of different constructions. However, *the French* are people, just like *the rich*, *the immoral* refers to something non-human, just like *the impossible*, and only *the nude* seems semantically rather marginal, and it is classified as an idiom by Payne and Huddleston.

Just how freely this construction can be used productively, however, remains hard to determine. Colour adjectives seem to be excluded, but *the black* and *the white* seem possible as racial terms, but in just those contexts *black* and *white* can be nouns by conversion (like *intellectual*) and have other grammatical options.

> the presence of poor whites was a constant threat, challenge and embarrassment to South African formations of white identity. (Thandiwe Ntshinga, *Poor Whites: A Threat, Challenge and Embarrassment to South African Formations of White Identity*, 2016. https://brill.com/display/book/9781848883833/BP000007.xml accessed 21 March 2024.)

Adjectives which do not seem to be possible in this construction include *ample, American* (unlike *French*!), *big, basic, flawless, icy*, but how far any of these are just not widely used and whether there are any generalizations over these unsystematic examples are questions that need to be considered further. All that can be said thus far is that there appear to be sufficient lexically determined gaps for us to say that this looks like a morphological construction rather than a syntactic one.

20.3   Example 2: Indicators of Composition

Another type of puzzle is raised by words like *brick, copper, cotton, iron, leather, steel, stone*. Such words are used as nouns, as in

> Cotton is grown in India and in the USA.
>
> We need cutlery made of steel.
>
> The stone for Stonehenge was brought from Wales.

At the same time, they have usages which appear to be adjectival in examples like

> We used to have a copper kettle.
>
> A stone wall enclosed the field.
>
> The facing is brick.

This means that these words cover the functions of both *wood* and *wooden*, both *wool* and *woollen*, where one member of the pair is a noun and the other an adjective, and so look as though they have a single form for two word-classes, which is a typical expectation when we are dealing with conversion. However, matters are not quite that simple.

The first point to consider is that there are words which fit neatly into neither the category like *stone* nor the category like *wool*. Consider *gold* and *silk*. *Gold* can be a noun as the name of a metal (*My ring is made of 18 carat gold*) and an adjective as a colour (*Their names were spelt out in gold letters*), and *golden* can also have both functions (*a golden crown, a golden beach*) or neither (*a golden oldie, a golden opportunity*). A *gold coin* means 'made of gold' (or, these days, often no more than 'the colour of gold' – *a gold coin donation* does not necessarily involve a Krugerrand), but *golden* in (*kill the goose that lays*) *the golden egg* also means 'made of gold'. It appears that each word has two polysemes, but that the polysemes of each are the same. The case of *silk* is rather easier, and more typical. The *-en* suffix creates an adjective, but an adjective whose meaning is 'resembling ~' rather than 'made of ~'. So *silken* is usually used of hair, or of a touch rather than of dresses or other clothing. *Silk*, on the other hand, can mean the material (*She bought some Indian silk*) or that something is made of that material (*silk stockings*). *Wooden* can mean 'made of wood' (*a wooden box*) or 'resembling wood and therefore not natural for a person' (*a wooden expression*). *Woollen* usually means 'made of wool', but in an expression like *woollen mill* is parallel to *flour mill* in the sense that the mill produces wool or flour, despite the lack of grammatical parallelism. Much of the complexity here is due to lexicalization. The suffix *-en* is no longer productive, and individual words have developed idiosyncratically, at least to some extent. This means that the forms with *silk, gold, wool, copper* are more likely to be semantically regular than the forms with an overt adjective.

The second point to consider here is that the relevant words do not behave like adjectives in allowing comparative forms or adverbs in *-ly* to be derived from them. We can see this as a function of their meaning (why would we need an adverb from *copper*?) or as a sign that they are not adjectives, but nouns. To the extent that comparatives or adverbs are required, the noun is first turned into an adjective, and then that adjective is used as a base: *silkier, silkiness, steeliness, stonier, woollier, woollily* and so on. Perhaps more importantly, many of these words are awkward in predicative position: *brick*, used above, is much better in predictive position than *stone*, for example.

The third point is that if we accept, for instance, *brick wall*, as a noun + noun sequence, then we expect any premodifying adjective to modify the entire unit, as in *tall brick wall*, where it is the wall and not the brick that is tall. However, when the first element alone is modified, it is modified by an adjective not by an adverb, and it is where the adjective + the first element is already fixed expression: a *red brick wall* is a wall made of red brick, an *Egyptian cotton towel* is made of Egyptian cotton rather than being (necessarily) an Egyptian towel. This behaviour is typical if these words are nouns; if they were adjectives we might expect **a redly brick wall*, parallel to *a beautifully slim figure*.

My conclusion is that despite their use in some constructions which make them look a bit like adjectives, these words are really nouns, and that we do not have to worry about deriving an adjective from a noun (or vice versa) here at all.

20.4   Example 3: Metonymy

As a final example, consider instances of metonymy, like

> The omelette in the corner hasn't paid yet.
> You don't often see a jogging hijab.

In both these cases, a person is referred to by something closely connected to them: the meal they ordered in a café or the headscarf they are wearing, and this is central to metonymy. Figures of speech like metonymy are not usually considered to be word-formation processes, because it is assumed that figures of speech are processed by general, non-linguistic, cognitive principles, and do not need to be dealt with explicitly in a grammar, because they transcend language and can be found, for example, in pictures or in music (consider the use of a piece of 1920s music on a film soundtrack to indicate a period in which the action is supposedly taking place) (Littlemore 2015). Unusually, though, conversion is often seen as a form of metonymy, even though it typically demands a change of word-class (Dirven 1999). We thus have two contrasting views of the link between metonymy and conversion: on the one hand, metonymy is not word-formation and not fundamentally linguistic, although it has many linguistic effects; on the other hand, conversion (which is a type of metonymy) is a word-formation process, a linguistic process. Furthermore, although metonymy does not usually cause a change of word-class when it applies in language, in conversion it typically does. Clearly, we have a problem of theoretical coherence here, one which can be solved by stipulation, although we would prefer an alternative solution.

One way to do this is to go back and look at the instances of coercion. Consider, for example, *British* versus *very British*. The two are cognitively close to each other, because being seen as British can suggest that there are several features that can give this impression, and if many of them are relevant, we have a case for seeing Britishness as being a cline. Reading a book is an activity in which the book plays a central and cognitively crucial role. One flash is a constituent part, and a defining one, in a series of flashes. The form *Rachel* (that is, the word itself) is what is shared by the people whose name is Rachel. In all these cases, we might be discussing metonymy, a figure of speech where one entity is used to provide access to another entity to which it is somehow related (Littlemore 2015: 4). That is, there is an argument for seeing many (and perhaps all) cases of coercion as cases of metonymy. If that is true, then coercion and conversion are just terms for subtypes of metonymy, and the differences between the two are just the ways in which the subtypes differ from each other. Depending on one's position, the differences or the similarities might be considered the most important factors.

Ironically, the biggest objection to such a view comes from within Cognitive Linguistics. Brdar and Brdar-Szabó (2014) claim that the term *metonymy* is being applied so freely that it becomes meaningless. Personally, I find an argument that says that metonymy is ubiquitous and so we should call it something else in part of its range a rather strange argument. Seeing the extensive scope of metonymy is part of its value. This does not, for me, imply that there is no point in having specific terms for subtypes of metonymy, but does imply that there is benefit in recognizing the overarching category.

20.5 Discussion

Although conversion is well recognized as part of word-formation, that does not mean that there is agreement on just what is part of conversion and what is not. The trouble with this is that it implies that while we may recognize conversion in some instances, our definition of conversion or our understanding of it is not sufficient to determine just what should count as conversion and what should not. Apart from the instances discussed here we have cases like *The enemy downed three of our planes*, where the verbal uses of prepositions is extremely rare and semantically unsystematic, cases like *I don't want to hear you effing and blinding* where the semantic regularity of the process meaning 'saying *f . . . ing* or *blinding*' is remarkably constrained and it is not clear whether we have verbs or nouns in the output, because *No effing or blinding* makes the relevant words look like nouns, and cases like *I'm feeling very under-the-weather* where a phrase appears to be the source of what might be considered a word (see further Section 16.3). It may be that we need better criteria for determining the limits of conversion.

Challenge

The construction illustrated in

> The rich are not like you and me

has long been a puzzle. It is sometimes referred to as 'partial conversion', but that does not really answer the question of whether or not it is a type of conversion. Calling it 'partial' draws attention to its syntactic restrictedness, which raises the question of whether conversion should be defined primarily by a shift in word-class or whether adopting the full set of features of the new word-class is part of the primary definition. This question is probably not resolvable. But we can consider whether the examples like *the French*, *the Dutch*, *the British* (but not *the American, *the Indian), meaning 'the people' is the same construction as the one with *the rich* or a separate one? Is being used with plural concord and meaning 'people' sufficient to link the two, as was done in this chapter? What evidence can you find in either direction?

References

Amade, Louis & Gilbert Bécaud. (1967). L'important c'est la rose. La Voix De Son Maître [His Master's Voice] – EGF 963

Andersen, H.C. ([1835–72] 1961). *Samlede eventyr og historier*. Jubilæumsudgave. Odense: Flensted.

Audring, Jenny & Geert Booij. (2016). Cooperation and coercion. *Linguistics* 54, 617–37.

Bauer, Laurie & Salvador Valera. (forthcoming). Conversion: A position paper. To be published by Oxford University Press.

Brdar, M. & R. Brdar-Szabó. (2014). Where does metonymy begin? *Cognitive Linguistics* 25, 313–40.

Dirven, René (1999). Conversion as conceptual metonymy of event schemata. In Klaus-Uwe Panther & Günter Radden (eds.), *Metonymy in Language and Thought*. Amsterdam: Benjamins, 275–87.
Littlemore, Jeannette. (2015). *Metonymy*. Cambridge: Cambridge University Press.
Nagano, Akiko. (2018). A conversion analysis of so-called coercion from relational to qualitative adjectives in English. *Word Structure* 11, 185–210.
Payne, John & Rodney Huddleston. (2002). Nouns and noun phrases. In Rodney Huddleston & Geoffrey K. Pullum (eds.), *The Cambridge Grammar of the English Language*. Cambridge: Cambridge University Press, 323–523.
Pustejovsky, James. (1995). *The Generative Lexicon*. Cambridge, MA: MIT Press.

21 Reflections on Back-Formation

A typical way of forming a new word is to take a known word and, using it as a base, add an affix. For example, we can find the verb *write*, add the suffix *-er*, and get *writer* (or, to be more precise, someone did this in the distant past, and the word that was formed by this method is still transparent in its formation today).

Historians of the language know that such a process is not always used. To cite a standard example, the word *editor* did not arise historically by adding the suffix *-or* to the verb *edit*. Instead, the English verb *edit* was formed by a process of deletion from the noun *editor*, which preceded it.

If we look at the words *writer* and *editor* from a twenty-first-century viewpoint they appear to be parallel formations: both have an agentive suffix added to a verb. The different pattern of formation has been made invisible with passing time. This has a couple of important results: the first is that it is difficult to find instances of back-formation, because they look just like regular formations; the second is that most examples of back-formation are within the domain of the etymologist. Knowing about back-formation, once sufficient time has passed, requires expert knowledge of a type that most speakers of the language do not possess. Moreover, even the experts can have trouble finding the appropriate information. Marchand (1969: 391) concludes from this that back-formation "has often diachronic relevance only". But, as is pointed out by Bauer (1983: 230), "back-formation is a synchronically productive process in English word-formation".

One of the results of relatively recent (or ad hoc) back-formation is that the output is often stylistically marked. It often sounds slightly jocular, even if the jocular overtones do not usually last particularly long – although *couth* from *uncouth* has retained its non-serious tone for several hundred years. Some recent examples are given below.

> On Saturday we houseclean (William Kotzwinkel. 1994. *The Game of Thirty*. Boston and New York: Houghton Mifflin, p. 183)

> You'd ... axe-murder the entire crew (Anne Rivers Siddons. 1980. *The House Next Door*. Collins, p. 38)

> Derik said, "At least we're being ... whatever that word is."

Lucas said, "What word?"
"You know..."
"Proactive," Sally said.
"So let's proact our asses over to Dalloglio's place." (John Sandford. 2002. *Mortal Prey*. New York: Putnam, p. 297)

"imagining your consternation," Leo said.
"I am indeed consterned," I said, not caring that it wasn't a word. (Jack Frederickson. 2013. *The Dead Caller from Chicago*. New York: Minotaur, p. 305)

fiddling with an electronic cigarette ... "Apparently, it's a cessation aid," Callow mumbled. "The only thing it's cessating is my will to live." (Jamie Doward. 2016. *Hostage*. London: Constable, p. 94)

Which of these instances of back-formation individuals find jocular may depend on how recent the formation is in the individual's experience. For the author, *surveille,* from *surveillance* still sounds non-serious, though it has become a standard form for many people. Just as euphemisms lose their euphemistic nature with regular usage over time, so old jokes regularly lose their jocularity with repetition. Damon Runyon's *more than somewhat* and Lewis Carroll's *curiouser and curiouser* were both originally jokes. We can thus possibly link the jocularity of recent back-formations to the fact that listeners are aware that they are unfamiliar (see Chapter 4). The unfamiliarity draws attention to the items, and one of the ways of reacting to the unfamiliarity is to see it as being deliberately jocular. The more familiar the back-formation becomes, the less it has the jocular effect and the more it becomes just a normal expression.

The logic behind the term 'back-formation' is that a rule of word-formation is, in some way, undone. Either affixation is cancelled or something that looks as though it is an affix is deleted (even if there is no real affix present, as with the verb to *cessate* which is not the basis of the noun *cessation*). There might, however, be a better way of viewing the process. Consider the word *surveillance*. *Surveillance* was borrowed from French. In French, it is derived from the verb *surveiller*, but the verb did not accompany the noun *surveillance* into English. English speakers thus had a noun with no corresponding verb. English does, however, have many words ending in *-ance* which do have corresponding verbs: *acceptance, allowance, assistance, assurance, clearance, conveyance, resistance* and so on. On the basis of a paradigm of this nature, the speaker can deduce that *surveillance* must be a comparable noun, and that therefore *surveille* must be the base verb. The verb *surveille* is already there, waiting to be recognized, it is not created when a perceived need arises. What back-formation really is, under this view, is an acknowledgement of a form which already exists in the paradigms of English word-formation. When speakers first use it, it is recognized as unfamiliar, but its unfamiliarity does not affect its grammaticality. This does not mean that speakers do not, on occasions, make historically false analogies. Given *orient* and *orientation* they can deduce that the noun is *orient*, the verb is *orientate* and the nominalization of that verb is *orientation*. Given *deduction* (which can correspond to the verb *deduce* or to the verb *deduct*), speakers can make the assumption that the verb *deduct* is just another way of saying *deduce*. They may not limit themselves to what linguists would call patterns of word-formation, but may see *pease* as the plural of *pea*, and thus create a new singular noun with a regular plural, because that form was already there in the language as a mass noun. The label of 'back-formation' comes from linguists who are aware that the etymology is not what the forms superficially suggest. From the point of view of the speaker, this is simply recognition of the patterns of morphology in the language, and using this knowledge where there is an apparent gap in their vocabularies. Perhaps back-formation would be better termed 'recognition of an unfamiliar base'.

One particular type of back-formation is the type illustrated by *houseclean* in the examples above. The earliest form is *housecleaner* or *housecleaning* (in some cases it will be clear which, in others it may not be), and since both *-er* and *-ing* are regularly (though not exclusively) attached to verbs it is assumed that there is a verb to *houseclean*. In principle, we might say that [house [clean-er]] has been reanalysed as [[house-clean] er] (Adams 1973: 106). This is one of the major ways in which compound verbs are created in English. Other examples are *breath-test*, *crash-land*, *gate-crash*, *head-hunt*, *sky-dive*, or, arising from a past participle rather than a present participle, *tailor-make* and perhaps *colour-code*. Adams (2001: 106–8) provides many other examples. The theoretical question is whether the new forms are really compound verbs. Historically speaking, there is no compound verb in *house-cleaner* which can be left over when the *-er* is removed. If the line suggested above is given credence, though, we can say that whatever the etymological analysis of such verbs suggests, speakers treat them as though they are compounds to which suffixes have been added. The analyst has to decide whether to follow history or speakers' intuitions. In this particular case, such a decision has downstream implications, at least in defining a compound.

Challenge

One of the major problems that back-formation creates is the one related to expressions like *house-clean*, discussed above. Should such forms be considered to be verbs, or should they be considered to be instances of back-formation and not verbs? This is related to questions about conversion, where, for instance, *a cuddle* (which comes historically from the verb *to cuddle*) can be seen as a morphologically simple noun or a morphologically complex instance of conversion. By extension, we can ask whether the verb *to carbon-copy* (from the noun *a carbon-copy*) is or is not a compound. Consider the implications of such questions, looking at what positions you are forced to adopt when you accept either point of view. Can you resolve the issue?

References

Adams, Valerie. (1973). *An Introduction to Modern English Word-Formation*. London: Longman.
  (2001). *Complex Words in English*. Harlow: Longman.
Bauer, Laurie. (1983). *English Word-Formation*. Cambridge: Cambridge University Press.
Marchand, Hans. (1969). *The Categories and Types of Present-Day English Word-Formation*. 2nd ed. Munich: Beck.

22 Reflections on Coordinative Compounds

English coordinative compounds cause continuing problems of description, including what subtypes should be recognized, whether all of the constructions that have been considered under the heading are words, whether they are compounds, and how their heads are to be determined (see Chapter 13). A full discussion of these questions is provided in Bauer (2023), but in that paper it is left to the individual reader to determine where the lines should be drawn. Here I want to consider whether we have evidence which may lead to a conclusion on the range of constructions that should properly be considered to be coordinative compounds.

At first blush, it seems odd that there should be any problem here at all. If we take a fundamental definition of a coordinative compound, then we can say that it is a compound (and for most authorities that implies that it is a word) whose elements are coordinated (linked semantically by a relationship meaning 'and', rarely 'or' or 'but'). Wälchli (2005) adds to this that coordinative compounds are prototypically used to denote instances of what he terms 'natural coordination', that is collocations of words which recur because their denotata are frequently found together in the world, or are seen as being of importance in the relevant culture. All languages have instances of natural coordination, but not all languages use coordinative compounds to mark the relationship. For instance, in English, *husband and wife* might be considered an instance of natural coordination, while *man and landlady* would not be, although both are marked with overt syntactic coordination. We know from Wälchli (2005) that coordinative compounds as a mode of expressing natural coordination tend to become more common as one moves eastwards across Eurasia. This may be enough to make it odd that there is such a plethora of possible types available in English.

At the same time, if natural coordination is a prototypical reading of a coordinative compound, this implies that there is room for a great deal of variation, so that many constructions that we might wish to call 'coordinative compounds' might show some looser form of coordination. Added to this, we have a question of how we can be sure to recognize natural coordination and, surprisingly, how to recognize coordination.

22 Coordinative Compounds

Consider, for example, the expression *soldier boy*. How are we to interpret this? If we think it means 'the person is a soldier and a boy' we have a gloss which implies coordination. If we think that it means 'a boy who is a soldier' we have a subordinative relationship, with an essive semantic relation holding between the elements. Then we might see *soldier boy* as similar to *woman doctor* (see Chapter 13 and below). But *soldier boy* has the gender-marking element second instead of first, so the equivalence is not total, and while a *woman doctor* is typically a woman, a *soldier boy* is not typically a boy, unless figuratively speaking (although *boy soldiers* are talked about, they are denoted by an expression that puts the gender/age marking first). To further complicate the issue, coordinate structures are usually semantically equivalent when their elements are reversed (at least in syntax). *Bread and jam* means the same, has the same denotatum, as *jam and bread*. If both *soldier boy* and *boy soldier* are coordinative, we would expect them to mean the same, but they do not. We might therefore conclude that at least one of them, perhaps both of them, is not a coordinative compound. The example indicates that identifying coordination is not necessarily obvious, and that therefore identifying potential coordinative compounds is not straightforward.

In what follows, various different types of construction that might count as coordinative compounds will be considered, and the question will be raised as to whether they really are coordinative compounds and whether they are compounds. The types discussed may not be exhaustive, but all are mentioned in the literature as being relevant.

The first type is a locative type illustrated by *Alsace-Lorraine*, *Budapest* and *Nelson-Marlborough*. Here we find the name of a locality being made up of the names of two pre-existing localities which, between them, indicate the extent of the new locality. Most such names in English are foreign names borrowed from the appropriate area, but even then alternative formulations of names built from similar elements are common: *São Tome and Principe*, *Czechoslovakia*, *SeaTac*. Relatively recently, however, some names of this kind have been established as anglophone names: *Minneapolis-St Paul*, *Newcastle-Gateshead*, *Otago-Southland*. There is no obvious reason for this change in formation pattern. They do look like genuine coordinative compounds: as names, they act as single words, the entire word denotes a discrete entity, the words contain no grammatical markers (such as *and*).

The next type is the type where the names of commercial entities are made up of the names of two or more historically earlier entities: *HarperCollins*, *Mercedes-Benz*, *Rank-Hovis*. Again the new entity is named by its origins, but it may not be clear whether anything remains of the original component parts. What makes these pairs seem slightly suspicious (and the same could be said of the place names) is that the output of the process is a name (definite and applied to one particular entity) rather than a word which can denote any one of a set of very similar entities; most nouns do not have unique reference, but may refer to any member of a set. It is not clear that this is material, since it follows from the usage of the word as a name. It is nevertheless interesting to compare this usage with the compound names of gods in the Sanskrit tradition. The Sanskrit word *mitrāvárunau* 'Mitra and Varuna' denotes a team made up of the two deities, not a new entity that arises from parts of both. Even though there is no necessity that every coordinative compound should show precisely the same type of interpretation, and the distinction could be entirely a matter of the pragmatics of putting two names together, nevertheless this may indicate that such commercial coordinative structures are not prototypical compounds of the dvandva type.

We do find some examples where we apparently have two nouns coordinated. Good examples are hard to come by in English, but at least the following are suggested in the literature as relevant examples: *dinner-dance, murder-suicide, trailer-truck*. There is also a much wider range of examples which are less clear, including *vowel segment, fighter-bomber, fridge-freezer, soldier ant*. It is difficult to discuss these, since each example is slightly different from the others. For some writers, things can only be coordinative compounds if the two (or more) element coordinated are of the same type. A *soldier ant* must thus be 'an ant that resembles a soldier' (a subordinative type) and not 'an insect which is both a soldier and an ant'. This might also suggest that a *trailer-truck* must be 'a truck which has a trailer' rather than 'a trailer and a truck as a unit'. Even *dinner-dance* could be interpreted as 'a dance at which dinner is served' rather than 'an occasion on which dinner is served and guests dance'. This may be interpreting the constraints on coordination too severely, though. *In the field I saw a soldier and an ant* seems to be a perfectly good instance of syntactic coordination. Because there is so much disagreement on which of these words is relevant, if any, it is dangerous to assume that any of these is a genuine coordinative compound, and it is certainly clear that being able to give a construction a gloss using *and* is not a reliable test for a coordinative compound.

One type that makes this particularly clear is the type illustrated by *woman doctor, boy scout* and *hen pheasant*. In such examples, a gloss such as 'the person is a woman and a doctor' is clearly possible, and some writers see this as sufficient for these to be viewed as coordinative compounds. But, as has been noted since the time of Panini, the real function here is ascriptive (or attributive), and the first element is a gender marker (in the case of *boy scout*, perhaps also an age-marker). That is the function is the same as in *male tiger, she-wolf, bull-calf*, and possibly also as *lioness*. These are thus not coordinative at all.

What Bauer (2008) calls the translative type and the co-participant type seem easier to deal with.

Translative: literal journey: *Paris–Rome* (flight), *east–west* (trajectory)

Translative: figurative journey: *English–French* (dictionary), *subject–verb* (agreement)

Co-participant: non-directional: *Arab–Israeli* (talks), *Manchester–Chelsea* (match), *father–daughter* (dance)

Co-participant: directional: *CEO–employee* (communication)

There are two reasons why these should not be seen as coordinative compounds, and the two are linked. Most obviously, the two elements in the translative series are not equally weighted: changing the order changes the message. Then all of these are based on prepositional usages. *Paris–Rome* is a snappier form of *from Paris to Rome*. *Manchester–Chelsea* means 'between Manchester and Chelsea', but allows for attributive usage. At the very least, if these are compound nouns, they are exocentric because the prepositional meaning is not shown (as well as because the expressions are not hyponyms of either element), but it seems more straightforward to see these as syntactic expressions.

Examples such as *Sapir–Whorf* (hypothesis), *Creutzfeldt–Jakob* (disease) are harder to exclude. The 'team' meaning we saw with the Sanskrit example is present, and if we assume that they act as adjectives, they must be grammatically, as well as semantically, exocentric. This does not prevent a coordinative interpretation.

Coordinative adjectival compounds, or at least some of them, seem rather easier to classify and to see as truly coordinative. This may be because they have a longer history in Germanic and in Indo-European more generally.

First, we have examples like *bitter-sweet, manic-depressive, obsessive-compulsive, shabby-genteel* (note the 'but' relationship in the last example, rather than the expected 'and' relationship). English does not have many of these, preferring, for example, *sweet and sour* to *sweet-sour*. They are not semantically homogeneous, sometimes indicating a hybrid, sometimes the extremes of something, and they are hyponyms of both elements.

The same is true of a series of expressions like *historical–social, political–religious, literary–historical*. This pattern is clearly productive, though the use of learned adjectives is slightly unusual.

The possibility of coordinative verbs is far more contentious. Although many examples have been suggested, such as *blow-dry, cough-laugh, drink-drive, fly-drive, freeze-dry, sleepwalk* and *stir-fry*, they are all problematic in one way or another. *Blow-dry* could be syntactic because it can be interrupted (*blow my hair dry*), *drink-drive* is nearly always used in the *-ing* form, *freeze-dry* and *stir-fry* can be seen as being types of drying/frying rather than the addition of two actions, and the *sleep* in *sleepwalk* might be seen as a noun. *Cough-laugh* is the best hope for a genuine coordinative compound (and *cry-laugh* is also attested), but even then, for medical people, there is a *cough/laugh* *syndrome* which is triggered by either a cough or a laugh, so that the meaning here is not entirely prototypical.

Other possible categories include compromises like *north-west* and *blue-green* (though English does not have many of either type, and prefers *bluey-green* or *bluish green* for the colour terms). Some languages have words like *red-white* meaning both red and white (e.g. in stripes), but English usually avoids these. Then there are mathematical coordinatives like *ninety-two* (in older English *two-and-ninety* was used), which might be syntactic because in *two hundred and ninety-two* there is overt syntactic coordination.

The most difficult category to deal with is the type illustrated by *actor-director, singer-songwriter, teacher-researcher* which denote a single entity viewed from two (or more) points of view (see also Chapter 13). The traditional Sanskrit dvandvas show two distinct entities which share some kind of function, so these are a distinct class from the semantic point of view. The overall expression is a hyponym of both elements, which matches the potentially coordinative adjectives, but it is not clear whether that should be a criterion, and if so, in which direction.

It seems that there are many types here which we can exclude, many types which are controversial member of the set, and hardly any that are clear-cut coordinative compounds. But that does not mean that the category cannot be applied to English. Just what counts, though, is often a matter of how the category of coordinative compound is defined for English.

One solution to the problems that have been raised here is simply to deny their existence. Anderson (1992: 316) says of coordinative compounds that they are "not really found in English", without explaining what he would do with the examples that have been cited here. Adams (2001: 3) is more explicit: anything that includes coordination breaks the right-hand-head rule (see Chapter 13) and therefore cannot be a compound, and must be a phrase. This is neat, though it fails to explore the possibility that it is the right-hand-head rule that is wrong, or at least incomplete. However, given the difficulties that face us if we try to determine which of these apparently coordinate structures might be compounds, perhaps this solution has much to recommend it – at least as long as we are dealing with English and not Vietnamese or Chinese.

Challenge

Consider the type illustrated by *singer-songwriter* or *director-producer*. Can you find any arguments either for or against the notion that these are compounds, that they are coordinative or that they are headed structures? What are the implications of your consideration?

References

Adams, Valerie. (2001). *Complex Words in English*. Harlow: Longman.
Anderson, Stephen R. (1992). *A-morphous Morphology*. Cambridge: Cambridge University Press.
Bauer, Laurie. (2008). Dvandva. *Word Structure* 1, 1–20.
  (2023). Coordinative compounds, including dvandva. In Peter Ackema, Sabrina Bendjaballah, Eulàlia Bonet and Antonio Fábregas (eds.), *The Wiley Blackwell Companion to Morphology*. Hoboken, NJ: Wiley.
Wälchli, Bernhard. (2005). *Co-compounds and Natural Coordination*. Oxford: Oxford University Press.

23 Reflections on the Irregularity of Prepositions

Although nouns, verbs and adjectives have regular functions in English word-formation, prepositions seem much more marginal in such uses, perhaps because of their predominantly grammatical function. Nevertheless, they do occur, at least sporadically, in a number of apparent cases of word-formation. In syntax, prepositions in English have several different functions. The prototypical use of prepositions is with a noun phrase, as in *on the street, in our house, down the chimney*. We also find the same forms used as adverbs in expressions such as *She was looking on, They all traipsed in* and *We jumped down*. Some authorities (Emonds 1972) talk about transitive and intransitive prepositions here. In verbs such as *She put on an angry expression, The soldiers fell in, I'll look up the answer* it may not be clear whether we should call the same forms 'prepositions', 'adverbs' or something else, and so some authorities prefer the term 'particle', perhaps to avoid the issue, although there is dispute in the literature as to whether prepositions in their core use of governing a noun phrase are a type of particle, and for some authorities 'particles' include the infinitival *to* (as in *to listen*), possibly words like *not* (also termed an adverb) and pragmatic particles like *oh*, or *like* (*She's like really bright*). I shall provisionally use the term 'preposition' here, but it should be clear that terminology in this area is not completely standardized. For a more sophisticated argument pointing out the difficulties of classification here, see Lee (1999).

For Chomsky (1970), the preposition is one of the four major word-classes, but that does not mean that it is like the others. Adjectives, nouns and verbs have lexical meaning, and typically denote states, entities and actions, while prepositions frequently have grammatical meaning, not necessarily predictable from any inherent meaning. For example, *We're going down the pub* (contrast *We're going down the river*) does not really make sense except idiomatically.

The class of prepositions is not a closed class. There is a set of prototypical prepositions, but there are also sequences of prepositions and expressions that function as prepositions though they are derived from words which belong to a different word-class. Examples of each type are given below.

23 Irregularity of Prepositions

> prototypical prepositions: above, across, after, at, before, by, down, for, from, in, near, of, on, out, past, through, to, under, up, via, with
>
> prepositional sequences: down from, into, onto, off of, out of, throughout, up to, within
>
> derived prepositions: concerning, excepting, excluding, following, given, including

Given this situation, we might expect to see word-formation processes which allow us to create prepositions, but we do not. As is shown in the few examples above, participles are used as prepositions as required. One possible analysis of this is that participles are changed into prepositions by conversion, but this implies that the participles, usually thought of as being inflected forms, can subsequently undergo conversion, usually considered a derivational process. The analysis is therefore not universally accepted.

Yet prepositions do seem to undergo conversion on some occasions. Examples are rare, however, and often very informal.

> prepositions as verbs: *to down* (a drink, an aeroplane), *to off* ('murder'), *to out* ('make something about a person – usu. their sexuality – public'), *to up* (the price; *to up and leave* 'suddenly depart')
>
> prepositions as nouns: *a by* (in cricket), *a down* ('bad opinion'), *an in* ('access', *the ins and outs* 'the details'), *the off* (*ready for the off* 'ready to start'), *an over* (in cricket), *up* (*ups and downs* 'vicissitudes'); *on the up and up* ('being increasingly successful')
>
> prepositions as adjectives: *down* ('depressed')
>
> prepositions in attributive position: *the down train* ('away from London'), *the up train* ('towards London'), *no through road*

There are also instances where the preposition might be analysed as coming from a homophone in another word-class: *above* (< adverb), *before* (< conjunction), *near* (< adjective), *past* (< noun), *round* (< adjective).

Even less frequently, we find prepositions being used as bases in overt derivational morphology.

> creating adjectives: *backward, downward, inward, offish* ('aloof'), *outward, upward*
>
> creating adverbs: *afterward(s), overly* ('excessively')
>
> creating nouns: *afters* ('course after the main course'), *downer* ('bad experience', 'drug that makes you relax'), *innie* ('type of navel'), *insider, outie* ('type of navel'), *outing* ('excursion'), *outsider, overage* ('surplus'), *rounders, underling, upper* ('drug that gives you energy')

Forms like *upper* (of a shoe, for instance) might be viewed as a comparative form or as an *-er* derivative (historically, it is a comparative, but it appears to have undergone conversion to a noun, which puts derivation further from the root than inflection), in *uppity* the <it> is not easily explicable.

What is striking about these examples is how few of the prepositions seem to be used in these ways. It is as if there is a core set of prepositions (not necessarily the most basic prepositions in grammatical usage) which can be used in these ways. It is also noticeable that many of these are not only informal but idiomatic.

This raises the question of whether there is any productive use of prepositions as bases in word-formation. Perhaps, rather than saying that there is conversion here, we should just say that word-classes are very fluid with this set of words, and should view the set of overt derivations from prepositions as being sporadic creations rather than the result of a strong pattern or rule of word-formation. This might help explain the low profitability of these patterns.

However, if that is the case, we need to explain why prepositions occur so much more frequently in compounds (and, not necessarily the same thing, when used as prefixes). Consider the indicative examples given below.

> as modifiers to adjectives (usually participial adjectives): *downgraded, inborn, near-sighted, outsourced, overearnest*
>
> as modifiers to nouns: *afterlife, by-product, by-road, down-light, off-side, overcoat, undershirt, upbeat, up-side*
>
> as modifiers to verbs (some of these might be considered prefixes): *downgrade, underplay, outsource, overlook, upchuck* ('vomit'), *upload*
>
> creating exocentric adjectives: *after-dinner, in-depth, near-death, off-centre*
>
> creating exocentric adverbs: *off-key, overnight*
>
> creating exocentric nouns: *afternoon, at-home, off-spring*
>
> creating exocentric verbs: *overnight, withstand*

If we put these things together, we get the distribution set out in Table 23.1. Looking at the material in this light (even though we could add more forms) gives a different perspective. It appears that some forms are pure prepositions, with no other use, while those words which have adverbial function also have the possibility of appearing in other functions. In other words, the core function here is adverbial, with some of the prepositions sharing form with adverbs. The use of *with* in examples like *withhold* is unexpected, but it is becoming more widely used as an adverb in *Are you coming with?* (originally from German). The forms used as bases for further overt word-formation are

23 Irregularity of Prepositions

Table 23.1 *Uses of forms that appear as prepositions*

Form	Adverb	In PhrVb	Conv to N or V	Modifier in Compound	Modifier in NP	Base for w-f
above	✓				above address	
across	✓	come across				
after	✓	look after	afters	afterlife		afters
at						
before	✓			beforehand		
beside						
by	✓	stand by		by-line		
down	✓	put down	to down	downhill	down payment	downer
from						
in	✓	drop in	an in	inlay	in thing	innie
near	✓		to near	near-side	near miss	
of						
off	✓	swear off	to off, the off	off-side	off day	offish
on	✓	get on		on-side		
out	✓	put out	to out, an out	outstay		outie
outside	✓		the outside		outside broadcast	outsider
over	✓	hold over	an over	overpay		overly
past	✓		the past		past time	
round	✓		to round, a round		round table	
through	✓	pull through			through train	
to	✓	come to				
under	✓	go under		underground	under surface	underling
up	✓	look up	to up, ups and downs	upkeep		upper
with				withhold		

more limited, apparently to spatial adverbs, though not all of them. Note that using the term 'intransitive preposition' in place of 'adverb' does not help here, since we still have to be able to refer to a class of prepositions which have both transitive and intransitive usage.

Because prepositions have a function as much as a meaning, it is adverbs which are used in word-formation, even when the adverbs share a form with prepositions. This goes some way to explaining some of the apparent irregularities in the use of things that look like prepositions in English word-formation. Not all gaps can be expected to be filled in a derivational process, and the use of these adverbs is still rather limited, more in some constructions than in others.

Challenge

The adverbs used as bases for further derivational morphology seem to be particularly restricted. Look for further examples, and determine whether this particular set can be defined in semantic or functional terms and whether the affixes used with them are restricted in any way.

References

Chomsky, Noam. (1970). Remarks on nominalization. In Roderick A. Jacobs & Peter S. Rosenbaum (eds.), *Readings in English Transformational Grammar*. Waltham, MA: Ginn, 184–221.

Emonds Joseph. (1972). Evidence that indirect object movement is a structure-preserving rule. *Foundations of Language* 8, 546–61.

Lee, David. (1999). Intransitive prepositions: Are they viable? In Peter Collins & David Lee (eds.), *Clause in English: In Honour of Rodney Huddleston*. Amsterdam: Benjamins, 133–47.

24 Reflections on Reduplication

Reduplication, the meaningful repetition of all or part of a word, is sometimes considered to be one of the few candidates for a universal process of word-formation. As we might expect, therefore, English does show some patterns of reduplication, but relatively few in comparison with some other languages. We can distinguish between various types of reduplication: the type where a whole word is repeated, and the types where a part of a word is repeated. When part of a word is repeated we find cases where consonants change and cases where vowels change. There are formal or semantic subtypes of each of these types.

24.1 Whole-Word Reduplication

Whole-word reduplication is rare in English, and restricted to a few semantic or stylistic types, mostly childish words, sometimes extending to slang words. Some examples are given below.

boo-boo	'mistake'
choo-choo	'train'
chin-chin	a toast, 'cheers' (originally from Chinese)
chuff-chuff	'train'
do-do	'faeces'
housey-housey	'bingo'; also without reduplication
mama	'mother'
no-no	'something forbidden'
papa	'father'
pee-pee	'urine, an act of urination'
poo-poo	'dismiss (e.g. an idea)'
putt-putt	'a form of mini-golf in which only putts are used'
quack-quack	'the call of a duck; a duck'
so-so	'indifferent, neither good nor bad'
wee-wee	'urine, act of urination'
woo-woo	'involving the supernatural'
woof-woof	'dog'
yo-yo	'child's toy'

This list may include more than one type, since *quack-quack*, for example, has stress on the first element if it means 'duck' but stress on the second element if it means 'the noise a duck makes'. *Mama* and *papa* have second-element stress, at least in isolation and naming parents, unlike, for instance, *do-do*. Some loan words like *dik-dik*, *gogo*, *juju*, *muumuu*, *pompom*, *tomtom* may not count as instances of reduplication in English, although their adoption may be due to the attraction of the reduplicative structure.

Repeated element compounds may also be included here, though it is not clear that the same morphological process is involved, since phrases as well as word-like elements may be repeated (see Chapter 11). These examples are rarely established. Some examples are given below.

> Think me up a way to earn some blunt, would you? Not earn-earn it, but come into it proper-like. (Grace Burrowes. (2017). *Too Scot to Handle*. New York: Forever, pp. 236–7)

> But I didn't know her-know her. (Kirsten Lepionka. (2017). *The Last Place You Look*. New York: Minotaur, p. 86)

It is often hard to draw the line between reduplication and syntactic repetition. Some examples of structures which are at least arguably syntactic (and thus not word-formation) are given below, but the classification is not always clear-cut.

aye-aye	positive response to an order
blah blah	indicating meaningless talk
bye-bye	'goodbye'
fifty–fifty	'equally likely'
ha ha	indicating laughter, or mock laughter
there there	used to comfort
yes yes	indicating emphatic agreement

Clearly syntactic repetition includes things like *It's very very interesting*, *It's a long long way*, *That's really really stupid*.

24.2 Repetition of Part of a Word: Consonants Change

Typically, what happens in words like this is that the initial consonant or consonant cluster of a word changes, so that the two parts of the new word rhyme. These constructions are therefore often called 'rhyme-motivated'. (For rhyme more generally, see Chapter 17.) In some instances, there is an ordinary word to which a rhyming element is added, but in many cases neither element is an independent word of English. Some examples are given below.

argy-bargy	'an argument'
arty-farty	'exaggeratedly artistic'
bow-wow	'dog, sound of a dog'
boogie-woogie	'style of jazz'
fuddy-duddy	'very conservative'
hanky-panky	'improper behaviour'
helter-skelter	'fairground ride'
hocus-pocus	magic word
hoity-toity	'very haughty'
hubble-bubble	'hookah'
itsy-bitsy (*or* itty-bitty)	'very small'
lovey-dovey	'demonstratively affectionate'
mumbo-jumbo	'gobbledygook'
namby-pamby	'lacking vigour'
piggy-wig(gy)	'nice pig'
roly-poly	'rolled-up, round'
super-duper	'excellent'
teeny-weeny	'very small'
wagger-pagger-bagger	'waste paper basket' (old Oxford University slang)
walkie-talkie	'hand-held radio'
willy-nilly	'whether you want to or not'

It is not entirely clear which element is the central element here and which element is the reduplicated element, and neither is it entirely clear what consonant is likely to occur in the reduplicated element. Labial consonants (including /w/) seem to be slightly overrepresented in the construction as a whole, but other consonants are certainly not excluded. Similarly, there seems to be some preference for plosives. The use of disyllabic elements is at least strongly preferred, if not required (consider *wham-bam*). The construction is not very productive.

Whether expressions like *(the screaming) hab-dabs*, *the heebie-jeebies* fit into this pattern or not may be controversial, since the plural marking seems to be an important factor in these words.

One very specific pattern, used almost exclusively in American English, where it derives from Yiddish, is the use of an introductory /ʃm/ cluster (note that this cluster is not generally allowed in English). The word with this cluster is usually written as a separate word from its base (often separated by a comma), which differentiates this structure from the others illustrated above which seem to be added to a base to create single words. Some examples are given below.

> Well, daughter/shmaughter, know what I mean? (Robert Wilson. 2015. *Stealing People*. London: Orion, p. 174)

"So you think she's dead?"

"Think, schmink. Her blood was in the kitchen." (John Lescroart. 2014. *The Keeper*. New York: Atria, p. 20)

Coincidences, smincidences. (Kate Medina. 2016. *Fire Damage*. London: Harper, p. 292) [note the unusual form, from a British publisher]

24.3 Repetition of Part of a Word: Vowels Change

Where the vowel in a stressed syllable changes, the constructions are said to be 'ablaut motivated'. Unlike the rhyme-motivated examples, these do not strongly prefer disyllabic elements, though they certainly occur. There are two major formal patterns, one where /ɪ/ alternates with /æ/ and one where /ɪ/ alternates with /ɒ/ (with appropriate replacements in American English). In some instances, all three can be found in the same expression. Some examples illustrating all three patterns are given below.

/ɪ/ ~ /æ/

chit-chat	'idle talk'
dilly-dally	'delay'
flim-flam	'trick'
kit-cat	'originally the name of a London club'
knick-knack	'small ornament'
mish-mash	'medley'
pitter-patter	'a faint sound, esp. of footsteps'
riff-raff	'undesirable people'
shilly-shally	'act indecisively'
tittle-tattle	'gossip'
zig-zag	'turn alternately left and right'

/ɪ/ ~ /ɒ/

clip-clop	'sound of a horse walking'
ding-dong	'fiercely contested, sound of bells'
flip-flop	'change direction, rubber sandal'
ping-pong	'table tennis'
sing-song	'an event where everyone joins in singing, lively pitch movement in speaking'
tick-tock	'sound of a time-piece'
tip-top	'very best quality'
wishy-washy	'weak, of poor quality'

/ɪ/ ~ /æ/ ~ /ɒ/

slip slop slap	slogan for avoiding skin-cancer

24 Reduplication

Although we can find occasional instances with different vowels (e.g. *bim bam boom*), the vowels in this construction are usually very restricted. Note, however, a few expressions such as

gewgaw	'bauble'
hee-haw	'sound made by a donkey; to make such a sound'
see-saw	'playground equipment'
fee-fi-fo-fum	expression attributed to fairy tale giants
ho-hum	'boring, ordinary; said to express boredom'
(oh) me, oh my	expression of amazement

24.4 A More Complex Pattern

There is a similar, if more complex, construction in English which has apparently remained unnoticed. It is unusual partly because it does not create nouns, adjectives or verbs, it is partly unnoticed because it is fairly rare, and it is not clear how regular it is.

Examples of the relevant construction(s) are provided below.

bippety boppety boo	Disney's *Cinderella*
blankety blank	a replacement for an expletive (BNC)
bumpety bump bump	
clickety clack	repeated clicking sound (e.g. of typing on a typewriter)
clippety clop	'sound made by horses'
dinkety bonk	a type of music (BNC)
flippety flop	a vocal representation of a tumbling movement
hippety hop	a representation of a repeated hopping movement
hoppity hop	as *hippety hop*
hoppity hoppity hoppity hop	extended version of *hoppity hop*
lickety split	'very quickly'
skippety-hop	a representation of the rhythm of the heart (BNC)
snippety snap	used to encourage speed (*Urban Dictionary*); a representation of the sound made by scissors
tickety boo	'in the best possible condition'

What these share formally is a first element with dactylic form ending in /əti/ (which in some varieties becomes [əri]) and a monosyllabic second element, with occasional reduplication of one element or the other. Sometimes the stressed vowels match, sometimes they fit with the usual ablaut patterns discussed above. Some of these forms have alternatives without the /əti/, such as *clip clop*, *flip flop*, but while *clip clop* remains a representation of a sound, *flip flop* does not necessarily remain a representation of movement, but may become a noun. The general construction type appears to be productive, but it is hard to find written examples.

24.5 Discussion

These constructions remain rather marginal in English, despite the familiarity of reduplication in many languages. The patterns of reduplication are also quite restricted, with initial consonants or consonant cluster and stressed vowels involved but not, for example, reduplication of initial or final syllables or the use of random vowels or consonants, which are common in many other languages. These constructions can be considered from the point of view of what remains the same, or from the point of view of what changes. What is particularly surprising in the English examples is how often the base is not an independent form. Finally, note that the same patterns of ablaut, at least, are found in fixed syntactic phrases such as *in dribs and drabs* 'a little at a time'.

Challenge

Choose any one of the patterns of reduplication discussed here, and consider whether it is better viewed as a matter of what is retained or better viewed as a matter of what is changed. What leads you to suppose you can tell? Have any patterns of English reduplication been omitted in this presentation?

Part VI

Historical Questions

25 Reflections on Dead Morphology

25.1 Introduction

There are certain patterns of word-formation which, although they once allowed the creation of new forms, now no longer seem to have that ability, despite the fact that some of the words created by the pattern still exist. Typically, speakers are not aware of these patterns, but occasionally there is some residual awareness, for at least some of the words involved. In what follows, these patterns are divided according to the word-class they once created, although alternative classifications would obviously be possible.

25.2 Creating Nouns

There are a few examples of ablaut-linking verbs with a corresponding nominal (Wescott 1970). Examples are provided below. Some of these are very old, and may never have been felt to be morphologically linked in English.

Verb	Corresponding noun
abide	abode
bind	band
bleed	blood
break	breech
breed	brood
drink	drench
feed	food
ride	road
shoot	shot
sing	song
sit	seat
write	writ

There are other examples where ablaut is a concomitant to affixation, which are not considered here.

There is a Germanic diminutive suffix -*ock* which can still be found in a number of English words, though its diminutive meaning has been lost in most of them. Some relevant words are listed below.

> bollock, bullock, buttock, haddock, hillock, paddock, pillock

It is not always clear what words contain this suffix from an etymological point of view, as there are similar-sounding suffixes from other sources, and because the relevant base is not always clear. Many of the words in the *OED* that are said to contain this suffix are now obsolete or extremely rare.

There is a Germanic diminutive suffix which comes down to English in the form -*en*. There are few remaining words with this suffix, and even then, it is not always clear whether this suffix is involved etymologically, or whether there is simply a coincidence of form. Potentially relevant words are given below.

> chicken, kitten, maiden

Another diminutive suffix, this one from French, has the form -*erel* or -*rel*, and is rarely recognizable as a suffix at all. Surviving words in which this etymological item may appear (although there is frequently some doubt) include those below. The newest derivatives with this suffix are from the seventeenth century.

> cockerel, dotterel, gomerel (Scottish), hoggerel, kestrel, mackerel, mongrel, pickerel, scoundrel, wastrel

There is a Germanic suffix -*t* which creates nouns. It is generally accepted as being a variant of the suffix -*th*, either positionally motivated (especially after <gh>) or regionally motivated (-*t* is a northern form). Alternation between -*t* and -*th* in the word *height/highth* may still be found regionally, and is used by Milton.

> over head up grew
> Insuperable highth of loftiest shade,
> Cedar, and Pine, and Firr (John Milton. 1667. *Paradise Lost*, Book 4)

The Germanic nominalizing -*t* has various etyma, which have merged by the time we get to English. Examples of -*t* on adjectives and verbs are given below. *Theft* is an unusual example on a nominal base.

> suffix -t on adjectival bases: drought, height
> suffix -t on verbal bases: draught, drift, flight, gift, might, plight, shrift, sight, thirst, thought, thrift, weight

The suffix -*th* (as in *truth* and *warmth*) is usually considered to be dead today. It is certainly difficult to find new forms, and where they are found, they are often made up by analogy with existing forms or are resurrections of older forms. Some speakers feel that *coolth* is innovative, but has been in continual use, usually jocularly, since the sixteenth century. There are many words which are etymologically the result of -*th* affixation which are not recognize as such today, or are only recognized by language professionals. Relevant words include *birth, death, dearth, filth, health, mirth, stealth, youth*. Part of the reason that such words are so obscure is that the vowel sounds have changed so much, and no longer reflect the original base.

25.3 Creating Adjectives

There is a very small set of adjectives related to a verbal base by ablaut.

Verb	Adjective
heal	hale, whole
fill	full

There is an etymological suffix, today spelled -*le*, which has left very few traces in English and which can no longer been seen as a suffix because its bases are no longer recognizable. Examples include *brittle, fickle, idle, little* and *nimble*.

The suffix -*ac* as in *cardiac* and *demoniac* is based on classical models, and shows some productivity in English, with words such as *hypochondriac* and *maniac*. The more recent *brainiac* is probably coined directly from *maniac*, and does not illustrate genuine suffixation at all.

25.4 Creating Verbs

There are patterns of ablaut that link transitive (or causative) and intransitive verbs, but these patterns are not predictable in the modern language and are very restricted in the number of items covered. There are other examples where ablaut is a concomitant to affixation, which are not considered here.

Intransitive	Transitive
fall	fell
lie	lay
rise	raise
sit	set

The suffix -*le* on verbal bases creates verbs which denote repetitive movements of small scale. Sometimes, it is sounds which are repetitive. There are many words in this class still in use, but many of them no longer have (in some cases, may never have had) an analysable base, which supports the notion that verbs that end this way may be viewed as monomorphemic. In some cases, the putative base has a long vowel, and the derivative a short vowel, which also masks the historical relationship. Selected examples, divided between verbs of movement and verbs of sound, are given below.

> verbs of movement: drizzle, scuttle, shuffle, sidle, sparkle, suckle, twinkle, waddle, waggle, wriggle
> verbs of sound: babble, cackle, crackle, giggle, gobble, mumble, prattle, rattle, rustle, sizzle, sniffle, tinkle, warble

There are some words which end in *-le* which probably do not contain the same suffix. Some examples are given below.

> bamboozle, puzzle, wheedle

A similar meaning is provided by *-er* in some verbs, particularly in words denoting vocalization of some type or the play of light. Examples are given below. In most of these, no base is currently recognizable, which explains the loss of productivity. In many cases, there has never been an independent base in English (although there may have been in older Germanic), and the *-er* is of questionable morphological value although it seems to have had the ability to carry meaning, perhaps as a phonaestheme.

> vocalization: chatter, gibber, jabber, mutter, snicker, snigger, splutter, stammer, titter
> play of light: flicker, glimmer, glitter, shimmer
> other: clamber, flutter, quiver, shudder, waver

There are several verbs of English which end in *-ish*, and which are derived from French *-iss* (in turn derived from Latin *-isc*). It is not clear that this was ever a suffix in English, but it is derived from a suffix. There are very few words where the removal of *-ish* leaves a recognizable base, and it is not always clear that any such base is relevant. Some examples are given below, some attached to what may once have been a base, some with no apparent base.

> possible base: banish, brandish, burnish, flourish
> no recognizable base: abolish, accomplish, demolish, establish, finish, furnish, languish, perish, punish, ravish

The prefix *be-* can be found in several sets of words, and it is marginally productive only when it co-occurs with a final *-ed* (as in *be-trousered*), and otherwise not productive. In some of its uses it is one of those prefixes which appears to be the head of its construction in the sense that it creates verbs from other bases. Examples of various constructions with this prefix are given below. Many of the words with prefix *be-* are now rare or archaic (e.g. *bedrench, bego, bespeak, bethink*) and some persist only – or mainly – as participles (e.g. *belated, beloved*).

25 Dead Morphology 191

    semantically opaque formations: become, befall, beget, behave, behold, belay, beseech, beset
    adjectival bases: becalm, bedim, belate, belittle, benumb
    connotation of scattered result or thoroughness of result: bedaub, bedraggle, besmear, bespatter, bespeckle, besprinkle
    nominal bases giving rise to verbs: bedevil, befog, befoul, bejewel, benight, besiege, bewitch
    with the meaning 'remove': behead
    creating transitive verbs: bedazzle, belie, bemoan, berate, bestir, bewail

The opaque words listed above are all formed on the basis of Germanic verbs, probably before the English period. Strictly, *begin* belongs here, but *gin* is no longer found in isolation in English. *Beseech* shows English palatalization of the final consonant in *seek*. *Behave* has become regular, suggesting the loss of connection with *have*; the others maintain their irregular past tense and past participle.

25.5   Generalizations

Some generalizations about why morphological patterns die out can be seen in the examples provided here. With patterns of apophony, there was no predictability in the alternating vowels by the time English emerged from Germanic so that new forms could not be created with confidence. The result was that, although ablaut remains a pattern which can be seen in conjugation of verbs, it is seen as mainly irregular and the overall idea of apophony as a way of forming words in English disappears. Many patterns of apophony are not even recognized as creating morphophonemic variation, only historical links.

If bases become unrecognizable, then affixation dies because the word cannot be analysed. We see this with the various *-le* suffixes, and with many examples of *-th*.

If the meaning of an affix becomes unclear, then the affix is likely to stop being used. The prefix *be-* provides a good example of this.

One very important point is that until the use of a particular morphological process exists only in non-transparent words, there is always the possibility that the process will return. Although it seems unlikely that *-th* will be resuscitated, while there are a few transparent instances such as *truth* and *warmth*, it remains a possibility, even though it could not then be used with to reconstruct established words like *depth* and *width*.

Challenge

Many English derivational suffixes disappeared at the end of the Old English period. For those who have studied Old English, consider the suffixes which vanished, and attempt to determine why they ceased to be productive. For those with little familiarity with Old English, look at those suffixes which persisted into modern English (use an etymological dictionary to discover relevant forms), and suggest reasons why those suffixes should have persisted. Are there general principles which mean that affixes are lost or persist?

References

OED. The Oxford English Dictionary [online]. oed.com
Wescott, Roger W. (1970). Types of vowel alternation in English. *Word* 26, 309–43.

26 Reflections on Compounds in English and in Wider Germanic

English is a Germanic language, but one which for various historical reasons has been strongly influenced by Latin and French. As a gross oversimplification, we might say that the basic vocabulary of English is Germanic, but that the refined vocabulary of English comes from French and Latin (with some of the technical vocabulary coming from Greek). The general patterning of how the language works, though, is Germanic. One part of that is that things that are called 'compounds' in English tend to function like the compounds in Germanic languages rather than like the compounds in Romance: they are right-headed (a *postage stamp* is a kind of *stamp*, just as in German a *Brief·marke* 'letter stamp' is a kind of *Marke*, while in French a *timbre-poste* 'stamp post' is a kind of *timbre*, following the left-hand element), the typical Romance structure of verb + noun as in French *garde-robe* 'keep dress' (i.e. 'wardrobe'), is not widely used in English and not used in German. In this chapter, the structure of compounds in the Germanic languages will be considered in rather more detail, and compared with the structure of compounds in English. It will be shown that the match is not as close as these brief introductory remarks might imply. For clarity of presentation in non-English examples, the decimal point is used to show boundaries between elements where this is not clear from the orthography, as was done in the *Briefmarke* example just above.

We can begin by considering compounds made up of an adjective and a noun, and the difference between a compound and a syntactic phrasal structure. Throughout Germanic, nouns have inherent gender (masculine, feminine or neuter in German or Icelandic, common or neuter in Dutch and Danish) and in indefinite phrases an attributive adjective agrees with its head noun, and we find so-called strong forms of adjectives.

'A big house' 'A big man' (nominative case, where this is significant)
Danish   German
Et stor·t hus   En stor mand   Ein groß·es Haus   Ein groß·er Mann

When there is a definite determiner, we find the so-called weak form of the adjective.

193

'The big house'   'The big man'
Danish   German
Det stor·e hus   Den stor·e mand   Das groß·e Haus   Der groß·e Mann

Due to various linguistic changes, the patterns do not work exactly the same way in all the Germanic languages, and there are exceptions to the general pattern, but this is a reasonable overall pattern for noun phrases. However, when the sequence of adjective and noun is a compound, the adjective appears in the stem form.

'A big city'
Danish   German
En stor·by   Eine Groß·stadt

Furthermore, any town which is big could be *en stor by* or *eine große Stadt*, but *en storby* or *eine Großstadt* puts it in a different class, it is, in English terms, a city. The compound also gets stress on the first element of the compound (Dutch has some exceptions: Don 2009: 375), while the syntactic phrase gets the stress on the noun. Compounds are written as single word, phrases as multiple words. In Dutch (Don 2009: 374) and German (Neef 2009: 388) the adjectives that can occur in these constructions are limited, largely to monosyllabic Germanic adjectives, although the constraint is hard to specify accurately. In Danish forms like *polar·eskimo* 'polar Eskimo' and *privat·kunde* 'private customer' are found, though they are rare. In Danish, but not in German, we also have another sign that the compound is a single word. We say *den store by* 'the big town' but *stor·by·en* 'big·town·the', where the postposed definite article is used only where the noun phrase contains just one word.

Some adjective + noun compounds are exocentric, that is they do not denote the entity normally denoted by the noun. In English, for example, a *redcap* is not a kind of cap, but is a kind of person/goblin/bird (depending on the dialect of the speaker or familiarity with the entities thus named). Examples from other languages are given below.

Language	Compound	Gloss of elements	Translation	Source
Danish	gul-bug	yellow-belly	'warbler (bird sp.)'	(Bauer 2009)
Dutch	rood-borst	red-breast	'robin'	(Don 2009)
Frisian	grou·kont	fat·arse	'person with a fat arse'	(Hoekstra 2016)
German	Rot-kehlchen	red-throat·DIMIN	'robin'	
Norwegian	raud·spette	red·spot	'flounder (fish sp.)'	

Now compare this with what happens in modern English. We do not have strong and weak forms of adjectives in English, only a base form, so that the syntactic distinctions cannot be shown in English. The only evidence we might have that English does not allow inflected adjectives in compounds, is that we cannot have inflected comparatives and superlatives in this position: *a blacker bird* is fine in syntax, but *a blackerbird is not a possible compound. Interestingly, both Danish and German have compounds with superlatives in them: Danish *største·belastning* 'maximum (lit. biggest) load', German *Höchst·geschwindigkeit* 'top (lit. highest) speed'.

There is, in English, a mismatch between the classificatory semantics and the stress (and orthography). While *blackbird* has stress on the adjective and classificatory semantics, *blue whale* has stress on the noun (as indicated by the orthography, though the orthography is not entirely reliable) and classificatory semantics. English also has a set of words with non-Germanic, non-simple adjectives with initial stress such as *dental hospital, dramatic society, primary school, solar system* (Bauer 2020).

As in the other languages, exocentrics are found in English.

The situation in English does not match the situation in the rest of Germanic because the patterns are more complex and less predictable in English. The productivity of the pattern is also not the same in English and in some of the other languages. Nevertheless, the central examples look very similar indeed.

We now move to look at noun + noun compounds. Noun + noun compounds are the default compounds in Germanic, and have been there since the earliest days of Germanic. Historians of the language generally divide these compounds into 'proper' and 'improper' compounds (in German *echt* 'genuine' and *unecht* or *eigentlich* 'real' and *uneigentlich*, with a range of translations in other languages, including English). The proper compounds (which appear to be considered genuine because they were the earliest type) may originally have had a noun-class marker following the stem (Harbert 2007: 30), but this was lost early, leaving stem + word compounds. The improper compounds carried an inflectional marker on the first element, typically a genitive marker. In later Germanic, this genitive marking becomes very much more common, but also less obviously genitive (Harbert 2007: 30). In some instances, the marker looks, to modern eyes, much more like a plural marker (perhaps especially in Dutch – Booij 2002: 179), or like an unmotivated form. Some of the apparent genitive markers are also used in places where they could not now occur as genitives. For example, German *Liebe·s·lied* 'love·LE·song' could not have an s-genitive on the end of a feminine noun, and *Liebe* is a feminine noun. Modern practice is thus to avoid classifying these as genitives, but to see them as semantically empty linking elements (hence the gloss 'LE' above). Once these are seen as semantically empty, it is not clear that there is any difference in type between the proper and the improper compounds (Chambers and Wilkie 1970: 60–1). The formal distinction is still alive in Faroese (Thráinsson et al. 2004: 204–8), and Icelandic with genitive singular and plural both found, but there still seems to be little semantic difference between proper and improper. In Frisian, the genitive compounds have second-element stress and the first element refers (that is a *koken·s·doar* 'kitchen·GEN·door' is the door of a specific kitchen, not a general type of door: Hoekstra 2016). It may be best not to consider these to be compounds. Apart from this example, the pattern of occurrence of the various linking elements (including no linking element) is typically a matter for discussion in teaching and descriptive grammars of nearly all the Germanic languages. Despite occasional examples which appear to show contrast (German *Land·mann* 'land man = farmer' vs. *Land·s·mann* 'land·LE·man = compatriot' and the same distinction holds in Danish) linking elements are likely to be predictable only on a probabilistic basis, influenced by various analogies (Krott et al. 2001).

One interesting use of the linking elements is that a linking element, perhaps most often an *s*-link, can be used to mark the constituency of a three-element compound. In compounds of the form [[[A][B]] C] a link may be added between elements B and C. This is reported from at least Danish, Faroese, German and Swedish (Bauer 2017: 140–1). Bauer (2009: 407) points out that at least for Danish this is no more than a tendency.

Semantically, Germanic compounds are typically right-headed, Danish *by·bus* 'town bus = urban bus' denotes a bus and not a town. This may or may not be definitional. Gender is typically also derived from the head element, although occasional exceptions are found. Similarly, the plural marker is usually, but not universally, inherited from the head. Otherwise, the semantic link between the elements is extremely free, except that the modifying element does not refer: a *Land·mann* is not a man connected with a specific piece of land, but a man connected with the land in general. Neef (2009: 395, citing Heringer) points out that German *Fisch·frau* 'fish woman' could mean any one of the following or others:

> a woman who sells fish
> a woman who has bought a fish
> a woman standing close to a fish
> a woman eating a fish
> a woman who looks like a fish

He concludes that, although some compounds have a more established meaning than others, in principle the compound cannot be understood without reference to the context. All that is given is that a compound of the form [A B] means 'a B having something to do with A'.

As with adjective + noun compounds, noun + noun compounds may also be exocentric. Some examples are given below.

Language	Example	Gloss	Translation	Source
Danish	storke·næb	stork beak	'pantograph'	(Bauer 2009)
German	Bücher·wurm	bookworm	'bookworm'	(Neef 2009)

They can also be coordinative, though these constructions are often controversial (see Chapter 22).

Compounds can be elements in compounds, occasionally leading to very long words, especially in technical language. This is discussed for English in Chapter 12.

Phonologically, compounds are stressed on the first element, and orthographically they are typically presented as a single word, though a recent spelling reform in Danish allows some separated spellings, so that the name of *Odense Banegård Center* 'Odense Railway Station' was controversial when the facility was opened. This convention is relatively new in German.

The greatest difference between the rest of Germanic and English is that there is no simple way to define a noun + noun compound in English. Stress on noun + noun sequences, while largely predictable from many factors, is not unified, the spelling is not consistent, and the semantic relationships between the elements are just as diverse as they are in the other Germanic languages. The various tests for a compound are difficult to apply and give inconsistent outcomes (Bauer 1998). Formally, a noun modifying another noun (whether we think of this as a compound or as a syntactic structure) is usually uninflected, but there is an increasing use of plural marking on the modifying noun. When this is found, some scholars see it as a sign that the construction is not a compound (Pinker 1999: 178–87), while others see unusually marked compounds (Bauer et al. 2013: 443). In either case, Bauer (2017: 143) concludes that the English forms are not linking elements. Where a genitive is found modifying a noun with an appropriate semantic reading, the tradition is not to call this a compound (but see Rosenbach 2006), but to see it as a syntactic construction. To add to the confusion, the use of an apostrophe to distinguish between a plural and a genitive is not standard: we find *girls school* or *girls' school*, *dogstooth* or *dog's-tooth*. The result is that it is hard to tell what constructions in English should be seen as comparable to compounds in other Germanic languages. This is despite the fact that there is much in common between the various languages, notably the semantics, including exocentricity.

Verb + noun compounds are standard in many Germanic languages.

Language	Example	Gloss	Translation	Source
Danish	fortælle·kunst	tell·art	'narrative art'	(Bauer 2009)
Danish	koge·punkt	boil·point	'boiling point'	(Bauer 2009)
Dutch	eten·s·tijd	eat·LE·time	'mealtime'	(Booij 2002)
Dutch	leer·boek	learn·book	'textbook'	(Don 2009)
Faroese	renn·i·skógar	run·LE·shoes	'running shoes'	(Thráinsson et al. 2004)
German	Web·fehler	weave·error	'flaw in weaving'	(Neef 2009)
German	Wende·punkt	turn·point	'turning point'	

Note that in Danish the verb is in the infinitive form, in German it is in the stem form, and in Dutch and Faroese it can have a linking element. While English does have compounds with base form verbs such as *think-tank*, *wait-time*, it is typical, especially in British English, to have an *-ing* form in such cases, as illustrated in the examples above. These forms are then most frequently interpreted as being nouns rather than verbs. Note that, for instance, British *draining board* is American *drain board*, and British *frying pan* is American *frypan* (Bauer et al. 2013: 477). Because of widespread conversion in English, the proper analysis of such forms is often difficult: is *boomtime* a case of a verb + noun compound or not?

Compound adjectives are quite common across Germanic, but there are relatively few patterns. We have a noun + adjective pattern which can be glossed as 'adjective like a/the noun'. As a subtype here we have the type where the noun acts as an intensifier, and the comparison is obscure or non-existent. Hoeksema (2012) calls these 'elative compounds'. Since these forms have right-element stress, they may not be compounds. We have a noun + adjective pattern where the noun is an argument of the adjective. We have a pattern with an adverb + noun (although the adverb often has adjectival form, but there are good reasons for thinking that adjective and adverb may be part of the same word-class in much of Germanic). There are verb + adjective compounds. Then there are various exocentric patterns where the head of the word is not an adjective, but the compound is used adjectivally. The various types are illustrated below, including English examples. Where no source is given, the words are sourced from dictionaries and experience.

Overt comparison

Danish	himmel·blå	sky blue	'sky blue'	
Dutch	fluister·zacht	whisper·soft	'as quiet as a whisper'	(Don 2009)
English	blood red			
German	himmel·blau	sky blue	'sky blue'	

Elative compounds

Danish	snot·dum	snot·stupid	'very stupid'	(Bauer 2009)
Danish	sten·rig	stone·rich	'very rich'	
Dutch	ape·trots	ape·proud	'very proud'	
Dutch	kei·leuk	boulder·funny	'very funny'	(Booij 2002)
English	shit hot		'very hot [usually not in temperature, but in approval]'	
German	blut-arm	blood poor	'very poor'	

Nominal argument

Danish	mad·glad	food·happy	'fond of good food'	
Danish	morgen·frisk	morning fresh	'refreshed by a good night's sleep'	(Bauer 2009)
Dutch	lood·vrij	lead free	'lead free'	(Booij 2002)
Dutch	milieu-vriendelijk	milieu-friendly	'green'	(Booij 2002)
English	ankle-deep			
English	word-final			
German	arbeit·s·scheu	work·LE·shy	'afraid of hard work'	
German	herz·zerreisend	heart·tearing	'heart-breaking'	(Neef 2009)
German	leben·s·gefährlich	life·LE·dangerous	'perilous'	

Adverbial

Danish	fri·t·stående	free·ADV·standing	'free -standing'	(Bauer 2017)
Dutch	dicht·bevolkt	thick·peopled	'densely populated'	(Don 2009)
Dutch	licht·grijs	light·grey	'light grey'	(Booij 2002)
English	dark blue			
Faroese	blíð·mæltur	soft·spoken	'softly spoken'	(Thráinsson et al. 2004)
German	voll·automatisch	full automatic	'fully automatic'	

Verb + adjective

Danish	stryge·fri	iron·free	'non-iron'	(Bauer 2009)
Dutch	koop·lustig	buy·cheerful	'acquisitive'	
English	go-slow			
Faroese	renn·vatur	drip·wet	'dripping wet'	(Thráinsson et al. 2004)
German	treff·sicher	hit·sure	'accurate'	(Neef 2009)

Where coordinative adjectival compounds are concerned, there are some common patterns in modern Germanic, and some interestingly different ones.

The coordinated learned adjectives (typically Latinate or Greek) occur in those languages that have such adjectives. Coordinated colour adjectives in most Germanic languages show the presence of both colours, while in English, coordinated colour adjectives usually show a hybrid between the two colours. Both sides have exceptions. But in Danish, Dutch and German there is a difference in stress between the two types, with initial stress reflecting the hybrid reading, and final stress reflecting the presence of both colours. In English, while *red-white* may occasionally be used to discuss the flags of Denmark, Austria or Poland, conjoined adjectives are usually preferred, so that the Danish flag is *red and white*. In English, the blended colour terms are rare, with adverbial modification of the colour term being preferred (*bluey-green, greenish-blue*) (Bauer 2010). Coordinated native adjectives (other than colour adjectives) are more common in the other Germanic languages than in English, where overt coordination seems to be preferred.

Coordinated learned adjectives

Danish	dialogisk-lyrisk	dialogical-lyrical	'dialogical-lyrical'	(Bauer 2009)
Dutch	pedagogisch-didactisch	pedagogical-didactic	'pedagogical-didactic'	De Haas & Trommelen (1993)
English	philosophical-historical			
German	wissenschaftlich-technisch	scientific-technical		(Fleischer & Barz 2007)

Colour adjectives

Danish	rød-hvid	red-white	'red and white'	
Dutch	rood·bruin	red·brown	'reddish brown'	(Bauer 2010)
Dutch	rood-groen	red-green	'red and green'	(Bauer 2010)
English	blue-green			
German	blau-grün	blue-green	'blue and green'	(Bauer 2010)

Coordinated native adjectives

Danish	døv·stum	deaf·dumb	'deaf and dumb'	(Bauer 2009)
Danish	bitter-sød	bitter-sweet	'bitter-sweet'	(Bauer 2009)
Dutch	doof·stum	deaf·dumb	'deaf and dumb'	(De Haas & Trommelen 1993)
Dutch	zoet·suur	sweet·sour	'sweet and sour'	(De Haas & Trommelen 1993)
German	taub-stumm	deaf-dumb	'deaf and dumb'	(Fleischer & Barz 2007)
German	süß·sauer	sweet·sour	'sweet and sour'	(Fleischer & Barz 2007)

Compound verbs are generally considered rare in Germanic, with the construction being apparently unknown in Gothic and sometimes controversial in other languages (Harbert 2007: 30). Nevertheless, examples are attested in older states of Germanic and can often be found in modern languages. The exception to the general rule is the phrasal verb (or particle verb), which is common. Some languages have a distinction between separable and inseparable verbs. Bauer (2009) cites Danish *til·falde* 'to·fall = fall to [e.g. *it falls to us to complete this*]' versus at *falde til* 'fall to = settle [e.g. *to settle in a new place*]'. Hammer (1991) gives examples of *tot·schlagen* 'dead·hit = kill' and *fest·stehen* 'firm·stand = be certain', where elements other than particles can be separated from the verbal stem in German. I shall not consider such complications here, but rather look at examples of compound verbs.

Language	Compound	Gloss	Meaning	Source
Danish	råd·spørge	counsel·ask	'seek advice'	(Bauer 2009)
Danish	små·bjæffe	small.PL·bark	'yap'	
Dutch	fijn·hakken	fine·chop	'chop up finely'	
Dutch	slaap·wandele	sleep·walk	'sleepwalk'	(De Haas & Trommelen 1993)
Dutch	snel·schrijven	quick·write	'take shorthand'	(De Haas & Trommelen 1993)
Dutch	stof·zuigen	dust suck	'vacuum clean'	(De Haas & Trommelen 1993)
English	cold-call			
English	pistol-whip			
Faroese	góð·kenna	good·know	'accept'	(Thráinsson et al. 2004)
Faroese	leið·beina	way·lead.to	'direct, instruct'	(Thráinsson et al. 2004)
German	frei·halten	free·hold	'keep unencumbered'	(Fleischer & Barz 2007)
German	kopf·stehen	head·stand	'stand on one's head'	(Fleischer & Barz 2007)
German	rad·fahren	bike·drive	'ride a bike'	(Neef 2009)
German	spül·bohren	rinse·drill	'to drill while rinsing with water'	(Fleischer & Barz 2007)
German	stehen·bleiben	stand·remain	'keep still'	(Fleischer & Barz 2007)
Old Scandinavian	bók·setja	book·set	'record'	(Haugen 1982)
Old Scandinavian	full-nøgja	full-satisfy	'satisfy'	(Haugen 1982)

As will be clear from some of the examples here, one of the problems with things that look like compound verbs in Germanic is that they are formed either by conversion from a compound noun or by back-formation, often from an agentive form. For some scholars (e.g. Marchand 1969, Booij 2002: 161) this means that verbal compounding is not productive. Where it is productive, it is often restricted. Adams (2001: 100–9) provides good coverage of compound verbs in English, but does not really see them as being created as compounds; Bauer (2017: 138), on the other hand, suggests that "verbal compounding is no longer marginal in current English".

Once a category of compounds has been established in the grammar of a language, things which may be marginal to the category are easily incorporated within it. Some typical examples are given below, sometimes included as compounds, sometimes not, depending on the analyst, but much more easily seen as compounds in wider Germanic than in English, where orthographic and stress criteria are not consistently relevant. The categories illustrated in Table 26.1 are not intended to be exhaustive, and gaps in the table do not necessarily indicate that relevant forms are not possible, nor does the presence of an example necessarily make the claim that it is (or should be considered) a compound rather than something else (perhaps a case of univerbation of commonly collocating elements).

The fundamentals of the compound are similar across Germanic, with differences of productivity in different traditions, and a few exceptional types that I have not dwelled on. One notable exceptional type is illustrated by *mann-skratti* 'deuce of a fellow, devil of a man', *karl·tötrið* 'old.man·poor.fellow' in Icelandic. This type is left-headed and is used only in emotionally charged language (Einarsson 1945: 180).

Much of what we find in English is recognizable from the dominating Germanic paradigms. The fact that compounds are classifying, that the semantics of noun + noun compounds is fixed only at the most general level, the fact that we find noun + noun constructions in great numbers, and also find adjectival compounds (much less in some of the languages) but find relatively few compound verbs, that the fundamental pattern is for stem + word with no inflection on the first element and the modifying first element does not refer to specific members of the class, all these are things that English shares with the Germanic pattern. But English has adjective + noun constructions like *red squirrel* which have the classifying semantics of Germanic compounds, but the superficial form of syntactic noun phrases, that English has many instances where learned adjectives are used as modifiers rather than using compounds (English *renal artery*, Danish *nyre·blod·åre* 'kidney·blood·artery', English *bovine tuberculosis*, Danish *kvæ·tuberkulose* 'cattle·tuberculosis', English *structural engineer*, Danish *bygning·s·ingeniør* 'building·LE·engineer'), the fact that the preferred interpretation of colour adjective + colour adjective compounds is different in English and in the other languages (and we can add conjoined place-names like English *London–Paris* and the equivalents in other Germanic languages where the English output is used attributively and

Table 26.1 *Other less frequent compound patterns in a range of Germanic languages*

Construction	Danish	English	Dutch	Faroese	German
Phrase+N	hvorfor-skal-man-op-om-morgenen-stemme why-must-one-up-in-the-morning-voice	soon-to-be-divorced wife	kat-en-mus·spel cat-and-mouse-game 'game of cat and mouse'		
Pronoun+N	hun·ræv she·fox 'vixen'	she-devil			Ich·form I·form 'first person singular'
Numeral+Adj	atten-årig 18-year.ly 18-year-old	four-dimensional	drie·dimensionaal three-dimensional		drei·stöckig three·floor.ed 'three storied'
Numeral+N	tre·dækker three-decker 'triplane'	six-pack	drie·tand three·tooth 'trident'	fimm·króna five·kroner 'a five-kroner coin'	Fünf·kamp five·struggle 'pentathlon'
Numeral+V	tre·dele three·divide 'trisect'			tví·býta two·divide 'divide in two'	
Prep+N	efter·år after·year 'autumn'	after-care			Vor·teil before·part 'advantage'
Prep+Adj	til·bøjelig to·flexible 'inclined to'	off-white	boven·natuurlijk above·natural 'supernatural'		unter·irdisch under·terrestrial 'subterranean'
Prep+V	op·råbe up·call 'announce'	download	uit·gaan out·go 'go out; originate with'		zu·setzen to·put 'add'
Prep+Prep	til·med to·with 'moreover'	into			dort·hin there·to 'thither'

the wider use in Germanic is for adverbial use – Bauer 2010), these all suggest systems which are importantly different. The same is true of the importance of stress in most of Germanic for defining a compound, as opposed to English, the clear perception of compounds as single words in most of Germanic, and the frequent analysis of forms like *forestry worker* as syntactic and not morphological in English (although there are also many who disagree). All these factors make it seem that while there may be central cases of overlap, there are more peripheral places where the two traditions diverge, and what is included as a compound may differ from one tradition to the other.

The importance of this is that general Germanic scholarship on compounds may not always transfer to the treatment of English, and it is hard to know whether this has done damage to the description of English or not. At the very least, it has meant that there is dispute in the literature on English about precisely where the boundaries of compounding lie. It is tempting to suggest that the differences arise through the influence of French on English vocabulary. For French, stress is not a relevant factor in determining whether something is or is not a compound; French has differing preferred patterns of marking the classifying relationship – either by using adjectives rather than nouns as modifiers or by using post-modifying prepositional phrases, as in French *chemin de fer* 'path of iron' corresponding to German *Eisen·bahn* 'iron·way' for 'railway'. While this seems eminently plausible, it is hard to prove, largely because some of the same descriptive problems arise in other Germanic languages as well. Whatever the cause of the differences, they mean that the analyst must not simply assume that what is said of other Germanic languages automatically applies to English.

Challenge

Constructions like *blue whale*, *red squirrel*, *white cell* seem to be halfway between compounds and syntactic structures: they are spelled and stressed like syntactic constructions, but their meaning is like the meaning of compounds, and like compounds they do not allow coordination of the adjective with another adjective while retaining their specialized meaning. Can you find any other aspects of their behaviour which might be helpful in determining their status? Whether you can or not, how do you think such constructions should be analysed, and how would you justify your position?

References

Adams, Valerie. (2001). *Complex Words in English*. Harlow: Longman.
Bauer, Laurie. (1998). When is a sequence of two nouns a compound in English? *English Language and Linguistics* 2, 65–86.

(2009). IE, Germanic: Danish. In Rochelle Lieber & Pavol Štekauer (eds.), *The Oxford Handbook of Compounding*. Oxford: Oxford University Press, 400–16.

(2010). Co-compounds in Germanic. *Journal of Germanic Linguistics* 22, 201–19.

(2017). *Compounds and Compounding*. Cambridge: Cambridge University Press.

(2020). *Blackbirds* and *blue whales*: Stress in English A+N constructions. *English Language and Linguistics* 25, 1–20.

Bauer, Laurie, Rochelle Lieber & Ingo Plag. (2013). *The Oxford Reference Guide to English Morphology*. Oxford: Oxford University Press.

Booij, Geert. (2002). *The Morphology of Dutch*. Oxford: Oxford University Press.

Chambers, W. Walker & John R. Wilkie. (1970). *A Short History of the German Language*. London: Methuen.

Don, Jan. (2009). IE, Germanic: Dutch. In Rochelle Lieber & Pavol Štekauer (eds.), *The Oxford Handbook of Compounding*. Oxford: Oxford University Press, 370–85.

Einarsson, Stefán. (1945). *Icelandic: Grammar, Texts, Glossary*. Baltimore: Johns Hopkins Press.

Fleischer, Wolfgang & Irmhild Barz. (2007). *Wortbildung der deutschen Gegenwartssprache*. 3. Auflage. Tübingen: Niemeyer.

Haas, Wim de & Mieke Trommelen. (1993). *Morfologisch handboek van het Nederlands*. 's-Gravenhage: SDU.

Hammer, A.E. (1991). *Hammer's German Grammar and Usage*. 2nd ed., revised by Martin Durrell. London: Arnold

Harbert, Wayne. (2007). *The Germanic Languages*. Cambridge: Cambridge University Press.

Hoeksema, Jack. (2012). Elative compounds in Dutch: Properties and developments. In Guido Oebel (ed.), *Intensivierungskonzepte bei Adjektiven und Adverben im Sprachenvergleich / Crosslinguistic Comparison of Intensified Adjectives and Adverbs*. Hamburg: Verlag dr. Kovač, 97–142.

Hoekstra Jarich, F. (2016). Frisian. In Peter O. Müller, Ingeborg Ohnheiser, Susan Olsen & Franz Rainer (eds.), *Word-Formation: An International Handbook of the Languages of Europe*. Berlin: De Gruyter Mouton, 2451–65.

Krott, Andrea R., Harald Baayen & Robert Schreuder. (2001). Analogy in morphology: Modeling the choice of linking morphemes in Dutch. *Linguistics*. 39: 51–93.

Marchand, Hans. (1969). *The Categories and Types of Present-Day English Word-Formation*. 2nd ed. Munich: Beck.

Neef, Martin. (2009). IE, Germanic: German. In Rochelle Lieber & Pavol Štekauer (eds.), *The Oxford Handbook of Compounding*. Oxford: Oxford University Press, 386–99.

Pinker, Steven. (1999). *Words and Rules*. London: Weidenfeld & Nicolson.

Rosenbach, Anette. (2006). Descriptive genitives in English: A case study on constructional gradience. *English Language and Linguistics* 10, 77–118.

Thráinsson, Höskuldur, Hjalmar P. Petersen, Jógvan Í. Lon Jacobsen & Zakaris Svabo Hansen. (2004). *Faroese: An Overview and Reference Grammar*. Tórshavn: Føroya Fróðskaparfelag.

Part VII

Questions Involving Inflection

27 Reflections on Inflection inside Word-Formation

27.1 Introduction

There are two apparently disconnected factors that seem to disallow inflectional affixes from occurring inside word-formation. The first is the general rule that derivational affixes appear closer to the root than inflectional affixes. To the extent that this rule holds, it bans any sequence of inflectional suffix + derivational suffix. The second is the observation that the first element in compounds is not inflected. We know this to be false, in the sense that it is an overgeneralization, so that discussions have been focused on explanations for the exceptions to the rules. It should be said that the constraint of inflection within word-formation is supposed to hold of English (and probably other languages as well), but not to be a universal. Many languages are reported to have internal inflections in compounds, including Finnish and Tariana.

> Finnish
> *auto·n·ikkuna* 'car·GEN·window' (Karlsson 1999: 242)
>
> *maa·lta·pako* 'country·ABL·flee.NMLZ' 'rural depopulation' (Sulala and Karjalainen 1992: 362)
>
> Tariana
> *ma:nakadru-ni* 'açai.tree.parrot-POSS' 'scarlet macaw' (Aikhenvald 2003: 132)

Many languages are reported to have inflectional affixes closer to the root than diminutive markers at least, but also with suffixes which are more obviously derivational (see Bauer 2003: 100).

> German
> *Kind-er-chen* 'child-PL-diminutive'
>
> Welsh
> *merch-et-os* 'girl-PL-diminutive'
>
> Dutch
> *muzikant-en-dom* 'musician-PL-NMLZ'

Of course, any theory that makes predictions about the sequencing of inflectional and derivational markers assumes the split morphology hypothesis (see Section 2.4), and that provides a useful starting point.

27.2 Inflection and Derivation in English

A good definition of inflectional morphology in English would presumably provide some behaviour that is shared by all inflectional affixes and not shared by any derivational affixes. While many such criteria have been suggested (see Plank 1994), it is noteworthy that Bauer et al. (2013: 29), like others dealing with English, stipulate where the boundary between inflection and derivation lies rather than providing a definition of the distinction. Their list of inflectional affixes (with which we might want to disagree) is as follows:

plural and possessive marking on nouns, third-person singular marking on present-tense verbs, past tense and past participle marking on verbs, present participle marking on verbs, comparative and superlative marking on adjectives and adverbs.

While this position reflects a certain consensus, it is far from a definitive list. Questions that could be raised about the list include: is the plural really inflectional (Beard 1982)? Is the comparative in English really inflectional (Matthews 1974: 48–9)? Is the possessive marker inflectional, or is it a clitic? Is adverbial *-ly* really derivational (Giegerich 2012)? Is ordinal *-th* (as in *fifteenth*) really derivational (Bauer et al. 2013: 536–7)? Are the participles still instances of inflection when the forms are used as adjectives or other word-classes? Is *n't* an inflectional affix (Zwicky and Pullum 1983)? More generally, we might ask whether it makes sense to ask about the application of the inflection–derivation divide to such forms at all.

These are all relevant questions, and they may not be questions which can be given a definitive answer. Furthermore, this does not exhaust the list of potential problems. This means that it would be possible to answer the whole issue by saying that it is not clear that the question makes any sense at all, and it therefore cannot be answered. However, in the present state of scholarship, the question does make sense, and the apparent restriction has been noted several times, so it is worth considering. In doing so, the ostensive definition of inflection used by Bauer et al. (2013) will simply be accepted as a starting point for the discussion. Future research may help refine the question a bit.

27.3 Inflection inside Compounds

We can illustrate the constraint by looking at comparative and superlative marking. If we accept that words like *blackbird* and *tallboy* are compounds (which is generally accepted, but not necessarily beyond question), then the constraint tells us that we should not be able to mark the comparative or superlative on the adjective within the compound. Since we cannot have *blackerbird or *tallestboy (or indeed other parallel words) the constraint seems to hold, and these inflectional forms are not allowed within compounds. In this particular case, though, the constraint is not (or may not be) restricted to compounds. Given *black market* and *tall order* 'difficult assignment' (which most would take not to be compounds), we cannot have *blackest market* or *taller order*, either. At least, we cannot have these if the semantic idiosyncrasies of *black market* and *tall order* are to be retained. They might be possible in environments in which the elements are entirely compositional, for example *He wrote three orders on the wall, in ever-increasing size. The tallest order was that no one was to go outside.* Such examples would not normally be seen as compounds, though. Just what the limits of the constraint really are may not be clear, but it does seem to hold within compounds.

But that is just one example. We also have to consider plural markers, possessive markers, third-person singular *-s*, *-ed* (and its irregular congeners) and *-ing*. Most of these seem to appear in compounds in some form or another.

First we must consider instances where the modifying element in the compound is a piece of syntax, as in *dad-needs-a-new-sports-car syndrome*, *grass-is-greener syndrome* (Bauer et al. 2013: 488). Here we find *needs* and *greener* inside the compounds. Are these counterexamples? Strictly speaking they are, though it depends on the care with which the constraint is formulated. But since the inflection is not a marker of the role of the first element, but arises instead from the piece of syntax that is transplanted inside the compound, such forms will be treated as irrelevant here.

The easiest of these to deal with may be the third-person singular *-s* on present-tense verbs. As far as I know, this never occurs within anything that might be thought to be a compound. Again, the constraint seems to work. The same is probably true of the past tense *-ed* (or irregular forms), though it may be hard to tell whether a past tense or past participle form is involved. We seldom find forms like *sangsong or *spentthrift.

The others are all problematic in one way or another. Some potential counterexamples are given below.

> plural: mice droppings, sales manager, sports bar, systems analyst
> possessive: bullseye, cat's-eye, foolscap, lambswool, menswear
> past participle: freedman
> present participle: humming bird, sleeping pill, washing machine

> ... in case anything social-media-worthy gets dragged up. (Gilly Macmillan. 2017. *Odd Child Out*. New York: Morrow, p. 159)

Of all of these, perhaps the plural is the most interesting and the most frustrating to deal with. One of the problems here is that within Lexical Phonology and Morphology it was suggested that irregular plurals could occur in the first element of compounds, but not regular ones, so that *mice-catcher* was permissible but not *rats-catcher, because the irregular plural was at Stratum I and thus available as a compound element, while regular plurals were added after compounding had applied (see Kirchner and Nicoladis 2009 for some discussion). The difficulty with this theoretical stance is that only some irregular plurals seem to be used in this way.

> "Missy, what are you looking for back there?" And she said, "I'm looking for mice manure." (Tony Hillerman. 1999. *The First Eagle*. London: Hodder Headline, pp. 60–1)

> Mice-free; mice population (used on Radio New Zealand National's *Morning Report*, 22 March 2018)

> Lice infestation is a parasitic skin infestation caused by tiny wingless insects. (www.msdmanuals.com/en-nz/home/skin-disorders/parasitic-skin-infec tions/lice-infestation accessed 25 November 2023)

As Kirchner and Nicoladis (2009: 95) point out, we do not find *teethbrush or *childrencare, even though we expect their referents to be used for more than one tooth or more than one child, and we can add that *feetpath, *geese-bumps and *menpower seem equally impossible, though *menfolk, womenfolk* are standard forms (these may be parallel to *gentlemen farmers* where both elements are plural). Latin and Greek plurals do not seem to be widely used in this way (we find, for instance, *bacterial growth* rather than *bacteria growth), but it is hard to be sure, partly because many such forms are unstable anyway. *Alumni association* is at least one common exception, and see *media-worthy* above. Plurals with voiced fricatives (e.g. *calf/calves*) do not appear to be used, but with zero plurals such as *deer-hunting* and *sheep-farming* it is impossible to tell whether there is a plural form involved or not, and the singular form seems more likely.

A rule which says that irregular plurals may be used in the first element of compounds as long as they end in /s/ seems far less motivated than a general rule based on Stratal Morphology. Moreover, it is not an obligatory rule: *mouse-droppings* and *louse-infestations* are equally possible forms. Overall, it seems that the use of irregular plurals in compound first elements has been overstated.

Regular plurals in the first element of compounds seem to be far more readily available. One set of these, perhaps the earliest examples, are those where the form in *-s* is not a simple plural of the unmarked noun. For instance, if there is such a thing as an *arm deal*, it might be a deal to buy prosthetic limbs, while an *arms deal* is one made to purchase weapons. This phenomenon accounts for forms such as *brains trust, clothes drier, draughtsboard, grassroots movement, mains power* and *savings bank*, among many more. On the other hand, it is by no means automatic that a final *-s* will be used in such cases. *Refreshment trolley* and *refreshments trolley* can both be found, *trouser press* is used rather than a form with plural *trousers*, a *card game* is the same as a *game of cards*, *wage bill* and *wages bill* are both found. Moreover, there is no clear justification for the variation that is found in such instances. Even in this particular set of circumstances, a form with no plural marking is, overall, more usual than might be thought.

In the mid-1960s reports start to appear in print of a new usage (or a rapidly increasing usage) of plural attributives or plural modifiers (Mutt 1967, Dierickx 1970) in English. Just when the trend began is difficult to say, but it was noticed at that point. These are usages such as *burns unit, careers officer, companies legislation, drugs problem, letters column, textiles industry*, which today do not seem at all out of the ordinary. If these are compounds, they break the rule about not allowing inflected forms in the first element of compounds. Even within this set of words, some are less innovative than others (and may seem more compound-like). The more established pattern includes many apparent compounds ending in *man*: *craftsman, marksman, salesman, sportsman, tradesman, yachtsman* and some with wider usage such a *sports jacket*. These do not seem to involve any genuine plural meaning (a craftsman may master only one craft, a yachtsman may sail on only a single yacht), and in most cases the singular and plural forms do not have different referents. Yet there does seem to be some tendency to use the plural form when a plural meaning is intended, so that *companies legislation* involves many or all companies, not just one, while *company policy* involves just one company. Previously, though, that would not have been enough to call forth a plural form. Whether this is the justification for the new usage or not, it is not clear why it should suddenly have gained traction. (For further discussion of this type, see Bauer 2017: 140–8, 2022: 157–62.)

If we are to uphold the postulated constraint against inflection in compounds, we would have to say that the relevant structures here are not compounds. Pinker (1999) does just that, in effect claiming that *sport jacket* and *sports jacket* illustrate two different constructions. Unfortunately, the only sign of the distinction may be that one has a plural noun and the other does not. However, in principle this remains an option (whether Pinker's analysis is used or some other), although it is one which looks as though it is circular.

The same thing may be true with possessives. The examples cited above look like compounds, and look like possessives whether or not the standard spelling involves an apostrophe. The spelling, though, as in other compounds, is a poor guide. A quick survey of four dictionaries gives the following range of spellings.

bugbane		
cowbane		
dogbane	dogsbane	dog's-bane
fleabane		
flybane		
foxbane		
		hare's bane
henbane	hensbane	
	ratsbane	rat'sbane
		wolf'sbane wolf's-bane, wolf's bane

These various spellings suggest that some genitive modifiers can be included in compounds, and that they are in variation with non-genitive modifiers. They also suggest some insecurity about such items, although the uninflected modifier remains the preferred option in most cases, and the frequency of the modifying noun may play a role. The underlying problem is that the genitive is not simply a marker of possession in English, but has multiple functions (as in many other languages). It can mark a determiner showing possession, it can show things that are not possession, and it can be used as a classifier for a following noun. Since an unmarked noun can also be used as a classifier, there is an overlap of functions, and the overlap of forms between a determiner and a classifier can also leave forms ambiguous on occasions. For example, *dog fennel* and *dog's fennel* are alternative names for 'mayweed', and *this woman's magazine* is classifying in *This woman's magazine contains no recipes or sewing tips* but possessive in *Every woman was told to bring a magazine to read, and this woman's magazine was The Economist*. It is the classifying genitives which might be thought to be compounds, perhaps especially those which are stressed on the first element (like *dog's fennel* and *menswear*).

It can be denied that genitives in attributive position create compounds (in which case there is some obligation to explain why these things are not compounds and what they are), or it can be denied that the genitive is an inflection. Either or both may be valid. But it certainly looks as though genitives create constructions which behave in a very similar manner to compounds. (For a more detailed discussion, see Rosenbach 2006.)

The participles may be less difficult to dismiss. It is absolutely true that the morphological process whereby *-ed* and *-ing* create adjectives and nouns is a puzzle (see Chapter 7), and equally puzzling just what the relationship is between those forms and the inflected forms of the verb is. But we may be able to ignore that puzzle, and say that nouns and adjectives can occur in the first elements of compounds, and that their form is irrelevant to this generalization.

Then *freedman* and *hummingbird* are just normal compounds, and we do not need to look at their internal constituency.

There is one potential problem here. While compounds like *hummingbird* are common, the *-ing* form is always a noun in them (in *hummingbird*, the *-ing* form could be interpreted as an adjective, but such cases are rare). Compounds with past participles in the first element are extraordinarily rare (as opposed to noun phrases with past participles in attributive position). Some of this could be to do with the problem of defining an adjective + noun compound in English (Bauer 2021), but we may not even have to look into that. Most English compounds of the form adjective + noun contain a monosyllabic adjective. Most past participles and all *-ing* forms are disyllabic or longer. In the spirit of Optimality Theory, all we need to say is that the length constraint overrules other constraints. However, that is not the end of the matter. First, we have apparent adjective + noun compounds with learned words in the first element, although they do not permit participles either: these are forms like *dental hospital, medical school, musical box, nervous system, operatic society, solar system* (Bauer 2021). The other problem is that irregular past participles are often monosyllabic and must be listed at Stratum I in the Level Ordering system, yet they do not seem to appear in compounds either: we do not find *blown-hair, *drunk-customers, *dug-gardens, *read-papers, and where we do find premodifying participles, we do not find a compound: *burnt skin, grown children, hand-fed piglets, home-grown vegetables, interesting lives. Knitwear* is a possible exception.

Overall, if we accept the presuppositions in the question of whether inflectional affixes can appear in the first elements of compounds, the answer is that they are limited rather than they do not occur. Why they are limited, and perhaps why those that can occur are exceptional, remain open questions.

27.4 Inflections inside Derivational Affixes

Inflectional affixes are found inside derivational affixes quite frequently, but not usually in productive usage and, in any case, not in many patterns. Some examples are provided below.

> with meaning-changing or obligatory *-s*: folksy, gutser, gutsful, gutsy, gutsiness, newsy, sudsy, woodsy
> with irregular plural: (see below)
> with plural *-s*: (see below)
> with possessive *-s*: not found
> with *-ed*: excitedness, presumedly, supposedly
> with *-ing*: interestingly, lovingness
> with comparative: betterment, betterness, lessen, worsen
> with superlative: mostly

One of my plainclothesers did get a little excited. (Jonathan Kellerman. 2010. *Deception*. New York: Ballantine. E-version, p. 244)

Her mom had taught her how to ... deal with handsy men. (Laura Griffin. 2019. *Desperate Girls*. London: Headline Eternal, p. 91)

both ... conceding the regular Unitedites' prior claim to the true dejection of defeat. (Martyn Bedford. 1997. *Exit, Orange and Red*. London: Bantam, p. 261)

Here, nearly all of the instances can be justified without a claim that inflection can precede derivation: the forms are not simply inflectional, the inflected form is irregular, the *-ed* and *-ing* create adjectives whose internal structure is irrelevant. Exceptions are found, but are rare.

27.5 Discussion

Although it could be argued that, as phrased, a ban on inflection inside word-formation in English makes too many assumptions and is too superficial to be a coherent constraint, it holds up fairly well. We might, for instance, argue that a simple dichotomy between inflection and derivation is not sufficient (Booij 1996), that compounds are not well enough defined to support the claim, that inflection is not well enough defined to be a usable category in such a context, and all those points are important, though not necessarily an exhaustive list of objections. Nevertheless, the limited instances of inflection inside word-formation that we find in English suggest that even if the constraint is not absolute, it holds as a default. The exceptions that require further exploration are the use of the plural and the genitive in the first elements of compounds. The matter of the genitive might come down to a definitional problem: if we have a classifying genitive does it form a compound or something else? The plural is much harder to dismiss. The development of plurals in this position may arise from instances like *arms deal*, where the *-s* is arguably not just a plural marker, but shows some features of a derivational affix, and instances like *sportsman*, although it is not clear why such a minor pattern should expand. We do not yet appear to have a good account of how such forms developed, although their increase seems to be a twentieth-century phenomenon (see, for example, the graphs in Bauer 2017: 145–7). Without a better appreciation of precisely what has happened, it will be hard to understand what motivated the development.

Challenge

It is clear that plural nouns can occur in modifying nouns in English, and in some cases the resultant construction is a compound. The case with foreign nouns (containing foreign plural markers) is less clear, probably because examples are rarer. What examples can you find of Latin or Greek plurals used attributively? (Other languages may be considered, but they are even more difficult to find and to analyse.) Are the examples you find compounds or not? How can you tell? Do your findings influence your view of plurals within word-formation? If so, in what way and why?

References

Aikhenvald, Alexandra Y. (2003). *A Grammar of Tariana*. Cambridge: Cambridge University Press.
Bauer, Laurie (2003). *Introducing Linguistic Morphology*. 2nd ed. Edinburgh: Edinburgh University Press.
   (2017). *Compounds and Compounding*. Cambridge: Cambridge University Press.
Bauer, Laurie. (2021). *Blackbirds* and *blue whales*: Stress in English A+N constructions. *English Language and Linguistics* 25, 581–600.
   (2022). *An Introduction to English Lexicology*. Edinburgh: Edinburgh University Press.
Bauer, Laurie, Rochelle Lieber & Ingo Plag. (2013). *The Oxford Reference Guide to English Morphology*. Oxford: Oxford University Press.
Beard, Robert. (1982). The plural as a lexical derivation. *Glossa* 16, 133–48.
Booij, Geert. (1996). Inherent versus contextual inflection and the split morphology hypothesis. *Yearbook of Morphology 1995*, 1–16.
Dierickx, Jean. (1970). Why are plural attributives becoming more frequent? In Jean Dierickx & Yvan Lebrun (eds.), *Linguistique contemporaine: homage à Eric Buyssens*. Brussels: Éditions de l'institut de sociologie de l'université libre, 39–46.
Giegerich, Heinz J. (2012). The morphology of *-ly* and the categorial status of 'adverbs' in English. *English Language and Linguistics* 16, 341–59.
Karlsson, Fred. (1999). *Finnish: An Essential Grammar*. 2nd ed. London: Routledge.
Kirchner, Robert & Elena Nicoladis. (2009). A level *playing-field*: Perceptibility and inflection in English compounds. *Canadian Journal of Linguistics/Revue Canadienne de linguistique* 54, 91–116.
Matthews, P.H. (1974). *Morphology*. Cambridge: Cambridge University Press.
Mutt, O. (1967). Some recent developments in the use of nouns as premodifiers in English. *Zeitschrift für Anglistik und Amerikanistik* 15, 401–8.
Pinker, Steven. (1999). *Words and Rules*. London: Weidenfeld & Nicolson.
Plank, F. (1994). Inflection and derivation. In Ron E. Asher (ed.), *The Encyclopedia of Language and Linguistics*. Oxford: Pergamon, vol. 3, 1671–8.
Rosenbach, Anette. (2006). Descriptive genitives in English: A case study on constructional gradience. *English Language and Linguistics* 10, 71–118.
Sulkala, Helena & Merja Karjalainenen. (1992). *Finnish*. London: Routledge.
Zwicky, Arnold M. & Geoffrey K. Pullum. (1983). Cliticization vs. inflection: English *n't*. *Language* 59, 502–13.

28   Reflections on Canonical Form

Canonical form is not something that is much discussed in present-day morphology, though it was familiar in the 1950s (see Hockett 1958). Part of the reason for the notion being ignored is probably that it has been replaced by arguments based on prototypes. Canonical form, though, may be worthy of some rehabilitation, since it allows us to focus on form rather than on the range of factors that make something prototypical in its category. A reformulation in other terms would be perfectly possible, but might not add much.

The notion of canonical form is that certain word-parts have typical shapes in different languages. For instance, although there are other patterns, there is a familiar pattern in Arabic in which the root is made up of three consonants, so that *katab* 'he wrote', *maktuub* 'office, writing place' and *kitaab* 'book' all share the root *KTB*, to do with writing.

Part of the reason that so many 'embellished clippings' (Bauer and Huddleston 2002) are two syllables long in English may be that there is a canonical form of two syllables for a basic word in English (though we would need rather more evidence to elevate this assumption to the nature of a hypothesis). Relevant words are *Aussie, cauli, drongo, Maccas* (this is what the hamburger restaurant McDonald's is called in Australia), *muso, piggie, preggers* and so on. However, there is one place in English where the idea of a canonical form really does seem to play a clear role.

Prefixes in English contain at least one whole syllable. They may contain more than one syllable (*epi-, mega-, mini-, super-* and, if you think these are prefixes, *cardio-, electro-, syntactico-*). Prefixes do not contain less than a syllable. In case this seems obvious, consider suffixes in English, which can contain just consonants, in words like *cats, loved, tenth*. It is worthy of comment that we do not have prefixes of this form.

Therefore, some morphological puzzles of English which will be illustrated immediately below do not contain single-consonant prefixes, because a prefix must contain a whole syllable and not just a consonant. The most often cited example here is that if we look at *ear* and *hear*, it might be thought that there is a prefix *h-* which creates verbs from nouns (even though there is no verb **heye*). Similarly, the relationship between *roquet* and *croquet* is not a matter of a prefix

28 Canonical Form

(it is not even clear what the prefix would mean in this instance). The relationship between *melt* and *smelt* in the sense of smelting ore) is also excluded, although there is an etymological link here. And the relationship between *ethane* and *methane* (or *ethanol* and *methanol*) is not a matter of a prefix *m-* (etymologically, there are distinct Greek elements *eth-* and *meth-* here). The four pairs cited here do at least have some meaning to relate them (however obscure); an indefinite number of other pairs of English have a putative prefix of non-canonical form and no serious meaning correlation: *owl* and *cowl*; *oast* and *toast*; *ray* and *pray*; *awe* and *flaw*. Perhaps most interesting, though, is that if we accept this conclusion, then the *shm-* that we find in (American English) *school-shmool, professor-shmofessor* (see Bauer et al. 2013: 413 and Section 24.2 in the present book) is not a prefix, but some other kind of word-formation – probably fixed consonantism associated with reduplication.

Another place where we might make appeal to canonical form is in the consonants used in suffixes. The consonant phonemes of English are set out below, as if they were set out in the chart of the International Phonetic Association, with places of articulation shown by the columns, manners of articulation shown by the rows, and voicing shown by position in the cell, voiceless consonants on the left, voiced on the right.

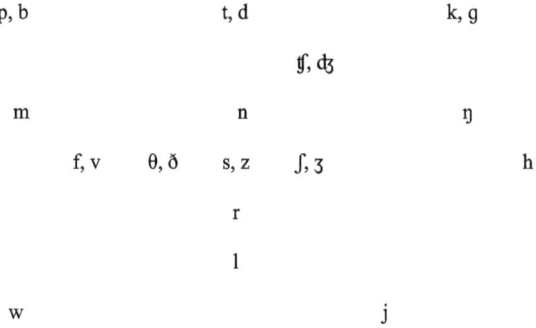

Now I want to consider some sets of affixes of English. Precisely what the inflectional affixes of English are is slightly controversial (see Section 27.2). The adverbial *-ly* in words like *apparently* is much discussed, and the ordinal *-th* in words like *ninth* is a possibility. The *-st* in *lovest* and the *-t* in *willt* have now vanished, as has *-eth* in the third-person singular of the present tense. The suffixes below are generally agreed to be inflectional.

> *-ed* (/t/, /d/, /ɪd/), *-s* (/s/, /z/, /ɪz/), the plural marker, *-er* (/ə(r)/), the comparative marker, *-est*, the superlative marker, *-en* and *-ren*, plural markers, *-en*, a past participle marker, *-s*, the third-person singular of the present tense, and *-ing*

220   Part VII Questions Involving Inflection

Just below, the consonant table is repeated, but this time those consonants found in the inflectional affixes are highlighted, and those mentioned in potentially inflectional suffixes are dimmed.

Consonants from inflectional suffixes

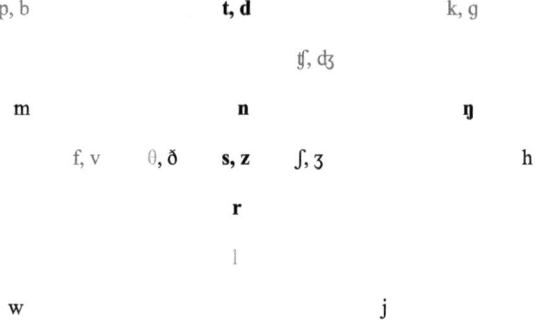

A glance at this version of the chart makes it perfectly clear that the /ŋ/ in *-ing* is way out of line. All the other consonants in inflection are alveolar – and even if we included old forms like *-eth* in *maketh*, they would be coronal (articulated with the tip and/or blade of the tongue).

What happens if, instead of looking at inflectional suffixes, we look at derivational suffixes? Here we must distinguish between those which are native to English, and those which have been borrowed, usually from French, sometimes from Latin or Greek (even then, often via French). The latter list is the longer one, and probably not a closed list. Both types are listed below.

> major native derivational suffixes: -dom (kingdom), -en (leaden), -er (killer), -ful (hopeful), -hood (neighbourhood), -ish (greenish), -less (useless), -ling (duckling), -ly (friendly), -ness (brightness), -ship (citizenship), -some (fulsome), -ster (youngster), -ter (laughter), -th (warmth), -ward(s) (backward(s)), -y (chilly)

> major borrowed derivational suffixes: -able (presentable), -age (marriage), -al (parental), -an (African), -ana (Victoriana), -ant (attendant), -ar (uvular), -ation (civilization), -ee (employee), -ese (journalese), -esque (Disneyesque), -ess (duchess), -ette (usher-ette), -ic (telepathic), -ify (justify), -ist (specialist), -ity (serenity), -ive (active), -ize (lionize), -let (piglet), -nik (folknik), -or (conductor), -ous (zealous), -y (telepathy)

If we now repeat the consonant table again with the consonants from these two lists highlighted, it will become clear that rather more consonants have been allowed in, and that there is no longer a clear-cut restriction. However, if we weight the various consonants by the number of times they recur in affixes, the same set would still be the most heavily weighted ones.

Consonants from native suffixes

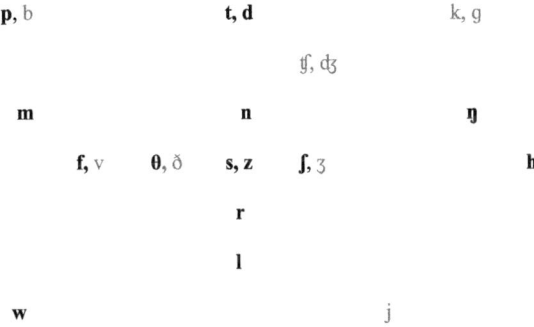

Consonants from borrowed suffixes

p, b		t, d		k, g	
		tʃ, dʒ			
m		n		ŋ	
	f, v	θ, ð	s, z	ʃ, ʒ	h
		r			
		l			
w			j		

If we move on and look at prefixes, there is even less pattern. It is not obviously possible to give a definitive list of prefixes (even native ones, because the status of things like *by-* may be unclear), but there do not appear to be motivated gaps in the consonants that may appear in them. Some prefixes are listed below to make the point, and only /ð/ seems to be systematically excluded. This is just one way in which prefixes are more word-like than suffixes.

Some illustrative prefixes of English

a- (atelic), ambi- (ambidextrous), ante- (antediluvian), arch- (arch-enemy), be- (bewitch), circum- (circumpolar), crypto- (crypto-communist), deca- (decapod), dis- (dislike), em- (embed), endo- (endocentric), extra- (extraordinary), giga- (gigabyte), hemi- (hemisphere), hepta- (heptagon), hyper- (hyperactive), multi- (multilingual), para- (para-legal), proto- (proto-language), quadr- (quadruped), step- (step-father), theo- (theocentric), vice- (vice-regal), with- (withhold), yotta- (yottabyte), zetta- (zettabyte).

If we conclude that the initial *s-* in *smelt* is not a prefix because of its form, we must also ask whether *-ing* is an inflectional suffix, since its form makes it appear an unsuitable member of that class. The argument for *-ing* being inflectional is that it meets the criteria for an inflectional affix: it is formally regular, it is semantically regular, it is productive, it does not change word-class, and it realizes one of the markers of tense/aspect, which are otherwise considered to be inflectional because they are required by the grammatical structure of the sentence. But this characterization is limited to the use of *-ing* that we find in examples like the following.

> I am enjoying retirement.
>
> She is managing well under the circumstances.
>
> It is raining.

The suffix *-ing* also occurs in two very different functions: creating adjectives and creating nouns.

> *Creating adjectives*
> A very interesting book.
> A rather surprising suggestion.
> Breaking news.
> This wine is disgusting.
>
> *Creating nouns*
> This building was designed by Sir Christopher Wren.
> His building so close to the boundary was illegal.
> Their constant moaning annoys me.
> Their accidentally killing the bird upset me.

The best way of dealing with these forms in a grammar is not agreed upon. There are several possibilities, not all equally attractive. Among the possibilities are (a) assume three homophonous affixes *-ing*, (b) view *-ing* as being a word-class changing inflectional affix, (c) see the adjectival and nominal uses of *-ing* as being derived by conversion from the verbal *-ing* form, (d) see the participle as being a separate word-class from noun, verb or adjective. All of these solutions have problems associated with them.

Among the problems is that the various *-ing* adjectives and nouns do not behave in the same way. Some of the adjectives allow premodification and give rise to *-ly* adverbials, others do not; some of the nouns allow modification by adjectives, while in other constructions they are modified by adverbs; some of the nouns act like action nominalizations, others do not. Some of this is predictable grammatical behaviour, some of it is lexical. For instance, adjectival *-ing* is less productive than nominal or verbal *-ing*.

An alternative way of looking at this is that *-ing* is fundamentally nominal (as is its origin), and fundamentally an action nominalization. Nouns can be used attributively and in predicative position, where they overlap in function with adjectives. The use of *-ing* to mark the continuous form then has to be described as a construction involving a nominal which has become idiomatized and so is not readily analysable in its modern form. Under such an analysis, *-ing* would no longer be an inflectional marker, and the lower productivity of adjectival uses of *-ing* than on nominal and verbal uses would be explained. This is a lot to derive from the canonical form of inflectional affixes, but the analysis might nevertheless have some internal, as well as historical, merit.

We can also look at the canonical form of words. It was suggested above that it might be the case that words are typically two syllables long in English. If we look at the words containing just one meaningful element (that is, a stem, but no affixes, so monomorphic or monomorphemic words), and look at the most common words in English, the average length of such a word is 1.4 syllables, with adjectives and verbs slightly shorter than nouns. Given that, by Zipf's law, rarer words will be longer than common ones, an approximation of two-syllable words being some sort of default length makes sense. If we look at derived forms (not compounds) in the first 1,000 most frequent words, in which a separation into base and affix makes clear sense in modern English, then the average length of the derivative is 2.94 syllables. We can deduce that, in common words, derivatives of the required nature usually contain only one affix, adding about one syllable to the length. Again, rarer words are likely to be longer. If inflected forms are also counted, the length of the words observed will also be slightly longer. These figures are made less reliable by the number of words, usually of Greek and Latin origin, which do not conform to the criteria used for derivatives here, and which are often longer. Given the existence of words like *institutionalization*, or *antidisestablishmentarianism*, it is clear that the average or expected length can be exceeded by a considerable amount, but the rarity of such forms indicates that the expected range is between about one and six syllables, with very few words going beyond those limits.

Challenge

Make a case for any one of the following possibilities: (a) that all *-ing* forms are verbal, and other word-classes are derived from that; (b) that all *-ing* forms are adjectival, and all other uses are derive from that; (c) that all-*ing* forms are nominal and that all other uses are derived from that; (d) that the three *-ing* suffixes are homophonous but distinct suffixes; (e) that one of the three uses of *-ing* is derived by conversion from one of the others. Compare and contrast any two of these solutions.

References

Bauer, Laurie & Rodney Huddleston. (2002). Lexical word-formation. In Rodney Huddleston & Geoffrey K. Pullum, *The Cambridge Grammar of the English Language*, Cambridge: Cambridge University Press, 1621–1721.

Bauer, Laurie, Rochelle Lieber & Ingo Plag, (2013). *The Oxford Reference Guide to English Morphology*. Oxford: Oxford University Press.

Hockett, Charles F. (1958). *A Course in Modern Linguistics*. New York: Macmillan.

29 Reflections on the Spread of Regular Inflection to Simple and Derived Forms

29.1 Introduction

If you have a noun like *mill* and from that you make a compound like *windmill*, then you expect that both *mill* and *windmill* will make their plural in the same way, by adding an *-s*: *mills*, *windmills*. What may be less clear is why you should have this expectation, except, perhaps, that it is clearly the majority pattern. Does the *-s* on *windmills* arise because the plural of *mill* is *mills*, does it arise because it is the plural of a compound, does it arise because complex words are inflectionally more regular than simpler words, or is there something else going on?

We can answer some of these questions fairly simply by giving examples. If we have *one tooth* and *two teeth*, but *one sabre-tooth* and *two sabre-tooths*, then it is clear that the plural of the compound does not follow automatically from the plural form of the second element. If we have *one wolf, two wolves* and *one timber wolf, two timber wolves*, it is clear that compounds do not automatically take a regular plural, or that complex words are automatically inflectionally more regular than simple ones. There is something more complicated going on. Various explanations have been given which are supposed to cover at least some of the cases. But if we look at what is going on here in detail, we find that there are no rules, and scarcely even tendencies. Somehow, our morphological rules (even the inflectional ones) have to be able to cope with irregularity.

29.2 Figurative Uses

When the personal computer was invented and was driven by an instrument known as a *mouse*, it immediately became important to know what the plural of *mouse* was. In the first years after the introduction of these tools, they were often referred to as *computer mouses*. More recently, *computer mice* seems to be preferred. The explanation that is often offered here is that figurative uses of a word can be inflected regularly, even if the word usually inflects irregularly. For this to be a reasonable explanation, there must be other supporting examples, and there are.

Bauer (2009) cites the following examples:

> Todd ... didn't need wilder gooses to chase. (Kevin J. Anderson and Doug Benson. 1995. *Ill Wind*. New York: Tom Doherty, p. 381)

> If it turns out that Qatar is innocent ... our gooses could be cooked. (John Sandford. 2001. *Chosen Prey*. London: Simon & Schuster, p. 300)

> And that's when those louses / Go back to their spouses / Diamonds are a girl's best friend. (Jule Styne, from *Gentlemen Prefer Blondes*, 1953)

The difficulty with these examples is that they do not seem to cover all the possible nouns. Although we cannot prove much from failing to find a particular example, it would seem odd to say *The new laws have no tooths*, where *tooth* is being used metaphorically, or to talk about *Chessmans*. Yet *Walkmans* was the plural of *Walkman* for many speakers when the device was first introduced. All we can say is that there are examples where figurative usage seems to license a regular plural for a normally irregularly inflected noun, certainly not that this is a rule of English morphology.

29.3   Names

If you visited Disneyland or Disney World, you might find yourself in a shop surrounded by stuffed toys, all representations of Disney characters. Under such conditions, you might say something like *Look at all these Donald Ducks!*, but what would you say if the character was Mickey Mouse? Speakers do not know. Both *Mickey Mice* and *Mickey Mouses* are found. We might argue that the regular plural is possible because these are not real mice, but involve a figurative use of the word *mouse*. A more likely explanation is that the relevant factor is that *Mickey Mouse* is a name.

Pinker (1999: 171–2) cites the example of the *Toronto Maple Leafs*, a hockey team, and sees this as a matter of seeing accumulations as different from the set of individuals that make up the accumulation. But he also cites the *Timberwolves*, a basketball team. He suggests it depends where you start: if you start from *Maple Leaf*, you get *Maple Leafs*, but if you start from *Timberwolves*, you can get one *Timberwolf* without having a team of *Timberwolfs*. The argument seems to allow for whatever outcome you find, which may be what is needed because there is certainly variation. Pinker (1999: 162) cites an example from J.R.R. Tolkien's *The Fellowship of the Ring*, where characters argue as to whether the Proudfoot family should be called the *Proudfoots* or the *Proudfeet*. This leads us to an alternative explanation, namely that since a Proudfoot is not a foot, that is that the compound is exocentric, it is the exocentricity that is crucial.

29.4   Exocentric Constructions

There is a now old-fashioned slang term meaning 'policeman', a *flatfoot*. But if you have multiple police officers, what do you then call them if you want to use that term? You can have one *sabretooth*, but usually two or more *sabretooths*, even if that animal has many *teeth*. Some real examples are provided below, some using irregular morphology, some using regular morphology.

> She's running around with lowlives. (Bill Pronzini. 2008. *The Laughter of Dead Kings*. London: Constable, p. 35)

> Native Americans have been living in this region for over ten thousand years. The Cheyenne, Kiowa, Shoshone, Blackfeet and, more recently, the Crows. (James Rollins. 2011. *The Devil Colony*. New York: William Morrow, p. 372)

> Can you do others? ... I mean animals, you know, or still lifes. Lives. (A.J. Finn. *The Woman in the Window*. New York: William Morrow, p. 90)

> "Isn't that what they call cops", he continued. "Flat foots?" (Nora Roberts. 1990. *Public Secrets*. New York: Bantam, e-version, p. 192)

Bauer (2009) gives examples from dictionaries – the *OED* and Gove (1966) – with umlaut and fricative-voicing plurals. The examples are reproduced below.

broadleaf	broadleafs
cloverleaf	cloverleafs, cloverleaves
coltsfoot	coltsfoots
cottonmouth	cottonmouths /ðz/
flatfoot	flatfoots, flatfeet
frogmouth	frogmouths /θs/, /ðz/
goosefoot	goosefoots ('plant'), goosefeet ('hinge, junction, etc.')
lowlife	lowlifes, lowlives
tenderfoot	tenderfoots, tenderfeet
waterleaf	waterleafs

Again, we see variation, with the regular plural a possibility, but not a necessity in such environments.

29.5   Conversion/Zero-Derivation as a Circuit Breaker

The verb *ring*, as of a bell, is irregular and its past tense is *rang*. However, if *ring* means 'to put a ring round' as in *ring the city* or *ring a pigeon*, then the past tense is regular, and is *ringed*. Kiparsky (1982: 12) draws attention to such verbs, and suggests that when the verb is derived from a noun (by a process of conversion/zero-derivation), the verb is always regular. That is, we have a process which we can write as follows, where the Ø-symbol is used to indicate the intervening conversion/zero-derivation, and where the output verb is always regular:

$$\text{ring}]_N + \emptyset > \text{ring}]_V$$

Kiparsky cites verbs such as *ink*, *link*, *wing* as being particularly significant here, since there is an opposing tendency to make verbs of this phonological make-up irregular. Pinker (1999: 158) adds more examples, but seeks out examples where the noun in the base of the process has a homophonous verb which is usually irregular. It is irrelevant to the question whether to *deflea* (an animal) sounds like *flee* which has an irregular past. On this basis, Pinker adds denominal verbs like *brake* ('apply the brakes'), *spit* ('put on a spit'), *string* (as in *to string beans* 'to remove the strings from' or *to string a violin* 'add strings to') all of which have regular past tense and past participle forms in line with the prediction. (There is a problem that the verb *string* as in *string a violin* also comes from a noun, but has a past *strung*; in the seventeenth century the verb was regular.) Note also the implication that the noun *ride* must come from the verb *ride*, rather than vice versa, because *ride* is an irregular verb. The same is true of the nouns *bid*, *bite*, *break*, *drink* and so on, and this probably feels right in terms of the semantics of the noun–verb pair.

Kiparsky pushes this further. Most complex verbs (whether made up of a preposition, which may be viewed as a prefix, and a verb or a noun and a verb or of two verbs) inflect in the same way as the verbal (second) element. *Outgrow* has *outgrown* because *grow* is the head of the new verb and inherits its inflection; *sunburn* inflects like *burn*; *cough-laugh* inflects like *laugh*. So *understand* has *understood*, like *stand* has *stood*, even though there is no literal standing. The metaphorical use of *stand* in *understand* is not enough to give it a regular inflection, and we do not, except possibly in child language, get *understanded. Yet the past tense of the verb *grandstand* is *grandstanded* (Kiparsky 1982: 12). But the verb *grandstand* is based on the noun *grandstand*, and so it functions just like *ring* (the city) mentioned above. Its past tense is *grandstanded*. In other words, we get the following pattern, where the Ø resets the inflection to regular inflection:

$$\text{stand}]_V > \text{stand}]_N + \text{grand} > \text{grandstand}]_N + \emptyset > \text{grandstand}]_V$$

Unfortunately, Kiparsky does not give other examples. But there are relevant cases.

blue-light]ₙ + Ø > blue-light]ᵥ   past participle *blue-lighted*
free-fall]ₙ + Ø > free-fall]ᵥ   past participle *free-fallen*
highlight]ₙ + Ø > highlight]ᵥ   past participle *highlighted* or *highlit*
jacklight]ₙ + Ø > jacklight]ᵥ   past participle *jacklighted*
moonlight]ₙ + Ø > moonlight]ᵥ   past participle *moonlighted* 'worked extra hours'
or *moonlit* 'illuminated by the moon'

searchlight]ₙ + Ø > searchlight]ᵥ   past participle *searchlighted*
spotlight]ₙ + Ø > spotlight]ᵥ   past participle *spotlit* or *spotlighted*
test-drive]ₙ + Ø > test-drive]ᵥ   past participle *test-driven*

The fact that there is not a wider set of appropriate verbs is unfortunate, and may invalidate the data; but the examples here (all from the *OED*) do not provide strong support for Kiparsky's position.

29.6 Back-Formation

One potential cause, which does not seem to have received previous comment, is back-formation. The verb *creep out* has a regular past tense and past participle, *creeped out*, which might be considered odd in that the past tense and past participle of *creep* are *crept*. But *creep out* does not seem to derive from the verb *creep*, from which its meaning cannot be deduced; rather it seems to derive from the noun *creeps* (as in *It gives me the creeps*) or the adjective *creepy*. Since a final suffix is deleted to give *creep out*, we appear to have back-formation here. The same might be true of *moonlight* ('work extra hours off the books for cash in hand'). Although the *OED* sees this as being derived from the noun *moonlight*, an alternative analysis is that it comes from *moonlighter*, by back-formation. This accounts for the meaning and for the usual regular form of the verb in this sense, although *moonlit* is sometimes found in this reading. Since back-formation is a relatively rare formation pattern, examples where this hypothesis can be tested are hard to find, but it seems plausible.

> Clury, who moonlit as a private investigator, had been loved by Jake. (William Bayer. 1994. *Mirror Maze*. New York: Villard, p. 36)

> Tracey would have match-maked her socks off. (Milly Johnson. 2019. *The Magnificent Mrs Mayhew*. London: Simon & Schuster, pp. 260–1)

29.7 Jokes

The native words of English that take ablaut plurals are all monosyllabic, if we take it that *woman* is etymologically a compound of *man*. The monosyllabic native words that end in <ouse> /aʊs/ are few in number, and most of them have irregular plurals.

   grouse grouse ('game bird')
   grouse grouses ('complaint')
   house houses (/haʊzɪz/ in standard English)
   louse lice
   mouse mice

Blouse (pronounced with /z/ in Britain) is French. *Scouse* is usually an adjective, but can also be a noun; its origin in *lobscouse* is obscure, but may be from Dutch. This leaves *spouse*, which, while it is also French in origin, no longer has the French form.

Given these parallels, we would not necessarily expect a new monosyllabic word with a spelling ending in <ouse> to take an umlaut plural, but the umlaut is the most common plural within this very restricted paradigm. Finding *spice* as the plural of *spouse* is thus, not entirely surprising, and the fact that *spice* has a homophone meaning 'condiment, like pepper' is irrelevant. That *spice* is not the usual plural of *spouse* is not entirely surprising, either. When it is used, it is always a joke plural (like *meeces* as the plural of *mouse*). As *meeces* shows, jokes do not have to conform to ordinary rules or patterns of formation, though they are better jokes the nearer they come to conforming to some pattern: conjugating *think* as *think* / *thank* / *thunk* is funny because it reflects an existing pattern and clashes with other lexemes in different forms.

This is different from the other examples in that the regular plural is not the one chosen for the joke, but we do find regular and irregular morphology in alternation with each other.

29.8 Conclusion

Although the regular inflection of forms which might be expected to show irregular inflection can be explained in many instances, by the factors mentioned above, all of them show that we cannot see this as an absolute rule, only as a tendency of different strengths in the different cases. These factors may allow regular inflection, but they do not demand it. This allows us to see a pattern, but does not seem to be compatible with the notion of a rule, since rule usually implies that what the rule describes is, at the very least, always available.

Challenge

There are not many verbs like *ring* which are irregular in some meanings, but regular when they are derived from a noun. How many can you find (including compound verbs)? Are there any with an overt nominalization marker? Are there any which become adjectives rather than nouns?

References

Bauer, Laurie. (2009). Facets of English plural morphology. In *Ročenka textů zahraničních profesorů / The Annual of Texts by Foreign Guest Professors*. Prague: Philosophical Faculty of Charles University Prague, 9–21.

Gove, Philip (ed.). (1966). *Webster's Third New International Dictionary*. Springfield, MA: Merriam-Webster.

Kiparsky, Paul. (1982). Lexical morphology and phonology. In Linguistic Society of Korea (ed.), *Linguistics in the Morning Calm*. Seoul: Hanshin, 3–91.

OED. The Oxford English Dictionary [online]. oed.com

Pinker, Steven. (1999). *Words and Rules*. London: Weidenfeld & Nicolson.

30 Conclusion

30.1 Introduction

This book has covered a wide variety of topics, not necessarily always from the same point of view. Some features will have been recurrent, though: a certain scepticism about the way in which theories assume languages work, where more data can show that things are not as straightforward as the theory suggests (see, for example, Chapters 5 and 15); a desire to clarify what individual technical terms mean (see, for example, Chapters 9 and 22), not necessarily to be prescriptive, but to point out that the same term does not always mean the same thing and that clarification may be helpful; an attempt to distinguish between things that always happen and things that may happen (see Chapter 29) because of a conviction that word-formation is extremely flexible in the way that it works; an attempt to point out areas where accurate descriptions are difficult. A handful of topics are so general that they cut across individual presentations and recur, and some of these are considered below.

30.2 Rules

What does a linguistic rule look like? In the late 1950s a rule was phrased as an instruction: given a particular input, this procedure is carried out, with an inevitable output. But such a view cannot hold for long. There are too many places where there are options as to what the output might be. Given a verb like *present*, we can say *He presented her with a medal, He presented a medal to her, A medal was presented to her, She was presented with a medal* and so on. Knowing what the verb is, what was presented and the gender of the presenter and presentee is not sufficient to determine the syntactic output. And while we might attempt to narrow matters down by looking at the information flow, for instance, a simple input–output view of a rule is of limited value. So then we say that the output can be anything that is permitted by the rules. Active and passive are both permitted, the subject of the passive sentence can be the person to whom something is presented or the object which is presented, and so on. As long as the output is licensed by a rule, it is fine. In either case, though, the rules are coercive. They restrict the possible outputs. Such a view makes sense: you cannot do whatever you like in organizing words into sentences, there are strong constraints, and errors can lead to incomprehensibility.

One of the things we learn by considering word-formation is that the outputs need not be something that is predetermined. The word *catanality* ('what cats have instead of personality') cannot be predicted from what we know about extant patterns of English word-formation, yet is attested. The verb *well-pay* (see Section 2.5) may not even be grammatical. Variability in outputs used to be described in terms of variable rules (following the work of Labov), but variable rules are not predictive, they are simply a descriptive statistical analysis of observed patterns in the past, so they cannot be used to tell us which form can arise, which means that, beyond a certain point, they do not help with what we find in word-formation. Analogy (see Chapter 8) might work, but nobody knows precisely how it works or how it can be instigated or constrained. At this stage, I see analogy working within paradigms as being a very promising way of making progress in word-formation and explaining the developments that arise, but that, too, will have weaknesses.

30.3   Ludicity, Technicality and Productivity

Catanality and *well-pay* illustrate the very strong ludic element that pervades the creation of new words, but of course there is also a lot of innovation in the technical and scientific areas, as new words are invented for new entities, new procedures, new theoretical concepts and the like. What these have in common is that the formations are considered and consciously formed. There is a line of thought in morphological studies, going back to Schultink (1961), which says that consciously formed words do not illustrate productivity. But sometimes the consciously formed words use the patterns that are also available for unconscious formations so that the distinction is hard to apply. There are certainly many unconsciously formed words produced by speakers, although the process by which they operate is not clear – which brings us back to the whole question of rules and analogies (see Sections 2.6 and 2.8).

These examples follow the normal anglophone tradition in word-formation studies of looking at the patterns of word-formation and what they mean. In the onomasiological approach to word-formation the view is different. As neatly encapsulated by Carstairs-McCarthy (2010: 258), the onomasiological approach turns

the world upside down. That is, the preoccupation of [scholars in this tradition] is not with structures and the meanings associated with them, but rather with meanings and the structures used to express them.

This throws a different light on productivity, and may also imply that all word-formation is consciously produced in that there is always a choice between a derivative, a compound, a phrase, etc. as a way of naming something. It also suggests a reason why rhyme (see Chapter 17) or alliteration may be relevant forces in word-formation, though it still requires the speaker to know, in some way or another, what patterns can be used to produce new words.

30.4 The Instability of Theoretical Constructs

Our inevitable experience of education leads us to believe that theoretical constructs and processes associated with them are well defined and fixed. It would probably be counterproductive for teachers to say we have a particular entity which we can define in any one of four different ways with different theoretical implications. Yet that is precisely the reality. It just requires sophistication in dealing with the subject matter to be able to see the differences, and evaluate the different variants. For the morpheme, we find Mugdan (1986) providing several different views of the nature of the morpheme, and we can still ask questions about whether further constraints are needed. There is less in the literature on the nature of the lexeme, but still no clear agreement (see Chapter 9). And a process like blocking raises almost as many questions as it provides answers (see Chapter 5). Theoretical constructs evolve, are refined, are sometimes rejected, and even then refuse to go away. Some of this is simply a by-product of our naming techniques. We do not want to go through the hassle of creating a new term for every minor adjustment we make to an existing idea, since a plethora of quasi-synonymous technical terms is difficult to deal with, and sometimes, when scholars do create new terms, it is not helpful. To my mind, this is the case for Allen's (1978) term the ISA criterion (*a side door ISA door*) to replace the established linguistic term of 'hyponymy' and related terms.

30.5 The Difficulty of Dealing with Data

Nigel Fabb cites the late Morris Halle as having said that "data is overrated" (https://linguistics.mit.edu/hallememories/). I'm not sure I agree, but I certainly think that data is (to continue the number agreement) extremely difficult to evaluate. The huge increase in the amount of linguistic data available to us through the internet has advantages and disadvantages. On the plus side, there is far more unedited material available for perusal than there used to be, so that what can be found is far less uniform in its style level. On the downside, every piece of data now has to be evaluated: who wrote it, was the writer being serious (and does it matter), is a typographical error involved (see Section 2.5), was a lapse of memory involved? In word-formation we have to ask whether attestation implies existence, whether a new formation of a particular type indicates productivity, whether a pattern has been misinterpreted or not, and so on. Some of the examples I have cited in this book come from publishing houses that seem to be particularly innovation-friendly, and it might not be clear to what extent a particular editor is letting innovative uses through while another might remove them. Of course, it might just be that I enjoy reading authors who happen to publish with certain publishing houses. Whatever we might conclude, it is very comforting if the collected examples tell a coherent story, even if it is one which is restricted to particular genres.

30.6 Insecurity about Processes

Although we can see repeated patterns in word-formation, and we can make hypotheses about the way in which the members of the pattern arise, it is remarkable how often we do not really know how the processes work. Back-formation (see Chapter 21) is a classic example. We can see examples which fit our prejudices about the process of back-formation, but there is so much variation in what we see that it is difficult to be sure how speakers actually process it, either in production or in analysis. Conversion (see Chapter 20) is another such process. A rather different case is provided by coordinative compounds (see Chapter 22). We can find plenty of examples which the analyst can gloss as instances of coordination, but it is not always clear whether this gloss is justified in the broader scale of things. Is every instance that can be glossed with a coordinating conjunction necessarily a matter of coordination, or is there genuine ambiguity between glosses such as 'A and B' and 'an A which is a B'? And this is before we start to ask whether something is or is not a compound, a matter where the answer may depend upon the definition we happen to have chosen to work with – which may be inevitable, but casts doubt on the ability of linguists to judge matters of classification. The insecurity might, in the short term, be a good thing, in that it proves that scholars are trying to solve a problem, but we must assume that the ultimate aim is to remove the insecurity. Some do this by changing the definition (see Chapter 7), others do it by changing our view of how to classify (see Chapter 7). Both can be helpful. What we need is a coherent view of how the various parts of the whole fit together.

30.7 Fuzzy Grammar

This book is largely written from the point of view of someone who believes that grammatical categories need to be clearly distinct from each other: we should know whether we are dealing with a noun or an adjective, with inflection or derivation, with a compound or something else. At the same time, dissatisfaction with such a system has been expressed because it does not seem possible – either within English or across languages – to determine which side of the dividing line we find ourselves on or even, in some instances, if there is a dividing line. Whether we get to this point of view by dealing with prototypes, canonical categories, problems with defining categories or some other route, the result is the same: we may be clear about what the most central, typical, canonical examples of a category (noun, word, compound, inflection) are, but we have no good way of circumscribing the categories clearly when it comes to the more peripheral members or potential members of the category. We have entered the area of fuzzy grammar (Aarts et al. 2004). All the problems we have with categories and their inconsistent behaviour push is in the direction of fuzzy grammar. As Sapir (1921: 38) puts it, "all grammars leak" (although people interpret that comment in different ways). What makes this awkward is that it is hard to see just how to deal – whether in a formal way or in a more intuitive way – with a system that works in this way. Yet it is crucial that we should know how to do this if we are to make progress with describing the way language works.

30.8 Summing up

It will probably be obvious that, although this book happens to deal with word-formation, the concerns that arise when we consider word-formation recur in almost any other study of linguistic structure. Calude and Bauer (2022), for instance, deal in depth with cases where it is not clear what is happening to certain English constructions diachronically, and where we do not know how best to describe the structure of the language from a theoretical point of view. The examples considered are different, but the overarching concerns are often very similar. In this, the study of word-formation is simply the study of linguistic structure in one specific field, and studying English word-formation merely a way of restricting the scope of the enterprise.

Challenge

Choose any issue that has been raised in this book that you find to be particularly contentious. Why is it contentious? If you wanted to provide a solution to the issue, what information would you need? Does a definitive evidence-based answer seem possible? How should your answer help define a fruitful approach to the study of word-formation?

References

Allen, Margaret R. (1978). *Morphological investigations*. Unpublished PhD dissertation, University of Connecticut.

Bas Aarts, David Denison, Evelien Keizer & Gergana Popova (eds.). (2004). *Fuzzy Grammar: A Reader*. Oxford: Oxford University Press.

Calude, Andrea S. & Laurie Bauer. (2022). *Mysteries of English Grammar*. New York: Routledge.

Carstairs-McCarthy, Andrew. (2010). Review of Rochelle Lieber & Pavol Štekauer (eds.), 2009. *The Oxford Handbook of Compounding*. Oxford: Oxford University Press. *Word Structure* 3, 252–60.

Mugdan, Joachim. (1986). Was ist eigentlich ein Morphem? *Zeitschrift für Phonetik, Sprachwissenschaft und Kommunikationsforschung* 39, 29–52.

Sapir, Edward. (1921). *Language*. London: Hart-Davis.

Schultink, Henk. (1961). Produktiviteit als morfologisch fenomeen. *Forum der Letteren* 2, 110–25.

Index of Topics

abbreviation, 22
ablaut, 184, 187, 189, 191, 229
accidence. *See* inflection
acronym, 16, 22, 30, 37, 90, 91, 144
affix, 5, 57, 64, 71, 84
   apparent deletion of, 165
   borrowing of, 151
   boundary, 122
   competing, 45
   derivational, 107
   homonymy of, 28, 84, 98
   repetition of, 100
   sequence of, 97
affixation, 28, 29, 37, 59, 122
   cancellation of, 165
   to syntactic bases, 131–132
affixoid, 57
affix-telescoping, 97, 99
alliteration, 142, 234
allomorph, 4, 5, 19
allomorphy, 4, 5, 20, 29, 127
A-morphous Morphology, 13, 86
analogy, 53, 64–68, 85, 196, 233
analysability, 18, 99, 189
Andersen, Hans C., 158
apophony, 16, 191
Arabic, 90, 218
assonance, 142
availability, 29, 39, 43

back-formation, 16, 22, 44, 146, 164–167, 201, 229, 235
backronym, 144
bahuvrihi, 26
base, 57, 64, 67
blend, 22, 105, 145
blocking, 28, 43–46, 48, 50, 51, 234
   domain or type, 44
   individual or token, 43
   inflectional, 43
   lexical, 44

token, 47
type, 47
borrowing, 47, 123, 141, 148–151
bound variant. *See* allomorph

canonical form, 218
canonicity, 6, 236
Carroll, Lewis, 165
Chinese, 172
clipping, 16, 30, 37, 145
   embellished, 145, 218
coercion, 155, 161
Cognitive Linguistics, 6, 14, 84, 161
coinage, 45, 51, 64
collocation, 81
competition, 46–48
composition. *See* compounding
compound, 22, 36, 37, 58, 71, 110, 168, 193–204, 209, 210–215, 225, 235
   appositional, 104, 172
   clipping, 145
   coordinative, 103, 168–172, 197, 199, 235
   co-participant, 170
   elative, 198
   genuine. *See* compound, proper
   identical constituent or repeated element, 100, 180
   proper vs improper, 195
   synthetic, 37
   tautological, 91–92
   translative, 170
   verbal, 104, 166
compounding, 1, 30
connotation, 83
conscious formation, 65, 66, 233, 234
Construction Grammar, 14, 158
conversion, 1, 16, 22, 60, 155–162, 175, 201, 227–229, 235
   partial, 162
coordination, 110
   natural, 168

238

Index of Topics

corpus, 2, 20, 22, 81, 113, 139
cranberry morph. *See* morph, unique
creativity, 64

Danish, 27, 100, 133, 193, 194, 195, 196, 197, 198, 199, 200, 201, 202
decomposition, 111
degemination, 123
derivation, 1, 15–16, 30, 88, 175, 215–216, 220
derivative, 1
diachrony, 30, 54, 164
dictionary, 2, 20, 22, 41, 77, 78
diminutive, 140–141, 188, 209
Distributed Morphology, 6, 13, 83
Dutch, 93, 111, 138, 140, 193, 194, 195, 198, 199, 200, 201, 209, 230
dvandva, 170, 172

elsewhere condition, 43
endocentricity, 58, 102, 104
etymology, 19, 32, 164, 166, 188, 219
euphemism, 165
Exemplar Grammar, 14
exocentricity, 26, 102, 103, 171, 194, 197, 227
expletive insertion, 24
extender, 5, 125

familiarity, 47
Faroese, 196, 198, 199, 201
figure of speech, 6, 22, 31, 37, 48, 103, 160, 169, 225
Finnish, 209
formative, 71
French, 91, 92, 104, 133, 134, 146, 148, 149, 151, 165, 188, 190, 193, 204, 220, 230
frequency, 20, 23, 46, 47, 78, 122, 125, 139, 141
Frisian, 194, 196
fuzzy grammar, 235–236

German, 24, 27, 30, 50, 107, 111, 140, 148, 151, 176
Germanic languages, 100, 133, 171, 193–204
Gothic, 200
grammeme, 71
Greek, 69, 120, 138, 148, 149, 150, 151, 193, 199, 212, 219, 220, 223

headedness, 6, 27, 58, 91, 100, 102–108, 110, 135, 158, 190, 193, 196, 202, 228. *See also* right-hand head rule
homonymy, 78, 84, 98
homophony, 150, 230
hyperonym, 102. *See also* superordinate
hyphen, 133
hypocoristic, 140

hyponymy, 26, 58, 59, 81, 82, 103, 104, 171, 234
hypostatization, 81

Icelandic, 193, 196, 202
idiom, 72, 87, 174, 176
infixation, 2
inflection, 15–16, 30, 44, 69, 88, 209–217, 219, 225–230
initialism, 1, 16, 24, 69, 91
institutionalization, 17, 31, 43, 45, 51
internal modification, 16
Irish, 141
Italian, 50, 140
item-familiarity, 39, 65, 99

Japanese, 2
Jerome, Jerome K., 28, 132

Kristofferson, Kris, 78

Latin, 69, 71, 86, 97, 148, 150, 151, 190, 193, 199, 212, 220, 223
Lear, Edward, 81
lemma, 16
level ordering, 43, 119, 215. *See also* Lexical Morphology
lexeme, 1, 14, 16, 69–73, 88, 127, 134, 234
  phrasal, 71
lexical item, 72, 145
Lexical Morphology, 6, 97, 119, 120, 212
lexicalization, 17, 119, 128, 160
lexicography, 16, 31
linking element, 148, 195, 196, 197
listedness, 72
listeme, 71, 72
ludicity, 41, 52, 66, 99, 142, 164, 189, 233

malapropism, 78
Mandarin, 35
Māori, 16, 93
metonymy, 84, 103, 160–161. *See also* figure of speech
Milton, John, 188
morph, 4, 5, 123
  unique, 27
morpheme, 3–5, 35, 102, 139, 223, 234
morphology, 1, 19, 30–31, 51, *et passim*
  expressive, 24
  marginal, 24
morphome, 128
morphophonemics, 21, 119–130, 144
motivation
  ablaut, 182
  rhyme, 180
multiple word expression (MWE), 17, 31, 48, 69, 134

name, 61, 93, 226
Natural Generative Phonology, 19
neoclassical compound, 16, 148. *See also* neoclassical formation
neoclassical formation, 36, 67, 84, 113, 148–151
no-phrase constraint, 28
norm, 50–51, 53–54, 128
Norwegian, 194
novelty, 39–41

onomasiology, 48, 233
onomatopoeia, 138
opacity, 18
Optimality Theory, 215
overabundance, 44

Panini, 13, 170
paradigm, 6, 14, 53, 78, 165, 233
participle, 15, 21, 62, 127, 210, 222
particle, 174
periphrasis, 45
phonaestheme, 16, 138–140, 190
phrasal verb, 16, 24, 69
plural modifier, 213
polysemy, 84
potentiation, 29
pre-emption. *See* blocking
prefix and prefixation, 1, 2, 14, 16, 20, 22, 29, 99, 124, 218. *See also* affixation
productivity, 2, 17, 20–21, 32, 39, 47, 50, 99, 132, 139, 151, 190, 233. *See also* availability, profitability
   marginal, 20
profitability, 39
prototype, 5, 58, 218, 236

reanalysis, 166
recursion, 97–101
redundancy, 20, 47, 90
reduplication, 2, 16, 107, 179–184, 219
repeated morph constraint, 28
resonance, 139
rhyme, 141–142, 234
right-hand head rule, 28, 102, 103, 105, 172, 196
root, 209
   bound, 112, 113
rule, 14, 17, 25, 31, 52, 120, 129, 139, 230, 232–233
   occupied slot. *See* blocking
   redundancy, 19
   variable, 233
   via-rule, 19
Runyon, Damon, 165
Russian, 50

Sanskrit, 170
separable vs inseparable verbs, 201
separation constraint, 29, 87

Shakespeare, William, 120
slang, 78
sound symbolism, 138
Spanish, 93, 104, 140
spelling, 14, 15, 20, 24, 61, 121, 122, 123, 126, 129, 133, 144–146
split morphology, 15, 17, 210
stratum, 119
structuralism, 13
suffix and suffixation, 1, 2, 16, 22, 71, 97, 107, 113, 209, 218, 219. *See also* affixation
superordinate, 25, 81, 82, 102
suppletion, 43
Swahili, 2
Swedish, 27, 133, 138, 196
synchrony, 17, 164
synecdoche, 103
synonymy, 43

Tariana, 209
tautology, 90, 100
Tolerance Principle, 139
Tolkien, J.R.R., 27, 226
transparency, 18
transposition, 36, 87

unitary base hypothesis, 28, 59
unitary output hypothesis, 28
univerbation, 67
Usage-Based Linguistics, 14

velar softening, 122, 144
Vietnamese, 172

Welsh, 93, 209
West Greenlandic, 35
Wodehouse, P.G., 78
word, 1, 14–15, 35, 69, 168, *et passim*
   actual, 51
   grammatical, 71
   lexical, 71
   manufacture, 146
   morphosyntactic, 14
   phonological, 14, 112
   potential, 51–53
   virtual, 51
word manufacture, 52
Word-and-Paradigm, 86
word-based hypothesis, 29
word-based morphology, 86
word-class, 59, 84, 102, 156, 198
word-form, 1, 70, 71, 72
word-formation, 1, 13, 14, 15, 32, 48, 160, 175, 232, *et passim*

Yiddish, 181

Zipf's law, 37, 223

Index of English Word-Forming Elements

a-[$_{A, ADV}$], 29, 114
a-/an-[$_{NEGATIVE}$], 221
-able, 98, 220
-ac, 189
-age, 50, 85, 87, 151, 220
-al]$_A$, 84, 97, 98, 149, 220. *See also* -ial]$_A$
-al]$_N$, 84
ambi-, 221
-an]$_A$, 98, 125, 220
-ana, 220
-ant, 220
ante-, 115, 221
anti-, 112, 113, 114
-ar, 84, 98, 220
arch-, 221
-ary, 98
-ate]$_V$, 19, 29, 71, 97, 98
-ation, 83, 97, 98, 220

be-, 114, 190, 221
by-, 84, 221

cardio-, 218
-ce, 21, 45, 46, 47, 165
circum-, 221
con-, 124
counter-, 60
crypto-, 221
-cy, 21, 45, 46, 47

deca-, 221
dis-, 112, 124, 221
-dom, 30, 220

-ed]$_A$, 127, 128, 214, 215
-ed]$_{PARTICIPLE}$, 127, 190
-ed]$_{PAST}$, 127, 211, 219
-ee, 64, 65, 83, 84, 220
-een, 141
electro-, 218
em-/en-, 4, 114, 221
-en]$_A$, 160, 220

-en]$_{DIMIN}$, 188
-en]$_{PARTICIPLE}$, 219
-en]$_{PL}$, 93, 219
-en]$_V$, 18
endo-, 115, 221
epi-, 218
-er]$_A$, 28, 45, 120, 122, 215, 219
-er]$_{DIMIN}$, 140
-er]$_N$, 5, 17, 28, 29, 60, 64, 65, 71, 84, 87, 98, 107, 108, 121, 148, 149, 164, 166, 176, 220
-er]$_{PL}$, 93
-er]$_V$, 19, 190
-(e)rel, 188
-ese, 220
-esque, 220
-ess, 84, 220
-est, 120, 219
-eth, 219, 220
-ette, 140, 220
ex-, 150
exo-, 115
extra-, 221

-fold, 84
for-, 114
-free, 112, 114
-ful, 98, 220

giga-, 221
grand-, 124

hemi-, 222
hepta-, 222
-hood, 84, 220
hyper-, 222
hypo-, 141

-ial]$_A$, 98
-ian]$_A$, 98, 125, 126
-ian]$_N$, 98, 123
-ic, 17, 45, 47, 97, 98, 121, 123, 149, 220

241

Index of English Word-Forming Elements

-ical, 45, 47, 97, 99
-ie, 140, 141
-ify, 98, 123, 220
il-, 124
im-, 124
in-, 20, 53, 114, 124
-ing]$_A$, 39, 214, 215, 222, 223
-ing]$_N$, 166, 211, 214, 215, 222, 223
-ing]$_V$, 39, 61, 90, 120, 219, 220, 222
-ion, 19, 50, 84, 97
-ish]$_A$, 47, 57, 98, 100, 112, 121, 220
-ish]$_V$, 190
-ism, 30, 98, 121, 123, 149
-ist, 97, 121, 123, 149, 220
-istic, 97, 99
-itis, 84
-ity, 84, 98, 121, 123, 220
-ive, 220
-ize, 84, 97, 98, 123, 150, 220

-kin, 140

-le]$_A$, 189
-le]$_V$, 121, 189
-less, 84, 112, 113, 220
-let, 140, 220
-like, 47
-ling, 140, 220
-ly]$_A$, 3, 35, 59, 124, 220
-ly]$_{ADV}$, 16, 30, 124, 127, 160, 210, 219

maxi-, 114
mega-, 100, 151, 218
-ment, 21, 29, 98, 151
meta-, 99
micro-, 100, 112, 114, 115, 141
mini-, 100, 112, 114, 115, 141, 218
mono-, 114
multi-, 222

-n't, 210
nano-, 141
-ness, 84, 98, 113, 124, 127, 220
-nik, 220

-o, 140
-ock, 188
-ola, 141
-ology, 149
-or, 98, 164, 220
-ous, 84, 121, 150, 220
over-, 84

para-, 222
poly-, 114

post-, 84, 112, 114, 115
pre-, 84, 112, 114
pro-, 112, 114
proto-, 222
pseudo-, 115
psycho-, 113

quadr-, 222
quasi-, 115

re-, 84, 100, 112, 150
-ren, 219
-ric, 30

-s]$_{3SG}$, 211, 219
-s]$_{ADV}$, 84
-s]$_{DIMIN}$, 84, 140
-'s]$_{GEN}$, 214
-s]$_{PL}$, 213, 215, 216, 219, 225
-scape, 84
-ship, 98, 220
shm-, 181, 219
socio-, 113
-some, 220
-st, 219
step-, 222
-ster, 220
sub-, 99, 115, 124
super-, 100, 112, 114, 115, 218
supra-, 112, 114
syntactico-, 218

-t, 188
-t]$_{2SG}$, 219
-teen, 84
-ter, 50, 220
-th]$_N$, 17, 18, 19, 21, 98, 188, 220
-th]$_{ORDINAL}$, 210, 219
theo-, 222

un-, 3, 20, 28, 100
-ure, 29, 98

vice-, 222

-ward(s), 220
-wise, 112
with-, 222

-y]$_A$, 121, 220
-y]$_N$, 121, 150, 220
yotta-, 222

zetta-, 222
-zza, 140

For EU product safety concerns, contact us at Calle de José Abascal, 56–1°,
28003 Madrid, Spain or eugpsr@cambridge.org.

www.ingramcontent.com/pod-product-compliance
Ingram Content Group UK Ltd.
Pitfield, Milton Keynes, MK11 3LW, UK
UKHW022124060326
468743UK00020B/3511